THIRD EDITION

Psychology A2

The Mini Companion

Mike Cardwell
Cara Flanagan

OXFORD

UNIVERSITY PRESS

OXFORD
UNIVERSITY PRESS

Great Clarendon Street, Oxford OX2 6DP

Oxford University Press is a department of the University of Oxford.
It furthers the University's objective of excellence in research, scholarship, and education
by publishing worldwide in

Oxford   New York

Auckland   Cape Town   Dar es Salaam   Hong Kong   Karachi   Kuala Lumpur   Madrid
Melbourne   Mexico City   Nairobi   New Delhi   Shanghai   Taipei   Toronto

With offices in

Argentina   Austria   Brazil   Chile   Czech Republic   France   Greece   Guatemala   Hungary
Italy   Japan   Poland   Portugal   Singapore   South Korea   Switzerland   Thailand   Turkey
Ukraine   Vietnam

Oxford is a registered trade mark of Oxford University Press in the UK and in certain other
countries

© Mike Cardwell and Cara Flanagan 2012

British Library Cataloguing in Publication Data

Data available

ISBN 978 019 912986 7

10 9 8 7 6 5 4 3 2 1

Printed by Bell & Bain Ltd, Glasgow

Paper used in the production of this book is a natural, recyclable product made from wood
grown in sustainable forests. The manufacturing process conforms to the environmental
regulations of the country of origin.

Acknowledgements
Project development: Rick Jackman (Jackman Publishing Solutions Ltd)
Editorial management, design and layout: GreenGate Publishing Services
Design: Nigel Harriss
Cover design: Patricia Briggs
Cover photography: Chris Cardwell

Images: © Shutterstock/Eric Isselée

105470

Contents

Introduction

This book is a mini version of *Psychology A2: The Complete Companion*. It contains only the basic information needed for the AQA specification 'A' A2 examination. There are no frills and no extras.

When a cook makes a special sauce he or she will boil the liquid for a long time so that it reduces in volume and produces something that is intense and flavoursome. That's what we have done here – producing the nuggets of knowledge necessary to enable you to focus on what you *must* learn in order to do well in the exam, as distinct from what you *could* learn. In order to make the most of the material presented in this book you should use it alongside the A2 *Complete Companion* or your own A2 textbook.

The A2 examination

The A2 examination consists of two papers:

Unit 3 (PSYA3) Topics in Psychology

50% of A2 Level marks

Duration: 1 hour 30 minutes

The exam paper contains eight questions, each worth 24 marks in total, one question drawn from each of the eight topics in the specification.

You must answer three questions from the following eight topics:

- Biological rhythms and sleep
- Perception
- Relationships
- Aggression
- Eating behaviour
- Gender
- Intelligence and learning
- Cognition and development

Unit 4 (PSYA4) Psychopathology, Psychology in Action and Research Methods

50% of A2 Level marks

Duration: 2 hours

The exam paper is divided into three sections:

Section A – Psychopathology

You answer one question chosen from:

- Schizophrenia
- Depression
- Phobic disorders
- Obsessive compulsive disorder

Section B – Psychology in Action

You answer one question chosen from:

- Media psychology
- The psychology of addictive behaviour
- Anomalistic psychology

Section C – Psychological Research and Scientific Method

One compulsory structured question

Organisation of this book

This book is organised along the lines of the specification, divided into topics, divisions and subdivisions. At the top of each page in this book you will see the following:

The chapter title, covering one of the topics above.

Each topic/chapter, divided into 3 sections.

Each section is further divided into one or more subsections.

Chapter 1

Biological rhythms and sleep

Biological rhythms
Sleep states
The nature of sleep and lifespan changes

Functions of sleep: Restoration explanations
Functions of sleep: Evolutionary explanations

Functions of sleep: Restoration explanations

Slow wave sleep (SWS)

SWS initiates body repair (Oswald).

Growth hormone

Important in childhood because it stimulates physical growth.

Important throughout lifespan for protein synthesis and cell growth (cells need to be constantly replaced).

If sleep (SWS+REM) is restorative, total sleep deprivation should have negative effects…

Case studies show some support, e.g. DJ Peter Tripp stayed awake for 201 hours and after 5 days he experienced hallucinations and paranoia; his brain rhythms looked like he was asleep.

Non-human animal studies show that lack of sleep may be fatal. Rechtschaffen *et al.* kept rats on a rotating disc and after 33 days they died, although this may have been due to stress rather than lack of sleep.

The examination questions

All A2 exam questions (except 'Psychological Research and Scientific Method') are worth 24 marks. These marks are divided into:
- 8 marks of description (AO1)
- 16 marks of evaluation/how science works (AO2/3)

An exam question might say:

*Describe and evaluate **one** theory of perception.*
(8 marks + 16 marks)

This means you should present 8 marks of description of the theory (about 200 words) and 16 marks of evaluation (about 400 words).

An exam question might say:

*(a) Outline **one** evolutionary explanation of group display in humans.* *(4 marks)*
*(b) Discuss **one** social psychological explanation of aggression.* *(4 marks + 16 marks)*

This means you should present 4 marks describing one evolutionary explanation of group display (about 100 words) and a further 4 marks of material describing one social psychological explanation (about 100 words), and finally 16 marks of evaluation of the social psychological explanations (about 400 words).

The examples on the left show several things:

The division between AO1 and AO2/3 is shown after each exam question – the first mark given indicates the maximum mark available for AO1 and the second mark shows the maximum mark available for AO2/3.

The AO1 and AO2/3 elements are also indicated by exam injunctions, such as
- 'describe' or 'outline' which indicate AO1,
- 'evaluate' or 'consider' which indicate AO2/3, or
- 'discuss' which indicates both.

Note that the wording of the questions is drawn from the specification.

There are three assessment objectives (AOs):

AO1 refers to knowledge and understanding.

AO2 refers to the application of this knowledge, including analysis and evaluation.

AO3 refers to an understanding and evaluation of the research methods used in psychology. Such material can be used as part of effective evaluation but is not required in order to be awarded full marks.

The topic covered on each page is divided into
- ● Description (**AO1**) on the left.
- ● Evaluation (**AO2/3**) on the right.

There is less AO1 than AO2/3 for each topic, reflecting the mark balance in exam questions.

A key feature of the AO2/3 material is the **IDA** points – 'IDA' stands for issues, debates and approaches. The mark scheme for Unit 3 rewards the use of issues, debates or approaches as part of your evaluation.

It is important to note that credit is only given to AO2/3 points that are elaborated, including IDA points. If you simply identify evaluative points (including IDA points) you will get only minimal credit.

There is an important thing to notice about the AO2/3 points given in this book – they begin with an emboldened title (such as *'However'* or *'There are individual differences'*). Such 'lead in phrases' are crucial in establishing that you are making an evaluative point (AO2/3) rather than just describing further research (which would be AO1). Use these phrases in your essays.

Biological rhythms and sleep

Division A   Biological rhythms

Circadian rhythms
Infradian and ultradian rhythms
Endogenous pacemakers, exogenous zeitgebers
Disruption of biological rhythms

Division B   Sleep states

The nature of sleep and lifespan changes
Functions of sleep: Restoration explanations
Functions of sleep: Evolutionary explanations

Division C   Disorders of sleep

Explanations for insomnia
Explanations for other sleep disorders

Specification

Biological rhythms and sleep	
Biological rhythms	• Circadian, infradian and ultradian rhythms, including the role of endogenous pacemakers and of exogenous zeitgebers in the control of circadian rhythms. • Disruption of biological rhythms, for example shift work, jet lag.
Sleep	• The nature of sleep, including sleep stages and lifespan changes in sleep. • Functions of sleep, including evolutionary and restoration explanations.
Disorders of sleep	• Explanations for sleep disorders, including insomnia, sleep walking and narcolepsy.

Chapter 1		Circadian rhythms
	Biological rhythms >	Infradian and ultradian rhythms
	Sleep states	Endogenous pacemaker, exogenous zeitgebers
Biological rhythms and sleep >	Disorders of sleep	Disruption of biological rhythms

Circadian rhythms

Last about 24 hours.

The sleep–wake cycle

External cues, e.g. darkness and the time on a clock, tell us when to go to sleep.

Free-running cycle maintains the sleep–wake cycle in the absence of external cues. It is governed by an internal (**endogenous**) clock.

In the absence of external cues, the internal clock governs the sleep–wake cycle.

Supported by temporal isolation studies that demonstrate the free-running circadian rhythm, and show that the cycle persists despite absence of light, for example:

- Siffre spent long periods underground with no daylight, radio, etc. He found that his sleep–wake cycle generally adjusted to a 24-hour cycle (but sometimes changed dramatically to as much as 48 hours).
- Aschoff and Wever placed participants in an underground WWII bunker with no environmental or social time cues. The participants' cycle was 24–25 hours (sometimes up to 29 hours).

However…

In early studies participants were exposed to artificial light, which may have affected their cycle; Czeisler *et al.* demonstrated that rhythms could be entrained using artificial light.

There are individual differences…

- Cycle length varies from 13 to 65 hours (Czeisler *et al.*).
- Cycle onset varies, there are innate patterns of waking and sleeping: morning types (rise at 6am and go to bed at 10pm) and evening types (rise at 10am and go to bed at 1am) (Duffy *et al.*).

Case studies lack validity…

Siffre's findings were based on one unique individual, so lack generalisability.

However… they have been confirmed by other studies.

On the plus side, he also used an experimental approach, and thus could demonstrate a causal relationship between external cues and sleep–wake cycle.

Cycle can be entrained (i.e. brought into phase) to some extent by external cues.

Supported by…

Folkard *et al.* gradually reduced participants' circadian rhythm using a quickening clock, but when the 'day' was reduced to 22 hours the participants' own rhythms took over again, showing a limit for control of internal rhythms by external cues.

IDA *Real-world application…*

Chronotherapeutics is the application of biological rhythms to the treatment of medical disorders, taking medication or engaging in specific activities at certain times of day.

For example taking aspirin at 11pm to treat heart attacks. Aspirin levels then peak in bloodstream at the time when heart attacks commonly occur (about 3am).

Core body temperature

Body temperature is generally lowest at 4:30am and highest at 6.00pm.

Such variation explains…

- Superior recall and comprehension in 12–13-year-old children working in the afternoon rather than the morning (Folkard *et al.*).
- IQ test results best at 7pm compared with 9am or 2pm (Gupta).

Post-lunch dip

Tiredness in the afternoon may appear to be due to the effects of having eaten, but it occurs even if you don't eat – due to a circadian temperature rhythm.

Cause or correlation?…

Giesbrecht *et al.* deliberately lowered core body temperature and showed that this caused lower cognitive performance. It is not clear whether the effect is due to the direct effects of core body temperature, or whether the high core body temperature leads to increased physiological arousal and this creates the effect (Wright *et al.*).

However…

Hord and Thompson found no link between body temperature and cognitive performance.

Hormones

Cortisol levels are lowest at midnight and peak at about 6am. When levels are high, this creates alertness – which explains why you can't think clearly when you wake up earlier than normal (your cortisol levels are low and therefore you aren't alert).

Melatonin and growth hormone levels peak at midnight.

IDA *A biological and determinist approach*

- All of these explanations suggest that our sleep–wake patterns are fixed, caused by internal mechanisms and/or external cues.
- The power of these biologically determined rhythms is illustrated by the case of a young man who was blind. Light did not reset his internally-set circadian rhythms, which made it very difficult for him to function in a world tuned into cues such as clocks and daylight (Miles *et al.*).
- However, there is some flexibility in the system. For example, we can decide to go to bed two hours later than usual and wake up at the same time the next day without too much difficulty (e.g. in the study by Folkard *et al.* one person did manage to keep to a 22-hour rhythm, which shows that other factors can override the internal clock).

Ultradian rhythms

Sleep stages

Descending the sleep staircase:
- *Stages 1 and 2* – relaxed, alpha and theta waves, heart rate slows, temperature drops.
- *Stages 3 and 4* – called deep sleep (or slow wave sleep, SWS), delta waves, metabolic rate slows, growth hormone produced.
- *REM sleep* (rapid eye movement) – associated with dreaming, desynchronised EEG activity similar to the awake brain, brain and eyes active but body paralysed (paradoxical state).

One cycle takes about 90 minutes; later in the night there is more REM sleep and less SWS.

There are age differences…
Babies don't have the same stages; they display quiet and active sleep, which are immature versions of SWS and REM sleep. Relatively greater amounts of REM sleep may be related to the considerable learning that is taking place.

Older people experience reduced SWS and an associated reduction in the production of growth hormone. This may explain some of the symptoms associated with old age, e.g. lower bone density (van Cauter *et al.*).

The link between REM sleep and dreams has been questioned…
Dement and Kleitman demonstrated that people awoken during REM sleep were often dreaming, but dreams are not exclusive to REM sleep, often occurring at other times as well.

Neurobiological theories of dreaming make the erroneous assumption that REM sleep equals dreams and explain the function of dreaming in terms of the function of REM sleep.

Basic rest–activity cycle

During the daytime there is also a 90-minute cycle of rest followed by activity.

Friedman and Fisher observed psychiatric patients over a 6-hour period, and noted a clear pattern of 90 minutes between eating and drinking 'episodes'.

The value of the 90-minute rhythm…
Ensures that biological processes in the body work in unison. Complex metabolic processes are active in many different parts of the body at any time and some coordination between these is advantageous.

Infradian rhythms

Monthly cycles

Menstrual cycle determined by fluctuating levels of female hormones that regulate ovulation.

Pituitary gland releases hormones (FSH and LH), egg ripens and triggers production of oestrogen and later progesterone to prepare the lining of the womb for a fertilised egg. If there is no pregnancy, progesterone levels fall and the lining is shed.

Can be controlled exogenously…
Russell *et al.* showed that pheromones can entrain menstrual cycles (by collecting sweat from one group of women and rubbing it on the upper lips of another group of women). This shows that biological rhythms can be entrained by exogenous cues.

May have negative effects…
Premenstrual syndrome (PMS) is associated with certain direct effects: anxiety, depression, mood swings and aggression.

Such behaviours were once considered 'all in the mind' but now there is a recognised biological cause.

Research evidence from Dalton showed that PMS led indirectly to lower academic achievement, suicide and crime.

IDA *A determinist approach…*
Both SAD (seasonal affective disorder) and PMS suggest that certain behaviours are inevitable – and this has been used as a legal defence, e.g. Ms English was placed on probation (rather than a custodial sentence) for the murder of her boyfriend because she was suffering from severe PMS (Johnson).

Males also have been found to have near-monthly rhythms for temperature and alertness levels (Empson).

People can 'will' their biological rhythms to change, e.g. people told to wake up earlier than normal had higher levels of the stress hormone ACTH (Born *et al.*).

Seasonal affective disorder (SAD)

A yearly cycle
People with SAD are depressed in winter and recover in summer.

May be due to the hormones melatonin and serotonin – more darkness means more melatonin, and more melatonin means less serotonin (because melatonin is produced from serotonin). Low levels of serotonin are associated with depression.

Could be explained differently…
SAD might not be an effect of infradian rhythms, but due to a disrupted circadian rhythm, similar to jet lag – happens because we go to bed earlier as it's darker earlier in winter and this puts rhythms out of phase.

IDA *Real-world application…*
Phototherapy developed to treat SAD by exposing sufferers to very strong light (6000–10,000 Lux).

However, benefits of phototherapy may be due to a placebo effect as, in one study, 32% improved with placebo alone (Eastman *et al.*).

Endogenous pacemakers

The suprachiasmatic nucleus (SCN)

The SCN is a cluster of nerve cells in the hypothalamus.

It receives information about light because it is located above the optic chiasma. Even when the eyes are shut, information about light is received by the SCN.

The 'rhythm' is produced by a negative feedback loop:
- One pair of proteins combine (e.g. CLK+BLMAL1).
- This combination then produces a second pair of proteins (e.g. PER+CRY).
- PER+CRY make CLK+BLMAL1 inactive.
- As levels of CLK+BLMAL1 fall, this means PER+CRY are reduced and then levels of CLK+BLMAL1 increase again.

One SCN is in each hemisphere, each divided into:
- *Ventral SCN*, relatively quickly reset by external cues.
- *Dorsal SCN*, less affected by light (Albus *et al.*).

The effect of the SCN has been demonstrated…
In animal studies, e.g. Morgan bred 'mutant' hamsters with 20-hour circadian rhythms. When their SCN was transplanted into the 'normal' hamsters they exhibited the mutant rhythm.

IDA *An issue is the use of non-human animals…*
Animals used in this research are permanently harmed, which can be justified if the research is regarded as important, e.g. it can be argued that it is important for understanding the effects of desynchronised biological clocks in shift workers and providing suggestions for how this might be overcome.

However…
Generalisations made from animal to human behaviour may not be justified as biological systems are different, and also humans have the power of cognitive control over their behaviour, at least in some situations.

This can explain the effects of desynchronisation…
Desynchronisation occurs in jet lag and shift lag, and occurs when the ventral and dorsal portions of the SCN are out of phase.
A study by Folkard observed the effects of isolation in a woman, Kate Aldcroft. While in a cave, her temperature and sleep rhythms became quite different and she experienced symptoms similar to jet lag.

The pineal gland and melatonin

The pineal gland receives signals from SCN, and as a result produces melatonin.
Melatonin induces sleep by inhibiting the brain mechanisms that promote wakefulness.

IDA *The evolutionary approach can help us understand…*
The adaptive nature of biological rhythms, e.g. anticipating daily environmental events. Chipmunks without functioning SCNs were found to be more likely to die, presumably because they were awake at night and making noise, which attracted predators (DeCoursey *et al.*).

Exogenous zeitgebers

Light

Light entrains the free-running biological rhythm.

This affects the SCN and other peripheral oscillators, e.g. Campbell and Murphy shone light on the back of participants' knees and reset circadian rhythms.

Peripheral oscillators contain CRY (cryptochrome), a substance that is sensitive to light.

One issue is whether artificial lighting is enough…
Early studies of biological rhythms exposed participants to artificial lighting and it was assumed this would not be bright enough to entrain rhythms (e.g. Siffre cave study).
However, Campbell and Murphy shifted rhythms with light on the back of knees.
Boivin *et al.* found that even normal artificial lighting does have an effect, although bright lighting is better for resetting circadian rhythms.

IDA *Real-world application…*
Living in an artificially lit world may disrupt melatonin production, so leading to increased incidence of cancer (Stevens).

Social cues

Social conventions entrain biological rhythms, e.g. mealtimes reset cells in heart and liver (Davidson).

Temperature

Cold temperature signals a time for reduced activity.
Warm temperature is the time for activity (sleep–wake).
In warm-blooded animals, such as humans, daily changes in body temperature are governed by their circadian clock and these temperature changes entrain other circadian rhythms (Buhr *et al.*).

Problems occur when the biological system fails…
Having a biologically governed system has adaptive advantages but when it goes wrong, it is difficult to override, e.g. *familial advanced sleep-phase syndrome* (FASPS) has been linked to a faulty PER gene, causing sleeping and waking at wrong times, and difficulty leading a normal life (Chicurel).
Physiological changes during adolescence may cause delayed sleep phase syndrome, leading to unusual sleep patterns.

There are advantages with this blended system…
In fact, endogenous and exogenous cues act as one system. Total isolation studies are artificial; in the real world both cues interact to enable internal synchronisation of physiological processes, but also external synchronisation with inevitable environmental changes.

Chapter 1

Biological rhythms >

Biological rhythms and sleep >

Circadian rhythms

Infradian and ultradian rhythms

Sleep states

Endogenous pacemakers/exogenous zeitgebers

Disorders of sleep

Disruption of biological rhythms

Disruption of biological rhythms

Shift work and shift lag

Alertness decreases when cortisol levels are lower in the middle of the night, when core body temperature is also lowest (circadian trough) (Boivin *et al.*).

Sleep deprivation is inevitable because sleeping during the day is disrupted by noises and daylight; sleep length is typically 2 hours less than normal (Tilley and Wilkinson).

Effects on health, e.g. shift workers are three times more likely to develop heart disease (Knutssen *et al.*).

IDA *Real-world application…*
Our society relies on shift work and therefore it is essential to understand and reduce the negative effects caused by working shifts.

Many major disasters (e.g. *Exxon Valdez*) can be blamed on errors arising from the disruption of biological rhythms that are associated with shift work.

An alternative explanation…
Shift work effects are not just due to the direct effects of disruption of rhythms, but indirectly to such things as the associated social deprivation and family disruption, e.g. divorce rates may be as high as 60% in shift workers (Solomon).

IDA *Real-world application…*
Research has found systems that have fewer negative effects.
- Non-fluctuating shifts are better, i.e. a week of working days, followed by a week of working nights (Gold *et al.*).
- Forward-rotating shifts (phase delay) are better than backward-rotating shifts (Bambra *et al.*).

IDA *Real-world application…*
Artificial lighting can be used to entrain circadian rhythms and promote wakefulness. Boivin *et al.* showed that very bright lighting can reset the biological clock. They found that, within three days, a group of participants exposed to a very bright light had advanced their biological clock by 5 hours, whereas exposure to an ordinary light advanced participants by 1 hour and dim lighting led to a 1 hour delay.

Laboratory experiments should be verified…
Laboratory experiments demonstrate causal relationships but should be confirmed by more natural studies. Boivin and James studied nurses at work, and found that exposure to bright lights promoted circadian adaptation – supporting their laboratory study.

Jet travel and jet lag

'Jet lag' describes the physiological effects of desynchronised circadian rhythms.

Symptoms include nausea, fatigue, disorientation, insomnia and depression.

It is estimated that the dorsal part of the SCN takes several cycles to adjust to large environmental changes.

Phase delay is easier to adjust to – the same as staying up later than usual or travelling east to west.

Phase advance is more difficult because you wake up when you're in a circadian trough – same as getting up earlier or travelling west to east.

For example, US baseball results were better for teams travelling east to west – they won 44% of their games over a three-year period compared to 37% wins for teams travelling west to east (Recht *et al.*). This suggests that the east to west teams suffered less from jet lag than the west to east teams.

An alternative explanation…
The effects of jet lag may be due to other factors related to travel, such as long hours of travel, annoyance caused by other passengers and low-oxygen cabin air.

IDA *Real-world application…*
Melatonin may reduce the effects of jet lag because it naturally induces sleep.

Herxheimer and Petrie reviewed ten studies and found melatonin was very effective if taken just before bedtime, but when taken at other times of day it may delay adaptation to local time.

IDA *Real-world application…*
Social cues also entrain biological rhythms, so one way to cope with jet lag is to eat and sleep at the right times. This may be because peripheral oscillators, which are found around the body, are reset by eating.

Fuller *et al.* found that a period of fasting followed by eating at the right time helps to entrain biological rhythms.

It is important to consider individual differences…
Some people are more affected by circadian disruption than others – Reinberg *et al.* found that people whose circadian rhythms adapt more slowly actually cope best with shift work/jet travel.

Biological rhythms	The nature of sleep and lifespan changes
Sleep states >	Functions of sleep: Restoration explanations
Biological rhythms and sleep >	Disorders of sleep	Functions of sleep: Evolutionary explanations

The nature of sleep and lifespan changes

Infancy

Duration

Babies sleep for about 16 hours a day, but not continuously.

They wake every hour or so (cycles less than adult 90-minute cycle).

Patterns of sleep

Active and quiet sleep – version of REM sleep and SWS.

About half of infant sleep is 'active' – more than adult ratio of REM:NREM.

Infants don't go immediately into SWS; they start with very light sleep and are thus easily awoken.

Circadian rhythm

By about six months most children have one main sleep–wake cycle, with a few naps during the day.

IDA A developmental approach…

The lifespan approach is important because it recognises that sleep patterns are not consistent but change as we age. This has led to new understanding of, for example, some of the effects of ageing.

IDA An evolutionary approach…

Suggests that infant sleep patterns evolved so that parents can get on with daytime chores.

Infant sleep patterns evolved because infants have small stomachs and must wake and eat regularly.

There is a reason why infants have large amounts of active sleep…

Active (REM) sleep is associated with the production of neurotransmitters and consolidation of memory – both apply to infant development.

This is supported by…

Research that shows that premature babies (whose brains are even less mature) spend 90% of sleep time in active sleep.

Childhood

Children typically sleep about 12 hours a day, and EEG patterns resemble adult patterns.

The amount of sleep gradually decreases.

Parasomnias common in childhood, such as sleep walking and night terrors.

IDA Cultural bias…

Psychologists make assumptions about sleep behaviour based on research with American and British samples. Tynjälä et al. found considerable differences in sleep patterns across European countries in children of 11–12 years, e.g. Israeli children sleep 9 hours on average. This shows that sleep duration is influenced by cultural practices. Our view of behaviour often ignores such influences.

Adolescence

Sleep duration increases in adolescence.

Boys often have orgasm and ejaculation during sleep.

Phase delay

Circadian rhythms shift so teenagers stay awake later and wake up later.

Adolescent sleep can be explained by hormone changes…

Adolescence is a time when there are major changes in sex hormones.

These changes disrupt sleep because hormones are predominantly released at night. Many 'symptoms' of adolescence (e.g. moodiness, lack of motivation) may be due to sleep problems.

A consequence of phase delay…

Schools should adjust their school day to fit delayed sleep phase syndrome, which is typical of adolescents and means they have poor attention spans in the morning (Wolfson and Carskadon).

Adulthood

Typically 8 hours per night, 25% of which is REM sleep.

Increasing frequency of sleep disorders such as insomnia and sleep apnoea.

Too much sleep is not necessarily a good thing…

Kripke et al. surveyed 1 million adults and found that sleeping for 6–7 hours was associated with reduced mortality, whereas an average of 8 hours had a 15% increased risk of mortality and sleeping more than 10 hours was linked to a 30% increased risk.

Correlational data does mean a cause has been demonstrated…

It is likely that underlying illness is an intervening variable.

Old age

Sleep patterns change

More difficulty going to sleep, and wake more frequently.

REM sleep decreases to 20% of total sleep time.

SWS decreases to 5% of total sleep time.

Phase advance: go to sleep earlier and wake earlier.

May nap during the day to satisfy sleep needs.

Reduced sleep is a consequence of…

Physiological changes, but also problems staying asleep, e.g. insomnia and reduced SWS means people are awoken more easily.

A consequence of sleep changes is…

Less growth hormone is produced (because less SWS), which may explain some of the symptoms of old age, e.g. lack of energy and lower bone density (van Cauter et al.).

Lack of sleep may also explain impaired cognitive functions.

IDA Real-world application…

Sleep quality can be improved through the use of melatonin. Melatonin induces sleep by inhibiting the brain mechanisms that promote wakefulness.

Chapter 1

Biological rhythms

The nature of sleep and lifespan changes

Sleep states > Functions of sleep: Restoration explanations

Biological rhythms and sleep > Disorders of sleep

Functions of sleep: Evolutionary explanations

Functions of sleep: Restoration explanations

Slow wave sleep (SWS)

SWS initiates body repair (Oswald).

Growth hormone

Important in childhood because it stimulates physical growth.

Important throughout lifespan for protein synthesis and cell growth (cells need to be constantly replaced).

Secreted to some extent during the day but mainly in SWS. This is demonstrated by reversing the sleep–wake cycle and then growth hormone is produced during the day when SWS takes place (Sassin et al.). The amount of growth hormone correlates with the amount of SWS (van Cauter and Plat).

Immune system

Body's defence against viruses and bacteria. Lack of SWS is associated with reduced immune functioning (Krueger et al.).

REM sleep

REM sleep initiates brain repair (Oswald).

Brain growth

Infants have a greater proportion of REM (i.e. active) sleep than adults, which suggests that REM sleep may be important to brain growth.

Siegel suggests that the amount of REM sleep in any animal is proportional to the immaturity of offspring at birth, e.g. platypus young are very immature and have about 8 hours REM, whereas dolphin young are very mature and have almost no REM sleep.

Neurotransmitter function

Siegel and Rogaski suggest that during REM sleep neurotransmitters are not produced, allowing neurons to regain their sensitivity.

Antidepressant drugs such as MAOIs abolish REM activity – and also replenish monomaine neurotransmitters, supporting the link between REM and neurotransmitter recovery (antidepressant drugs increase neurotransmitter levels).

Memory

REM sleep may permit memories to be sorted and discarded if unwanted (Crick and Mitchison).

REM may be important in the consolidation of procedural memory (memory for *doing* things), whereas SWS is important for semantic and episodic memory (memory for events and meanings) (Stickgold).

If sleep (SWS+REM) is restorative, total sleep deprivation should have negative effects…

Case studies show some support, e.g. DJ Peter Tripp stayed awake for 201 hours and after 5 days he experienced hallucinations and paranoia; his brain rhythms looked like he was asleep.

Non-human animal studies show that lack of sleep may be fatal. Rechtschaffen et al. kept rats on a rotating disc and after 33 days they died, although this may have been due to stress rather than lack of sleep.

However…

Sleep-deprived individuals may actually be getting some sleep, e.g. laboratory observations have found that sleep deprivation for more than 72 hours results in periods of microsleep while participants are apparently awake (Williams et al.), i.e. sleep-deprived participants are only apparently awake but experiencing some of the benefits of sleep.

Another case study (Randy Gardner) found no psychotic symptoms after 11 days without sleep and there are reports of individuals (e.g. Hai Ngoc) who haven't slept for years with no ill effects. However, such individuals may be experiencing microsleep.

There are methodological issues…

Case studies relate to unique individuals, and other sleep studies often use volunteers who also might have unique characteristics (e.g. have less need for sleep than the norm) – so results might lack generalisability.

Non-human animal studies might lack generalisability because animals have different sleep requirements to humans.

If SWS is important, SWS deprivation should have negative effects…

Demonstrated in 'rebound effects' – when people are deprived of SWS they show need for more SWS on subsequent nights.

Acoustic stimulation is used to wake sleepers as soon as brain waves show SWS (Ferrara et al.).

If REM sleep is important, REM sleep deprivation should have negative effects…

This is supported by research evidence that shows that REM deprivation results in as much as 50% more REM sleep on subsequent nights (Empson).

If sleep (SWS+REM) is restorative, exercise should increase the need for sleep…

Exercise should use up proteins, etc., necessitating more sleep for restoration. Shapiro et al. found that marathon runners slept 2 hours longer after a race.

However…

Horne and Minard found that a series of exhausting tasks led people to go to sleep faster but not for longer.

IDA The evolutionary approach…

The main alternative to restoration theory is the evolutionary approach, which claims that sleep has no specific benefit except protection (to conserve energy or keep an animal safe from predators), rather than performing some specific biological function as claimed by the restoration approach.

The restoration approach doesn't explain, for example, why some species sleep one hemisphere at a time (e.g. dolphins). Nor does it explain why lack of consciousness is necessary.

It looks like environmental pressures are important in shaping sleep processes, which can be explained by the evolutionary approach.

Chapter 1

Biological rhythms | The nature of sleep and lifespan changes
Sleep states > | Functions of sleep: Restoration explanations
Biological rhythms and sleep > | Disorders of sleep | Functions of sleep: Evolutionary explanations

Functions of sleep: Evolutionary explanations

Energy conservation

High expenditure of energy

Warm-blooded animals (such as birds or mammals) use energy to maintain temperature.

This is especially true for small animals with a high metabolic rate (such as mice).

Predicts a negative correlation between body size and sleep…

Supported by… Zepelin and Rechtschaffen, who found smaller animals sleep more than larger animals, although there are exceptions, e.g. sloths, who are large and sleep a lot.

However, not supported by… Capellini et al. who found a positive correlation. This study used carefully selected, standardised data and therefore may be more reliable than older evidence.

Benefit of sleep

Sleep provides period of enforced inactivity to conserve energy, such as hibernation (Webb called it the *hibernation theory of sleep*).

Therefore small animals should sleep lots to conserve energy.

Energy only conserved in NREM sleep…

In REM sleep the brain is relatively active so energy may only be conserved in NREM sleep.

Suggests that… Only NREM (not REM) sleep evolved for energy conservation. More primitive animals (e.g. reptiles) only have NREM sleep, supporting the view that NREM sleep evolved first (for energy conservation) and REM sleep evolved later (to maintain brain activity).

If this is correct we would expect… A negative correlation only between body size and NREM sleep. Supported by Allison and Cicchetti but not by Capellini et al.

Foraging requirements

Time spent asleep (conserving energy)
is constrained by time needed for eating.

- Herbivores (e.g. cows) have to spend a lot of time eating because their food is poor in nutrients.
- Carnivores (e.g. lions) can afford to sleep a great deal.

Predicts a trade-off between foraging needs and sleep…

Capellini et al. found that animals with a greater need for foraging (because of high metabolism or diet low in energy) had lower sleep rates, supporting foraging needs as an explanation for sleep patterns.

Predator avoidance

Time spent asleep (conserving energy) is
constrained by risk of predation (being eaten).

- Predators can sleep for longer .
- Prey species are in danger when sleeping. However, if sleep is vital, then it is best to be done when the animal is least vulnerable, i.e. at night when they can hide.

Predicts a trade-off between predation risk and sleep…

Alison and Cicchetti found that species with a high risk of predation did sleep less. Though there are exceptions, e.g. rabbits (high risk of predation) slept as much as moles (low risk of predation).

However…

Capellini et al. found the relationship is complex, e.g. animals that sleep socially sleep fewer hours – but ought to sleep more because there is safety in numbers.

Waste of time

Sleep is wasting time

Meddis proposed that sleep is what animals do when they have nothing else to do with their time (e.g. when not eating, mating, hiding from predators, etc.).

For most animals this means sleeping at night and sleeping out of sight (e.g. in a burrow) because they are not as vulnerable while they are asleep.

Being awake is dangerous

Siegel also pointed out that being awake is dangerous, not just because of predation, but also because an animal is more likely to be injured.

The best adaptive strategy is to sleep as
long as you can.

For example, the little brown bat (small mammal, high metabolism) should sleep little. However, it has a very specific diet of insects that are around for a short time each day and the little brown bat is awake only then.

IDA The evolutionary approach…

Suggests that sleep must be adaptive in some way, otherwise why do all animals do it, but their patterns of sleeping differ? This suggests that these patterns are in some way adaptive to the species' environment.

The 'phylogenetic signal' provides key support…

The fact that animals that are close together on the phylogenetic scale share close similarities in their sleep patterns supports the view that such patterns have evolved through adaption to environmental pressure.

Capellini et al. concluded that foraging and predation risks act as selective pressures (i.e. a demand resulting in one set of genes being favoured over another).

IDA The restoration approach…

Restoration theory suggests that sleep evolved not just to occupy wasted hours, but because vital functions are performed.

Horne proposed a way to combine both approaches:
- Core sleep (= SWS), essential for bodily restoration.
- Optional sleep (= REM and some NREM sleep), dispensable but useful for occupying unproductive hours.

Explanations for insomnia

Short-term insomnia

Insomnia lasting a few weeks tends to be caused by immediate worries, e.g. exams or a recent death in the family.

Long-term insomnia

Lasting more than four weeks (a DSM definition).

Long-term insomnia is divided into primary and secondary insomnia:

Primary insomnia

- Difficulties sleeping that are not directly associated with any other health condition or physical cause (such as drug abuse or medications).

May be due to:

- Bad sleep habits, e.g. drinking coffee in the evening, having naps during the day.
- Expectations of sleeping problems because of previous cause, e.g. depression. The original problem has disappeared but there is still an expectation of sleep problems, which acts as a self-fulfilling prophecy leading to continuing sleep problems.

Secondary insomnia

Sleep difficulty is a symptom of of something else, i.e. insomnia is secondary to this other conditions, such as:

- Medical, e.g. heart disease, circadian rhythm disorder (leads to sleep at inappropriate time), rheumatism (makes it more difficult to sleep) or parasomnias such as sleep walking (disrupt sleep).
- Psychiatric, e.g. depression.
- Environmental, e.g. too much coffee, shift work.

IDA *Real-world application…*

The distinction between primary and secondary insomnia is important when deciding on treatment, because either you should treat the insomnia (if it is primary insomnia) or you should treat the underlying cause (in the case of secondary insomnia).

For example, in the case of insomnia arising from depression it might be unhelpful to treat only the insomnia.

However…

It is not always clear whether insomnia is simply a symptom of the main cause (i.e. secondary) or in fact primary. A survey of 15,000 Europeans found that insomnia often preceded depression, i.e. was primary. This suggests that insomnia *should* be treated (Ohayon and Roth).

Insomnia is studied because it has important consequences…

- Cognitive impairment – Zammit *et al.* found that patients experienced problems with concentration, memory and problem solving.
- Accidents – The National Traffic Safety Administration estimates that 1500 deaths annually are related to sleepiness/fatigue (Zammit *et al.*). The effects of tiredness have also been linked to industrial accidents as a result of shift work (see page 10).
- Psychological disturbance – Breslau *et al.* found that insomnia was also associated with increased risks for drug and alcohol abuse.
- Immune system underfunctioning – Savard *et al.* found *fewer* immune cells in the bodies of people with chronic insomnia compared with good sleepers. This would make insomniacs more vulnerable to physical illness, (although stress may be an intervening variable, causing both insomnia and immune system underfunctioning).

IDA *Nature and nurture – genetics and environment…*

Spielman and Glovinksy distinguished between risk factors that predispose, precipitate or perpetuate insomnia.

- Genetic factors (nature) predispose an individual to insomnia.
- Environmental stressors (nurture) trigger or precipitate primary insomnia (the diathesis-stress model of vulnerability + stress).
- Perpetuating factors include expectations of having difficulty sleeping, leading to a self-fulfilling prophecy.

There is evidence supporting teenage insomnia as a major problem…

A survey of 4000 11–17-year-olds showed that 25% experienced insomnia and 5% said it interfered with their ability to function (Roberts *et al.*). A year later 41% reported continuing problems with insomnia.

Research complications…

The large number of factors that may contribute to a person's insomnia makes it very difficult to conduct meaningful research – having so many factors leads to only small overall effects. This means that research is unlikely to uncover clear solutions to the problem, though one possibility is described below.

IDA *Real-world application…*
The cognitive approach…

Attribution theory is an example of the cognitive approach in psychology. It concerns the way we think about the causes of our own (and other people's) behaviour. In the case of insomnia, if a person believes they cannot sleep because of insomnia this produces self-fulfilling expectations i.e. they don't sleep as a result.

Attribution therapy suggests that an individual needs to think differently about the causes of their behaviour i.e. learn to make a different attribution about why they are not sleeping.

Storms and Nisbett tried this with insomniacs. They gave the insomniacs a pill and told them it would either stimulate them or make them sleepy. Those insomniacs who expected the pill to stimulate them went to sleep faster because they attributed their usual bedtime arousal to the pill and therefore relaxed more.

Explanations for narcolepsy

Psychological explanations

Lehrman and Weiss (1943) suggested that sudden attacks of sleepiness disguise sexual fantasies.

Little research support...

Psychological explanations have had little support and are now not generally included when considering the causes of narcolepsy.

Biological explanations: Malfunction of REM system

Makes sense because classic symptoms of narcolepsy match REM sleep characteristics, for example:

- Paralysis (lack of muscle tone).
- Intrusion of REM-type sleep (hallucinations) into daytime.

Therefore narcolepsy may be related to malfunction in system that regulates REM.

There is some research support for the malfunction of REM...

Vogel observed sleep patterns during narcoleptic episodes in one patient, and found (as predicted) that REM patterns were present at the beginning of each episode.

Siegel recorded activity in brainstem of narcoleptic dog, and found the same activity during cataplexy as found in REM sleep.

However...

Generally there is little research support for the REM malfunction explanation.

Variant of HLA

HLA (human leukocyte antigen) is part of the body's immune response.

Honda et al. found increased frequency of one type of HLA in narcoleptic patients.

More than 90% of people suffering from narcolepsy with cataplexy have been found to have the HLA variant HLA-DQB1*0602 (Stanford Medical Center).

Linking HLA to hypocretin...

Some variants of HLA increase the likelihood of autoimmune conditions. This may result in reduced numbers of hypocretin cells in the hypothalamus, and so lead to narcolepsy (Mignot).

There is research support for the role of hypocretins...

Lin et al. found narcoleptic dogs had a mutation in a gene on chromosome 12, which affects hypocretin production.

Findings from dogs confirmed in humans, e.g. narcoleptics had lower levels of hypocretin in their cerebrospinal fluid (Nishino et al.).

However...

Mutation in hypocretin (orexin)

The neurotransmitter hypocretin plays a role in keeping people awake.

Hypocretin is produced by cells in the hypothalamus. In narcoleptics a large number of these hypocretin cells are missing, resulting in low levels of hypocretin. .

Hypocretin loss in humans is not linked to inherited factors because narcolepsy doesn't run in families and not concurrent in MZ twins (Mignot).

Low levels of hypocretin likely to be due to brain injury, diet, stress or auto-immune attack (body's immune system turns on itself).

IDA Real-world application...

The role of hypocretins may lead to a treatment for narcolepsy, although it would need to be an artificial drug as the hypocretin molecule is unstable (is broken down before it reaches the brain).

Alternatively it may be possible to transplant normal hypocretin cells.

Explanations for sleep walking

Due to incomplete arousal

Sleep walking is a disorder of arousal, the sleep walker is asleep but engaged in tasks normally associated with being awake.

EEG recordings during sleep walking show delta waves (typical of SWS) plus beta waves (typical of awake state).

Person in SWS is awakened but arousal is incomplete.

IDA Nature and nurture – genetics and environment...

The evidence for a genetic basis for sleep walking:

- Prevalence of sleep walking in first degree relatives is ten times greater than in the general population (Broughton).
- There is 50% concordance for sleep walking in MZ twins compared with only 15% in DZ twins (Lecendreux et al.).
- Gene identified for sleep walking (DQB1*05) (Lecendreux et al.).

Risk factors

Sleep walking increased by sleep deprivation, having a fever, stress, alcohol and psychiatric conditions (Piazzi et al.).

Hormonal changes in puberty and menstruation may also be triggers but possibly only for genetically vulnerable individuals.

The environmental component acts as a 'stressor' as in the diathesis-stress model, for example:

- Sleep deprivation led to an increase in sleep walking in vulnerable individuals (i.e. those who had past experiences of sleep walking) (Zadre et al.). Levels of sleep walking rose from 50% to 90% after 25 hours' sleep deprivation.
- Children have higher levels of SWS which acts as a diathesis.

Why children?

Possibly because children have more SWS or because the system that usually inhibits motor activity in SWS isn't fully developed in children (and may be underdeveloped in some adults) (Oliviero).

One study did find that adult sleep walkers showed signs of immaturity in the relevant neural circuits.

IDA Real-world application...

Sleep walking is occasionally used as grounds for a defence in murder trials. In on case (Jules Lowe in 2003) expert testimony gave evidence that the defendant was prone to sleep walking as a consequence of insane automatism, a psychiatric condition.

Perception

Division A Theories of perceptual organisation
Gregory's top-down/indirect theory of perception
Gibson's bottom-up/direct theory of perception

Division B Development of perception
Perceptual development: Infant studies
Perceptual development: Cross-cultural studies

Division C Face recognition
Bruce and Young's theory of face recognition
An example of visual agnosia: Prosopagnosia

Specification

Perception	
Theories of perceptual organisation	• Gregory's top-down/indirect theory of perception. • Gibson's bottom-up/direct theory of perception
Development of perception	• The development of perceptual abilities, including depth/distance, visual constancies. • Perceptual development, including infant and cross-cultural research.
Face recognition and visual agnosias	• Bruce and Young's theory of face recognition, including case studies and explanations of prosopagnosia.

Chapter 2

Theories of perceptual organisation >

Development of perception

Perception > Face recognition

Gregory's top-down/indirect theory of perception

Gibson's bottom-up/direct theory of perception

Gregory's top-down/indirect theory of perception

Perception as hypothesis formation

A top-down process

According to this view, perception relies on stored knowledge to make sense of the physical information received by the senses.

This is necessary because the physical information is often inadequate.

Perception is based on an interaction between:

• knowledge stored in the brain
• sensory data.

A hypothesis or inference is developed based on previous knowledge and then tested against reality.

There is research support for this...

Hypotheses, once formed, are tested against reality. For example, Khorasani et al. found that the Müller-Lyer illusion had less effect once participants were told about the illusion.

However...

This is not true for all visual illusions, e.g. Necker cube reversals continue even after reality-testing (Shopland and Gregory).

This suggests that hypothesis testing may sometimes, but not always, contribute to the final perception.

Role of previous knowledge and expectation

Internal expectations are based on past experience

For example, people who are shown false playing cards (black hearts or red spades) 'see' brown or purple because expectations distort perception (Bruner et al.).

Expectations generally produce accurate perception

For example, a table viewed from any angle still looks rectangular (because of our expectations) even though the retinal image is rarely that shape.

There is research support for this...

Participants were shown a contextual scene, e.g. a kitchen. In this context participants often mistakenly identified a potentially ambiguous object such as a mailbox as a loaf of bread (Palmer). The kitchen context led to an erroneous hypothesis, which affected what was seen.

The digits 1 and 3 are perceived as the letter B when viewed in the context of a set of letters but as the number 13 in a set of numbers (Bruner and Minturn).

IDA Real-world application...

The effect of expectations can explain real-world events such as the error made by the US Navy in mistaking an Iranian passenger jet for an enemy aircraft about to attack and shooting it down with a missile, resulting in the death of 260 people.

Visual illusions

'Misapplied' hypotheses lead to errors of perception, e.g. visual illusions.

These are not accidental mistakes of perception but, rather, are 'lawful' and illustrate normal perceptual processes.

Examples

• Converging lines are used in two-dimensional (2D) paintings to suggest perspective.
• Necker cube – the red dot appears at front or back depending on which hypothesis about the shape is accepted.
• Müller-Lyer illusion – arrow with outward fins looks longer because equivalent to corner of a room, and thus looks farther away. The arrow with inward fins is equivalent to nearer corner of a building.

There is research support for Gregory's explanation of the Müller-Lyer illusion...

People who don't live in carpentered environments (e.g. live in round huts) are less likely to perceive the illusion, which might be because they are not used to seeing corners of rooms or edges of buildings.

Strengths of the top-down approach...

Can explain how the perceptual system copes with ambiguous situations and/or incomplete data.

Can help in the design of computer systems to 'see' the world, such systems are programmed to draw on experience.

Limitations of the top-down approach...

May not explain much of real-world perception because it is based on situations with ambiguous/incomplete data.

Can't explain why visual illusions persist even when you know the reality; reality testing should lead to the formation of new hypotheses.

Some concepts of the theory are imprecise, e.g. hypothesis testing doesn't explain what information is selected from the retinal image (Marr).

IDA The bottom-up approach

Gregory's top-down approach can be contrasted with Gibson's bottom-up/direct theory, which suggests that physical data are sufficient to explain perception.

See also 'Reconciling Gibson and Gregory' on the next page.

Gibson's bottom-up/direct theory of perception

The optic array

A bottom-up process
According to this view, the pattern of light received at the senses (the optic array) provides sufficient information for perception.

Perception is simply the detection of information.

Optic flow
As we move forward, objects straight in front remain stationary, whereas objects to the side flow past; the further away, the faster the flow.

The importance of movement
Perceptual information is received as the observer moves around the environment.

Ecological aspects of perception
Perception can only be understood by observing how it operates in the environment (i.e. ecological).

For example, depth/distance is indicated by texture gradient (objects further away have a finer texture).

Such information can be picked up directly.

The role of invariants in perception
Some aspects of the environment don't change as we move about (i.e. are invariant).

Examples of such invariants:
- Texture gradient, for example stones on a beach are larger and more spaced apart if they are nearby whereas they are smaller and more closely together when distant.
- Horizon-ratio relation – the proportion of an object above and below the horizon line is constant for objects of the same size standing on the same ground.

Using the optic array

Resonance
Animals 'pick up' perceptual information from the environment in the same way that a radio picks up radio waves.

Picking up information = resonance.

Affordance
The meaning of an object is directly perceived and tells you how the object can be used, i.e. its action potential.

For example, a handle looks like something to be grasped, i.e. it 'affords grasping'.

The concept of affordance links perception and movement, as objects afford potential for action.

The usefulness of perception
Perception is not simply the detection of information, but the detection of useful information. It enables an animal to respond to its environment in an adaptive way.

Biological motion demonstrates direct perception...
(Perception of movement directly from a changing array of dots.)

Johansson placed small lights on a moving body, and found that observers 'saw' movement from changing array of lights.

Even young babies (Fox and McDaniel) and animals (Blake) respond appropriately when shown changing dots, which suggests this is an innate ability.

Time-to-contact demonstrates direct perception...
(Judging the responses to be made when approaching an object.)

Long-jumpers change stride length as they approach take-off (Lee et al.).

Gannets close their wings at a constant time when they are making a vertical dive into water (Lee).

Both examples support the view that perception is directly perceived from the environment.

Movement can be shown to be important in perception...
Wraga et al. showed that the Müller-Lyer illusion disappeared when participants walked around a three-dimensional (3D) version.

Visual illusions can demonstrate direct perception...
Gregory's indirect approach explains visual illusions as an example of a misapplied hypothesis, but the direct theory can also explain them.

For example, the Ames room illusion has been explained in terms of top-down processing (expectations about rectangular rooms), but could also be explained in terms of horizon-ratio relation because the illusion persists even without walls and floor.

IDA Nature and nurture...
Gregory's theory suggests that perception can be explained in terms of experience (nurture), whereas Gibson's theory is related to innate mechanisms (nature). Research on pages 19–20 can be used to support these two positions.

IDA Real-world application...
Principles of direct perception have been successfully applied in designing autonomous robots that learn about the meaning of objects in their environment (Şahin).

Strengths of the bottom-up approach...
This approach highlights the richness of data in the optic array.

Examples described show that direct theory can explain some aspects of perception.

Limitations of the bottom-up approach...
Cannot explain research related to the role of previous knowledge and expectation (see previous page).

Best for explaining the evolution of perceptual abilities in a species but not the development of perceptual abilities in an individual, e.g. an African bushman can only learn the affordance of a red pillar box through personal experience.

IDA The top-down approach...
Gibson's direct theory can be contrasted with Gregory's top-down approach, which suggests that physical data are not sufficient to explain perception.

Reconciling Gibson and Gregory...
Bottom-up processes function in good visual conditions (e.g. daylight), whereas top-down processes function in ambiguous visual conditions.

Ventral stream of visual processing deals with object recognition (top-down) whereas dorsal stream deals with spatial/movement perception (bottom-up).

Perceptual development: Infant studies

Depth perception

Monocular cues (using one eye)

Dynamic cues (e.g. motion parallax) appear before static cues (e.g. occlusion), i.e. cues from movement versus cues from a static position. For example:

- Gibson and Walk found motion parallax was the most likely cue in the visual cliff studies. Infants (with a patch over one eye) refused to crawl over the side of the display, which looked deeper (in reality covered with glass).
- Hofsten et al. showed that three-month-old infants used motion parallax. They assessed perception using the habituation method – infants habituated to (got used to) three rods while being moved about, and later showed more interest in three equidistant rods (matching the effect of motion parallax).
- Granrud and Yonas found a response to occlusion around the age of 6 months.

Binocular cues (using both eyes)

Bower et al. tested retinal disparity by presenting different information to each eye so a 3D image appeared. Infants of 1 week responded by trying to grasp the object, showing depth perception.

Age-related changes in the use of perceptual cues.

For example, the use of shadows for depth perception tested by displaying two toys, one apparently closer because of shadows (one eye covered to remove binocular cues). Older infants (30 weeks old) responded, whereas younger infants (21 weeks old) didn't (Yonas et al.).

Visual constancy

Shape constancy (shape of object 'looks' the same despite differing retinal images).

Infants aged 2 months conditioned (being rewarded) to prefer a rectangle slanted at 45 degrees, later showed preference for this shape even when the retinal image was different, showing shape constancy (Bower).

Size constancy (an object, such as an apple, looks the same size despite different retinal images due to distance).

Infants habituated to certain cubes. When shown two cubes that had the same retinal size but one was more distant, they still responded to the new one, thus showing size constancy (Slater et al.).

Pattern perception

Newborn infants showed a preference for face-like patterns (Fantz).

They also showed a preference for complex patterns once their visual acuity (focus) has matured (Brennan et al.).

Criticisms have been made of the visual cliff studies...

The infants tested were 6 months old and had plenty of sensorimotor experience and therefore depth perception may be learned, not innate.

However...

Campos et al. tested 2-month-old infants by measuring their heart rates; the infants showed fear (raised heart rate) when wheeled over the (apparent) deep side of the visual cliff.

Further support...

The young animals tested (e.g. day old chicks and young goats) avoided the deep side suggesting depth perception is innate.

This research suggests many aspects of perception are innate...

The fact that many perceptual abilities are apparent at birth (or once the visual system has matured sufficiently) supports perception as an innate, bottom-up process (the nature position).

However, this is not true for all perceptual processes...

- Perceptual completion (bridging gaps in retinal image, e.g. Kanizsa triangle) is not displayed in 2-month-old infants (Ghim).
- Occlusion (part of object hidden) – at about 3 months infants treat the objects as if they were separate (Slater et al.).

This shows that... Some aspects of perception require knowledge about object properties (e.g. perceptual completion), as top-down theorists would argue (the nurture position).

Bottom-up theorists counter-argue...

That seeing the 'hidden' parts in such illusions is part of cognitive development (learning to differentiate between items) rather than part of the perceptual process.

IDA *Nature-nurture debate...*

It may not be nature or nurture, but both. Blakemore and Cooper showed that kittens that were deprived of certain visual experiences (no exposure to either vertical or horizontal lines) subsequently appeared blind to lines whose orientation matched the ones to which they had not previously been exposed. Further research found that the brain cells used to detect relevant line orientation had actually disappeared (Hubel and Wiesel).

This research demonstrates that innate visual mechanisms in the brain are shaped by experience – nature and nurture.

IDA *Problems with studying nature and nurture in infants...*

It is not always easy to decide what counts as an innate process (nature). A process is present at birth is not always innate – an infant has experiences in the womb and may learn to coordinate some sensorimotor processes.

Equally, just because an ability appears later in development it doesn't necessarily mean it is due to learning (nurture), because some innate abilities only appear when the nervous system is sufficiently mature.

There are methodological problems studying infants...

The conclusions from infant studies presume that we are actually testing infant abilities, whereas all of the techniques used rely on assumptions, e.g. assuming that an infant will express surprise at a novel object (the basis of the habituation method).

Infants might simply respond to subtle cues from the researcher (investigator bias), or might be sleepy and that's why they fail to show interest rather than because they were habituated.

Infants also have very poor visual acuity (the ability to focus). This means they may not be really seeing very much, or might mean they are actually more capable than they appear to be.

IDA *Real world application...*

Visual deprivation in children can result in permanent damage unless corrected early enough. Banks et al. found that children born with squint eyesight do not develop binocular vision and depth perception is impaired. If corrective surgery is performed before the age of four, the cells of the visual cortex are still available to develop binocular vision.

Perceptual development: Cross-cultural studies

Depth perception

Forest dwellers

Kenge, a Bambuti pygmy (forest dweller), interpreted distant buffalo as being insects. This shows lack of experience with depth cues (Turnbull).

The use of pictorial cues

Hudson tested children in South Africa using pictures that looked 3D because of the use of depth cues such as occlusion, linear perspective and object size.

European children, by the end of primary school, could use depth cues (e.g. could correctly identify which animal was nearer) but the Bantu children couldn't interpret the pictorial depth cues.

Jahoda and McGurk tested depth perception using cues such as texture gradient, linear perspective and size. Participants had to arrange a 3D model to represent the position of two girls in the picture. They found (1) the more depth cues available, the better participants performed, (2) the older the children the better they did, (3) Scottish children did better than Ghanaian children but all children showed some ability to interpret depth cues.

Visual constancies

Shape constancy

Zulus who live in rural areas without windows could not 'see' the *trapezoid window illusion* (window appears to swing back and forth instead of around because it is shaped like a trapezium). Urban Zulus could see the illusion, indicating that experience leads to shape constancy (Allport and Pettigrew).

Size constancy

Zulus were found to be less susceptible to the Müller-Lyer illusion (Segall *et al.*). This may be because they lived in circular huts (not a carpentered environment) – Gregory suggested that the illusion may be due to experience with edges of rooms and buildings, and Zulus would lack this.

IDA *Conclusions from classic cross-cultural studies support the nurture approach…*

The studies described on the left are from the 1960s (with the exception of Jahoda and McGurk). These studies suggest that many perceptual abilities are due to experience because people from different cultural groups, who each have different experiences, appear to have different perceptual capabilities. In this research the IV is cultural/perceptual experience and the DV is perceptual capabilities. This supports the view that perception is a top-down, learned process.

However…

More recent research (post-1970) has found contrary evidence. For example, Page repeated Hudson's research using a different style of questioning (asking 'Which is nearer to you, the antelope or the elephant?', instead of 'Which is nearer to the man, the antelope or the elephant?'). Zulus could cope better than in Hudson's study.

The studies on pictorial depth cues appear to be contradictory…

Hudson found experience did matter, whereas Jahoda and McGurk concluded experience mattered less.

One possible explanation for this is…

Some 2D pictures are more difficult to interpret. Deregowski proposed an important distinction between images:
- Epitomic illustrations provide poor or no information about depth, as in Hudson's pictures (and also e.g. a silhouette).
- Eidolic illustrations look 3D because they use more easily interpreted cues (e.g. texture gradient), as in Jahoda and McGurk's pictures (and also impossible figures, e.g. three-pronged trident).

This explains why there were more 3D responders on Jahoda and McGurk's task.

Another explanation is…

The difference between cultural groups may be because of using culturally relative depth cues rather than innate depth cues.

For example, Europeans use converging parallel lines to represent distance. This is a cultural convention (developed in 15th-century paintings) as opposed to a true reflection of reality – it is true that parallel lines converge but only at infinity and the horizon of our visual field is rarely at infinity (Berry *et al.*).

There are methodological problems with cross-cultural studies…
- Imposed etics – Using tests or procedures developed in one country/culture which may not be valid in the other culture, such as using the trapezoid illusion to test people unaccustomed to 3D pictures which therefore might not make sense to them.
- Representativeness – The group of participants tested may not be representative of that culture.
- Language – Participants and investigators, who rely on translators, may not understand each other.
- Natural experiments – The IV (cultural) is not specifically manipulated and therefore we cannot claim that it causes changes in the DV, we can only conclude that there is an association between experience and ability.

IDA *An alternative, biological perspective…*

These studies are all conducted assuming that the physical process of perception is the same in all people. However, the pigmentation of the retina has been found to vary with skin colour and is linked to difficulties in perceiving edges of objects (*retinal pigmentation hypothesis*). High pigmentation, found in African people, could explain why they are less likely to 'see' certain visual illusions.

IDA *Non-human animal research…*

Using evidence from non-human animal studies raises ethical issues about physical harm. It also raises issues about generalisability because human perception is different, e.g. influenced by cognition.

Bruce and Young's theory of face recognition

A serial model

Each stage or node is accessed one after the other (serially). At any time only some of the units (or nodes) are activated.

Step 1: Structural encoding

The details of a person's face are encoded as specific information about the features and expressions on the person's face.

Step 2: Route A – Familiar faces

- *FRUs (face recognition units)* – information about familiar faces, activated if there is a match.
- *PIN (person identity node)* – information about a person's identity, e.g. occupation, their interests, etc.
- *NRU (name recognition unit)* – person's name retrieved.

Names can only be accessed once the person has been identified; there is no direct link from face to name. Consistent with the fact that people rarely remember a name without knowing any personal identity information, whereas the opposite is common.

Activation of any of these three nodes may draw on the *cognitive system* to decide whether the match is close enough to constitute recognition or merely a 'resemblance'.

Step 2: Route B – Facial expressions

- *Expression analysis* – work out the meaning of facial expressions.
- *Facial speech analysis*, e.g. use lip movements to understand what someone is saying.
- *Directed visual processing* – processing other facial information.

This route is used when dealing with unfamiliar faces, which accounts for the finding that some people with brain damage can match familiar faces but not unfamiliar faces (Malone *et al.*).

Step 3: The cognitive system

All of the units/nodes are linked to the cognitive system, which provides information as required.

This might be information about stereotypes (e.g. actresses tend to be attractive) or information about the people we know (e.g. who you are likely to see in your local shopping centre).

There is research evidence to support the model…

Participants kept a diary for 8 weeks of their mistakes when recognising people. They could often recall information about a person but not their name, and not vice versa, supporting the serial nature of the model (Young *et al.*).

In another study Young *et al.* found participants were faster at identifying whether a particular face was that of a politician than identifying the politician's name.

Research on prosopagnosiacs shows that they can decode emotional expressions, despite being unable to recognise faces. Deficits of emotional understanding are located in a different region of the brain (the amygdala) than object recognition (Groome).

However, not all research has not confirmed the model's predictions…

For example, Stanhope and Cohen found that participants could retrieve names for faces, despite having no information about personal identity (PIN).

Strengths of the theory…

The theory generates precise predictions that can be tested, which can further our knowledge of face recognition.

The theory makes clear distinction between the way familiar and unfamiliar faces are processed.

Limitations of the theory…

The details of unfamiliar face processing are vague.

Other components of the model, such as the cognitive system, are also not clearly specified.

An updated model…

Burton and Bruce produced a connectionist model (*IAC model*). This model proposes that face recognition involves a large number of nodes (FRUs, PINs, etc.) with complex connections rather than serial links.

This matches the behaviour of the nervous system – lots of interconnected neurons, which fire when activated by sufficient incoming links.

IDA Real-world applications…

Assisting police in recognising unfamiliar faces (Identikit pictures).

Designing machines that will recognise faces for security, e.g. facial *cognitive biometric systems* (measure biological characteristics and match them against a database).

Are faces special?…

If face recognition is nothing more than object recognition, there is no need for a special model.

Face recognition is special…

- Studies have shown that infants have an innate preference for face-like stimuli, not just complex patterns (Fantz, Goren *et al.*).
- It makes adaptive sense to have a dedicated face processor because faces are important, e.g. recognising an enemy or decoding emotional expressions.
- The *fusiform face area* (FFA) is active when processing faces and not as active when identifying other objects (Kanwisher and Yovel).

Face recognition isn't special…

- Research on prosopagnosia suggests that face recognition isn't unique, i.e. is not different to object recognition generally.
- Some research has shown that the FFA is also active when recognising other objects, e.g. bird experts identifying birds or when trained to recognise *Greebles* (computer-generated novel objects) (Gauthier *et al.*).
- Face processing may simply be a form of expert object recognition.

Chapter 2

Theories of perceptual organisation
Development of perception
Bruce and Young's theory of face recognition

Perception > Face recognition > Visual agnosia: Prosopagnosia

An example of visual agnosia: Prosopagnosia

Case studies of prosopagnosia

Inability to recognise faces
PS – 52-year-old woman with damage to the lateral part of both occipital and temporal lobes. She could recognise objects but not familiar faces. She could recognise faces using peripheral cues (e.g. haircut or a person's posture) (Busigny et al.).

Inability to recognise faces and objects
NS – 40-year-old man with damage to the occipito-temporal junction area. He could perform some object and face recognition tasks normally, such as identifying an unfamiliar target face from a selection of faces. He did not experience the inversion effect (Delvenne et al.).

Partial face recognition ability
Mr W – A farmer who could recognise his individual cows and dogs but not people. Mr W could answer questions about individual facial features and could match unfamiliar faces to a matching face from a selection). He couldn't match photos of familiar faces and couldn't recognise himself in a video recording (Bruyer et al.).

There are problems with the use of case studies...
Inevitably the study of abnormal behaviour relies on case studies (because such behaviours are rare).
- Each case study involves an individual with unique patterns of brain damage. This makes it difficult to make generalisations about what behavioural deficits might be linked to which areas of the brain.
- Just because an area of the brain (such as the FFA) is associated with an inability to recognise faces, doesn't mean that part of the brain is responsible. It may be that the FFA acts as a relay station.
- Difficult to fully and reliably test any individual to be certain what they can and cannot do. This is due to many things – different methods used by different researchers; brain damaged patients may be slower all round and also may have developed strategies to deal with their deficits, both of which obscures their underlying problem.

Contradictory evidence...
It is difficult to reach firm conclusions from case studies because there are contradictions, e.g. some prosopagnosic farmers cannot recognise their individual cows (Assal et al.) or individual sheep (McNeil and Warrington), whereas the opposite was true for Mr W.

IDA Ethical issues...
The privacy of individuals in case studies is usually protected by using their initials (e.g. HJA), although it is relatively easy to discover a person's true identity.

There are concerns about psychological harm from research participation because patients such as PS are subjected to intensive testing to fully establish what they can or can't do, and this continues for many years.

Explanations of prosopagnosia

Acquired versus developmental
Most cases of prosopagnosia are due to brain damage (acquired prosopagnosia) but sometimes present from birth and are genetic (developmental prosopagnosia).

Duchaine et al. studied 10 prosopagnosic family members who showed normal facial emotional recognition but had some difficulties with object recognition.

Damage to a face processing unit
fMRI scans of PS indicated that damage to the FFA and OFA (fusiform face area and occipital face area located in the temporal and occipital lobes) in the right hemisphere underlies prosopagnosia (Rossion et al.). PS only had face recognition problems which suggests that face and object recognition have different causes.

Holistic processing failure
Farah suggested a continuum:
- At one end: the ability to decode structure (feature analysis, a configural process).
- At the other end: the ability to compute relationships among the parts (a holistic process).
Prosopagnosia results from problems with the latter, alexia is an example of problems with the former, difficulties with object recognition lie across both.

There is support for a unique face processor...
Research with developmental prosopagnosics (Garrido et al.) found a weaker response in their FFA when shown faces.

Duchaine et al. found that one developmental prosopagnosic (Edward) performed normally on a Greeble training task, indicating that face recognition differs from object recognition.

However...
Most prosopagnosics have difficulty with both face and object recognition. Humphreys and Riddoch argue that faces are simply complex objects and therefore require more skills for recognition. We would expect that patients with minimal object recognition wouldn't have prosopagnosia as well, which is generally what has been found.

Holistic processing failure is supported by research...
The fact that many prosopagnosics are not susceptible to the inversion effect suggests that they are not using holistic processing (Busigny and Rossion).

However...
HJA showed some evidence of holistic abilities (Groome), yet face inversion did not affect his performance (Boutsen and Humphreys).

PS had intact global processing on the Navon task (assesses global versus local processing) (Busigny and Rossion), suggesting that prosopagnosia is not due to a failure of holistic processing.

Links to Bruce and Young model...
Edward could describe a face but not remember information about a face; problem was with face recognition units (FRUs).

CB could say whether a person was familiar but not provide any information about them or name them; damage to PIN and NRU.

IDA Real-world application...
Insights from research can offer help to people with agnosias, if only to help them realise that their problems are not imaginary.

Relationships

Division A   Romantic relationships
The formation of romantic relationships
The maintenance of romantic relationships
The breakdown of relationships

Division B   Human reproductive behaviour
Sexual selection
Sex differences in parental investment

Division C   Effects of early experience and culture
The influence of childhood on adult relationships
The influence of culture on romantic relationships

Specification

Relationships	
The formation, maintenance and breakdown of romantic relationships	• Theories of the formation, maintenance and breakdown of romantic relationships: for example, reward/need satisfaction, social exchange theory.
Evolutionary explanations of human reproductive behaviour	• The relationship between sexual selection and human reproductive behaviour. • Sex differences in parental investment.
Effects of early experience and culture on adult relationships	• The influence of childhood on adult relationships. • The influence of culture on romantic relationships.

Chapter 3

Relationships >	Romantic relationships	>	The formation of romantic relationships
	Human reproductive behaviour		The maintenance of romantic relationships
	Effects of early experience and culture		The breakdown of relationships

The formation of romantic relationships

Reward/need satisfaction theory

We are attracted to people who provide us with direct reinforcement

Rewarding stimuli lead to positive feelings and punishing stimuli lead to negative feelings (operant conditioning).

Therefore:

• We enter into some relationships because that person creates positive feelings in us, which makes us feel happy, secure, etc.

• We do not enter into relationships with some individuals because they create negative feelings in us, making us feel unhappy, threatened, etc.

We are also attracted to people who are associated with pleasant events

They *acquire* positive value because of their association with something else that makes us happy (classical conditioning).

A relationship is likely to succeed when the positive feelings outweigh the negative feelings, and is likely to fail when the negative feelings outweigh the positive feelings.

There is research support for this…

An experiment by Griffitt and Guay found that participant rating (for liking) of an experimenter was highest when the experimenter had positively evaluated the participant, producing positive feelings in them.

IDA *This theory is culturally biased…*

This theory does not account for cultural and gender differences in the formation of relationships, suggesting that this is not a universal explanation of the formation of relationships.

• Lott suggests that, in many cultures, women are more focused on the needs of others than on receiving reinforcement.

There is a lack of mundane realism…

Most of the studies in this area have been lab studies, which don't necessarily show the principles of need satisfaction in real life.

However…

Some studies (e.g. Caspi and Herbener) have been conducted on real-life couples and have tended to support the claims of this theory.

There is research support for this…

In the Griffitt and Guay study, onlookers who witnessed the experimenter's evaluation were also more likely to be liked by the participant when the onlooker had witnessed a positive evaluation of the participant than a negative one.

In these conditions, participants gave the same ratings of 'likeability' to both the experimenter and onlooker, supporting the claim that attraction may be influenced through association with a pleasant event, and this makes the formation of a relationship with that person more likely.

Similarity

Similarity (of personality and attitudes) promotes liking

• We first sort potential partners for dissimilarity, avoiding those who are too different.

• From those remaining, we can then choose those who are most similar to ourselves.

• We are therefore more likely to form relationships with people similar to ourselves.

Personality

We are more likely to be attracted to those with similar rather than dissimilar or complementary personality traits.

Married couples with similar personalities are more likely to be happy than those with dissimilar personalities (Caspi and Herbener).

Attitudes

If partners' attitudes toward important issues differ, the process of attitude alignment may occur, as one or both partners modify their attitudes to produce similarity.

There is research support for this…

Lehr and Geher carried out an experiment to test whether attitude similarity would be important in determining whether someone would be liked more. Descriptions of an imaginary stranger had varying degrees of similarity with the participant's own attitudes.

The imaginary stranger was liked more (and seen as more suitable as a potential date) if he or she was similar to the person doing the rating.

IDA *There is an evolutionary explanation for this…*

Aron *et al.* suggest that the brain reward system associated with romantic love evolved to focus courtship energy on specific individuals.

Similarity is important in the formation of relationships because…

• By ruling out dissimilar people, we lessen the chance of being rejected as a partner.

• When people share our attitudes and beliefs, it tends to validate them, which is also rewarding.

But…

Rosenbaum suggests that *dissimilarity* rather than similarity is the more important factor in determining whether relationships will (or won't) form.

There are cultural similarities…

This 'dissimilarity-repulsion' hypothesis has been tested and supported across a number of different cultures including Singapore and the USA. By demonstrating cultural similarities, this suggests that sorting prospective partners initially according to *dissimilarity* is a universal phenomenon.

Chapter 3

Romantic relationships	>	The formation of romantic relationships
Human reproductive behaviour		The maintenance of romantic relationships
Relationships > Effects of early experience and culture		The breakdown of relationships

The maintenance of romantic relationships

Social exchange theory

People exchange resources (e.g. form relationships with others) with the expectation that they will earn a 'profit' – i.e. rewards exceed costs incurred.
- Rewards include: being cared for, companionship and sex.
- Costs include: effort expended developing a relationship, financial investment and time wasted.
- Commitment to a relationship is dependent on its profitability, with less profitable relationships being more vulnerable to termination.

There are limitations...
The main criticism concerns the selfish nature of the theory, i.e. the claim that people are only motivated to maintain relationships out of selfish concerns. It is possible that the principles of social exchange theory apply only in individualist cultures, which are characterised more by individual concerns.

IDA *There is a cultural bias in this theory...*
Moghaddam suggests that social exchange theory would only apply to relationships in Western cultures, and only to short-term relationships among individuals with high mobility (e.g. students).

Long-term relationships within less mobile population groups (e.g. in non-Western cultures) are more likely to value security rather than personal profit.

This suggests that social exchange theory does not represent a universal explanation of the maintenance of relationships, i.e. it is culturally biased.

We develop a comparison level (CL) against which new relationships are judged. It is the product of experiences in previous relationships plus expectations of the current relationship.
- If potential profit from a new relationship exceeds the CL, then it will be judged worthwhile.
- Comparison level for alternatives (CLA) – potential increase in rewards from new partner minus costs of ending current relationship.

There are limitations...
The theory does not explain why people leave relationships despite having no alternative, nor does it suggest how great the disparity in CL has to be for it to become unacceptable.

There is evidence of profit and loss in real-life...
The concept of CLA can be used to explain why some women stay in an abusive relationship. Rusbult and Martz argue that when investments are high (e.g. children, financial security) and alternatives are low (nowhere else to live, no money), this might be considered a profit situation, and so the woman might choose to stay in the relationship.

IDA *Real-world application...*
Importance of positive exchanges highlighted in Integrated Behavioural Couples' Therapy (IBCT) (Jacobsen *et al.*), which helps partners break the negative exchanges that cause problems in their relationships.

Equity theory

People strive to achieve fairness in relationships and feel distressed if they perceive unfairness.
Inequitable relationships exist when a person perceives that they:
- Give a great deal in a relationship and get little in return.
- Receive a great deal and give little in return.
Both are inequitable relationships and would leave them feeling dissatisfied. The greater the inequity the greater the dissatisfaction.

There is research support for this...
Stafford and Canary surveyed 200 married couples concerning equity and relationship satisfaction. They found that:
- Relationship satisfaction was highest for spouses who perceived their relationships to be inequitable.
- Satisfaction was lowest for spouses who perceived themselves to be most under-benefitted in their relationships.

Limitations of this theory...
Clark and Mills argue that a concern for equity may only characterise relationships between colleagues or business associates rather than relationships between friends or lovers (romantic relationships).

They claim that romantic relationships are governed by a desire to respond to the needs of the partner rather than any concerns about equity.

Ratio of inputs and outputs
An equitable relationship is one where one partner's benefits minus their costs equals the other partner's benefits minus their costs.

Perception of inequality in a relationship motivates a person to try to restore it (e.g. by changing perceptions of relative inputs and outputs) or end the relationship.

There are gender differences in the importance of equity...
Steil and Weltman studied married working couples. They found that the women generally rated their husbands' careers as more important than their own.

They concluded that because women tend to seek less for themselves in a relationship, this makes equity a less relevant explanation of relationship satisfaction in real-life relationships.

Because of this, it challenges the universality of equity as a determinant of relationship satisfaction.

Chapter 3

Romantic relationships	>	The formation of romantic relationships
Human reproductive behaviour		The maintenance of romantic relationships
Relationships	>	Effects of early experience and culture	The breakdown of relationships

The breakdown of relationships

Reasons for relationship breakdown (Duck)

Lack of skills

Some people lack the interpersonal skills to make relationships mutually satisfying. These include being poor conversationalists and poor at indicating interest in others. Others then find them unrewarding and the relationship breaks down.

There is research support for this explanation...

Boekhout et al. found that extramarital affairs were typically a direct reaction to a perceived lack of skills and/or stimulation in the existing relationship.

Undergraduates judged sexual boredom and the need for excitement as the main reasons for infidelity among males, and lack of attention and emotional dissatisfaction as the main reasons for infidelity among females.

Lack of stimulation, e.g. boredom

Often quoted when breaking off a relationship. People expect relationships to change and develop; if they do not this is seen as sufficient justification to end the relationship.

Despite this...

Long-distance relationships are increasingly common in our mobile society, and yet Holt and Stone found there was little decrease in relationship satisfaction provided that lovers are able to reunite regularly.

This suggests that people use different management strategies to successfully maintain long-distance relationships.

Maintenance difficulties

Some circumstances (e.g. going away to university or a military tour of duty) make maintenance of relationships difficult to manage because partners do not see each other often enough. This places a strain on relationships, which may be responsible for their breakdown.

IDA Real-world application...

The importance of social skills deficits in relationship breakdown has led to the development of training programmes to enhance relationship skills.

For example, Cina et al. compared couples who had received relationship skill training with those who did not. The 'trained' couples later reported much higher marital satisfaction compared to couples in the control group.

A model of breakdown (Duck and Rollie)

Relationships that are inequitable or where there are reasons for breakdowns as outlined above, are likely to create dissatisfaction in one of the partners. This may lead to:

Breakdown
One partner becomes dissatisfied with the relationship.
Threshold: I can't stand this anymore.

▼

Intrapsychic processes
Person broods on their partner's faults and on relational 'costs'.
Threshold: I'd be justified in withdrawing.

▼

Dyadic processes
Person confronts their partner and begins to discuss their feelings and the future.
Threshold: I mean it.

▼

Social processes
Dissatisfaction spills over to friends and family and so speeds partners toward dissolution.
Threshold: It's now inevitable.

▼

Grave-dressing processes
Partners construct a representation of the failed relationship that avoids putting them in an unfavourable light.
Threshold: Time to get a new life.

▼

Resurrection processes
Each partner prepares themselves for new relationships by redefining themselves and building on past experience.
What I've learned and how things will be different.

There is research support for this explanation...

Tashiro and Frazier surveyed undergraduates who had recently broken up with a romantic partner. They typically reported that they had not only experienced emotional distress, but also personal growth. Breaking up with their partner had given them new insights into themselves and a clearer idea about future partners (i.e. resurrection processes).

This model is important because...

It emphasises the value of communication in relationship breakdown. Paying attention to what people say and the ways in which they talk about their relationship gives a clue as to the stage they are at and therefore appropriate repair strategies that might be employed.

IDA Ethical issues in breakdown research...

Carrying out research in such a sensitive area raises significant ethical issues because participants may experience distress when revisiting the issues that led to the breakdown.

This means the researcher faces the dilemma of pursuing valuable information or terminating a study to prevent the participant experiencing further distress.

Gender differences...

Women are more likely to stress unhappiness and incompatibility as reasons for dissolution of their relationships (Brehm and Kassin).

Women have more desire to stay friends after a relationship has broken up, whereas men want to 'cut their losses' and move on (Akert). Men are more likely to cite 'sexual witholding'.

Sexual selection

Inter- and intrasexual selection

Intrasexual selection

Members of one sex (usually males) compete with other members of their own sex for access to members of the opposite sex (mate *competition*).

Whatever traits lead to success in this competition will be passed on to the next generation.

Intersexual selection

Members of one sex (usually females) show preferences for members of the opposite sex who possess certain characteristics (mate *choice*).

These indicate the chances of the mate being able to give protection and support to offspring which makes them more attractive as a potential mate.

A non-evolutionary explanation…

Some critics reject sexual selection as an explanation for male preferences for younger women. An alternative explanation is based on the need for social power; younger women are easier to control and are therefore preferred as mates.

Kenrick *et al.* rejected the claim that males consistently prefer younger women (a fundamental claim of sexual selection theory), finding that teenage males are most attracted to woman that were actually five years older than them, even though the older women appear to show no interest in them!

Mate-choice in real life…

Many of the studies carried out in this area have been restricted to expressed mate preferences rather than real-life mate choice.

However…

A study of actual marriages (Buss) confirmed that men do indeed choose younger women.

Statistics also show that men who divorce and remarry tend to choose women who are increasingly younger than they are.

Short-term mating preferences

Parental investment theory claims that men evolved a greater desire for casual sex and would ideally seek sex earlier in a relationship.

Female behaviour would not be subjected to the same evolutionary pressures.

In contrast to women, men appear to lower their standards in the context of short-term mating opportunities and show a marked decrease in attraction following sex (Buss).

There is research support for this…

Clarke and Hatfield's study with students on a college campus provides compelling evidence that men have evolved psychological mechanisms to ensure success in short-term mating, including a desire for sexual variety, the tendency to seek sex early in a relationship and a willingness to consent to sex with strangers.

IDA *Gender bias in short-term mating preferences…*

Although parental investment theory predicts that men more than women would have a preference for casual sex, Greiling and Buss suggest that women may also profit from short-term mating as a way of leaving a poor-quality relationship or to produce more genetically diverse offspring.

Long-term mate preferences

Sexual selection should favour high levels of choosiness in *both* sexes.

Poor mate choice is disadvantageous for both sexes who will have wasted valuable resources, but is particularly disastrous for women.

Women have an obligatory biological investment in their children, therefore are predicted to be very particular in their choice of mate. Therefore women are attracted to men who:
- Are able to invest resources in her and any offspring.
- Are able to protect her and any offspring.
- Show promise as a good parent.
- Are sufficiently compatible to ensure minimal costs to her and offspring.

Men are attracted to women who display signals of fertility, an indication of their reproductive value (e.g. youth and physical attractiveness).

There is research support for universal sex differences…

Buss explored mate preferences among men and women in 37 cultures. The main results were:
- Women more than men desired mates who were good financial prospects (i.e. had resources or ambition).
- Men placed more importance on physical attractiveness in a mate, cues to a woman's fertility and reproductive value.
- Men wanted mates who were younger than them, an indication that men value increased fertility in potential mates.
- Both sexes valued intelligence in potential mates (linked to parenting skill), kindness and dependability.

Mate choice varies with the menstrual cycle…

Research (Penton-Voak *et al.*) suggests that female mate choice is not constant and varies across the menstrual cycle. For short-term relationships, women show a preference for masculinised faces (indicative of highly efficient immune system) and for long-term relationships they show a preference for slightly feminised faces (suggesting kindness and cooperation in parental care).

The importance of fertility…

This was demonstrated in a study of lap dancers. Miller *et al.* calculated the tips earned by lap dancers at various stages of their menstrual cycle. Those in the most fertile stage of their cycle (i.e. in oestrus) earned twice the value of tips compared to girls who were not in oestrus.

Chapter 3

Romantic relationships
Human reproductive behaviour   >   Sexual selection
Relationships   >   Effects of early experience and culture   Sex differences in parental investment

Sex differences in parental investment

Maternal investment

Why sex differences?

Males can opt out of parental investment in a way that females cannot. The investment made by females is much greater than that made by males. This may be explained by the greater parental certainty for females.

Why do human females invest more?

Human young are born earlier in development compared to most other species, therefore are relatively immature and dependent on their mothers for much longer. Human mothers make a greater prenatal (through pregnancy) and postnatal contribution (through childcare).

The costs of maternal investment

Compared to males, costs for females are especially high. This results in a difference in the potential maximum reproductive success of the sexes, making random mating all the more costly for human females.

Extra-marital affairs are a consequence of greater female investment...

The expense of childrearing means that females want to ensure good quality offspring. One way to achieve this is to marry a man with good resources, but shop around for good genes through extramarital affairs with attractive men with good genes but no resources. Baker and Bellis estimate that about 14% of the population are products of such extramarital matings.

The benefits and risks of cuckoldry...

The benefits women could obtain by this type of behaviour include receiving additional social support from another male and higher quality genes for their children. The risks of cuckolding a partner include the possibility of abandonment and the use of mate-retention strategies by the current partner (Daly and Wilson).

There is research evidence for sex differences in investment...

Geher et al. exposed male and female undergraduates to various parenting related scenarios. They found clear differences in ANS arousal to those parenting scenarios that emphasised the costs of parenting. Compared to females, males showed significantly increased heart rate when presented with these scenarios. Consistent with predictions from parental investment theory, researchers concluded that males appear biologically less prepared than females to confront issues associated with parenting.

Paternal investment

Males invest less

- The minimum obligatory investment made by human males is considerably less than that of females. A woman can produce only a limited number of offspring, whereas a man can potentially father an unlimited number of offspring.
- Females must carry the developing embryo inside them for nine months, whereas males can walk away after conception.
- Indiscriminate mating, therefore, could cost a woman a great deal in terms of time and resources, whereas indiscriminate mating tends to be much less costly for a man.

Paternal investment and cuckoldry

Males must protect themselves from cuckoldry. Because human males make a considerable investment in their children (through the provision of resources), they are concerned about the fidelity of their mates. They try to ensure that their care is not misdirected towards non-relatives.

Sexual and emotional jealousy

Infidelity posed different adaptive problems for males and females, with males trying to avoid investing in offspring that were not their own. Men are more jealous of the possibility of sexual infidelity (to avoid cuckoldry) while women are more jealous of the possibility of a shift in emotional focus (and the consequent loss of resources).

Investment by grandparents

Consistent with greater paternity uncertainty of males, differences in investment between maternal and paternal grandparents have been found (Michalski and Shackelford). Grandparents appear to invest more in the maternal line than paternal line.

Males do invest...

Joint parental care is desirable because of the obvious benefits of successful reproduction. In any situation where males can increase the success of childrearing, it will pay them to do so. Research (e.g. Reid) supports the claim that human males do contribute to parenting by providing resources (e.g. a stable food supply), and this investment allows the family to live in healthier environments, resulting in a decrease in infant and child mortality.

IDA Insights from non-human species...

We can gain some insight into the origins of human parental behaviour through a comparative analysis of parental investment in closely related species such as chimpanzees and bonobos. In both species, males show little parental investment, suggesting that the emergence of male parenting in humans is likely to be the contribution of cultural learning.

Parental certainty is not always an issue for human males...

Some studies have contradicted the assumption that investment by fathers would always be greater if they know the child is biologically theirs. Anderson found that fathers appeared not to discriminate between stepchildren and their own children in terms of financial investment and time spent with the child.

There is evidence for sex differences in jealousy...

Buss et al. found that male students indicated more concern about sexual infidelity, whereas female students expressed more concern about emotional infidelity. When respondents were asked to imagine scenes of sexual or emotional infidelity – the men showed a much greater physiological response for situations involving sexual rather than emotional infidelity.

However...

Harris found that men tended to respond with greater arousal to any sexual imagery. This challenges the view that sex differences in jealousy are an adaptive response in males and females.

IDA Evolved characteristics...

Rowe suggests that an explanation of paternal investment based on evolutionary factors alone is severely limited. Men's parental behaviour depends on various personal and social conditions, e.g. the quality of the relationship with the mother, personality characteristics of the father, and childhood experiences such as parental divorce (Belsky).

Chapter 3

Romantic relationships
Human reproductive behaviour | Influence of childhood on adult relationships
Relationships | > | Effects of early experience and culture | > | Influence of culture on romantic relationships

Influence of childhood on adult relationships

Parent–child relationships

Attachment, caregiving and sexuality

Shaver *et al.* claimed that romantic love in adulthood is an integration of three behavioural systems acquired in infancy:

- **Attachment** – Later relationships are a continuation of early attachment styles because the behaviour of the infants' primary attachment figure promotes an internal working model of relationships. In extreme cases may lead to an attachment disorder.
- **Caregiving** – Knowledge about how one cares for others, learned by modelling behaviour of primary attachment figure.
- **Sexuality**, e.g. individuals who suffered from an insecure-avoidant attachment are more likely to hold the view that sex without love is pleasurable.

Effects of childhood abuse

Physical abuse in childhood has a number of negative effects on adult psychological functioning. These include increased rates of depression, anger and anxiety (Springer *et al.*).

Sexual abuse in childhood is associated with psychological impairment in adulthood. Many victims have difficulties forming healthy adult relationships.

Individuals who have experienced **both forms of abuse** develop a damaged ability to trust people and a sense of isolation from others (Alpert *et al.*), which inhibit the development of romantic attachments in adulthood. van der Kolk and Fisler found that individuals who suffered childhood abuse were more likely to form disorganised attachments, which led to difficulty in regulating emotions.

There is research support for the importance of attachment style…

Fraley conducted a meta-analysis of studies, finding correlations from .10 to .50 between early attachment type and later relationships. Fraley suggested that one reason for low correlations may be because anxious-ambivalent attachment is more unstable.

However, attachment type may be determined by the current relationship…

This might explain why happily married individuals are securely attached. Significant relationship experiences may alter attachment organisation, e.g. Kirkpatrick and Hazan found that relationship break-ups were associated with a shift from secure to insecure attachment.

Research supports the continuous influence of attachment…

Simpson *et al.* carried out a longitudinal study, spanning more than 25 years, with participants studied in infancy, early childhood, adolescence and adulthood. The findings supported the claim that the expression of emotions in adult romantic relationships can be related back to a person's attachment experiences during earlier social development.

IDA *Studies of non-human animals can overcome the ethical difficulties of deprivation studies with human infants…*

Experiments involving social deprivation are not possible with human children because of the ethical issues involved. However, study of non-human primates has provided compelling evidence of the necessity of peer interaction for adequate adjustment. Suomi and Harlow found that rhesus monkeys reared with inadequate peer contact showed social inadequacies as adults.

Research supports the influence of childhood abuse on adult relationships…

Berenson and Andersen found that abused children have a difficult time developing adult relationships. Adult women who were abused in childhood later displayed negative reactions toward people who reminded them of their abusive parent. This process of transference could lead individuals abused in childhood to use inappropriate behavioural patterns learned from their relationship with an abusive parent in subsequent interpersonal relationships.

IDA *Determinism in the development of adult relationships…*

Research such as the Simpson *et al.* study above appear to indicate that early experiences have a fixed effect on later adult relationships, This is not the case as Simpson *et al.* also found plenty of cases where participants were experiencing happy adult relationships despite not having been securely attached as infants.

Interactions with peers

Childhood friendships

Qualter and Munn – Children develop a sense of their value through interactions with others, which in turn determines how they approach adult relationships.

Nangle *et al.* – Children's friendships are training grounds for adult relationships. Having a friend to confide in promotes feelings of trust, acceptance and a sense of being understood, which are important in later adult relationships.

Adolescent relationships

Romantic relationships in adolescence help to redirect intense interpersonal energy away from parents and towards a romantic partner, and allow adolescents to experience an emotional and physical intimacy that is different from that experienced with parents.

Madsen – some dating in adolescence is advantageous for adult relationship quality, but too much can be maladaptive.

There are gender differences in the nature of peer relationships…

Research has demonstrated gender differences in childhood relationships. Richard and Schneider found that girls have more intimate friendships than boys. Other research (e.g. Erwin) has found that boys' relationships tend to be more competitive, a fact attributed to the greater emphasis on competitive play activities. In contrast, girls are more likely to engage in cooperative and sharing activities.

However…

Erwin claims that sex differences in the experience of childhood relationships have been over-emphasised, and that the many similarities in male and female relationships in childhood tend to be overlooked.

Romantic relationships in adolescence can have negative effects…

Haynie found that romantic involvement increased deviance in adolescents by as much as 35% and Neemann *et al.* found negative effects on academic achievement.

The claim that dating in adolescence can result in poorer quality adult relationships is challenged by…

Roisman *et al.* found no effect of romantic experiences at age 20 on relationships at age 30. There is no consistent evidence that adolescent romantic relationships are the 'building blocks' of adult relationships.

Chapter 3

Romantic relationships
Human reproductive behaviour | Influence of childhood on adult relationships
Relationships | > | Effects of early experience and culture | > | Relationships in other cultures

Relationships in other cultures
Western and non-Western relationships

Voluntary or non-voluntary relationships

Western cultures are predominantly urban, ensuring relatively easy social and geographical mobility, and therefore interaction with a large number of people. This leads to a high degree of choice over who people interact with on a voluntary basis.

Non-Western cultures lack these urban settings, therefore people have less social and geographical mobility, interaction with fewer others on a daily basis, and therefore less choice over who they form relationships with.

Individual or group-based relationships

Attitudes in individualist cultures, where individual interests are more highly regarded than group goals or interests, are consistent with the formation of relationships based on freedom of choice, whereas collectivism leads to relationships that may have more to do with the concerns of family or group.

The importance of love

Levine et al. compared 11 cultures using a questionnaire and found that a higher proportion of respondents from collectivist cultures than individualist cultures were willing to marry in the absence of love. This suggests that love is seen as a comparative luxury in collectivist cultures.

Moore and Leung, in a study of romantic love among Australian students, found differences between Anglo-Australian and Chinese-Australian students in their attitude to romantic relationships, love and loneliness. Attitudes to romantic love were endorsed by both groups.

Cultural differences in loneliness

Seepersad et al. suggest that, compared to young adults in non-Western cultures, young adults in Western cultures would experience a greater degree of loneliness because of their high desire for romantic relationships.

A strong emphasis on the importance of romantic relationships in Western cultures may amplify individual's feelings of loneliness.

Seepersad et al.'s study found that Korean students relied more on family to satisfy their social network needs, whereas US students relied more on friends and significant others.

There is research support for this...

Epstein found that in societies with reduced mobility, non-voluntary (arranged) marriages seem to work well, with low divorce rates and surprisingly high levels of love between the partners.

Myers et al. also found no difference in marital satisfaction between Indian couples in arranged marriages and non-arranged marriages in the USA.

However...

A Chinese study (Xiaohe and Whyte) found that women who had married for love were happier than women who were in arranged marriages.

IDA Evolutionary explanation for universal love...

Pinker claims romantic love is a 'human universal' that evolved to promote survival and reproduction among humans.

Jankowiak and Fischer support this claim with their finding that romantic love existed in 90% of the 166 non-Western cultures they studied.

Voluntary relationships are not necessarily the most successful...

Although we might expect relationships based on love to produce more compatible partners than relationships based on family or financial reasons, this may not necessarily be the case.

For example, parents may be in a better position to judge long-term compatibility than young people who are 'blinded by romantic love' and who ignore areas where they may be incompatible.

Despite this, however, Xiaohe and Whyte's Chinese study found that freedom of choice in relationships appeared to promote marital stability rather than instability, suggesting greater long-term compatibility in non-arranged marriages.

The consequences of increasing urbanisation...

Attitudes toward romantic relationships may be better explained by the greater urbanisation and mobility found in Western cultures rather than Western/non-Western cultural differences. For example, the increase in divorce rates in India is attributed to the thriving middle class rather than within the country as a whole.

IDA Cultural bias in representations of romantic relationships...

The influence of US romantic comedies may create a warped sense of the 'perfect' relationship and present a culturally biased view of romance to young people. Being exposed to highly idealised views of relationships creates the impression that these are 'normal'.

A questionnaire study by Johnson and Holmes found that people who had watched US romantic comedies tended to have views of relationships that reflected the themes portrayed in the films. For example, these films tended to suggest that love and commitment exist from the moment people meet, whereas in real life this is a far more gradual process.

There are methodological problems with research in this area...

Research into cultural differences in relationships may be limited by the research method adopted within a study. If any aspect of the study (e.g. a measure of 'love' or 'satisfaction') is interpreted differently within one culture compared to another, this creates a cultural bias that invalidates any conclusions that might be drawn.

The need for indigenous psychologies...

The methodological problems in cross-cultural research has led some psychologists to suggest the development of indigenous psychologies. This would involve using explanations and research methods designed specifically for that culture rather than the culture of the researcher. This would mean studying aspects of relationships that are meaningful within a particular culture without imposing aspects from other cultures.

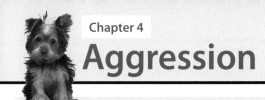

Aggression

Division A   Social psychological approaches to explaining aggression

Social learning theory
Deindividuation
Institutional aggression

Division B   Biological explanations of aggression

Neural and hormonal mechanisms in aggression
Genetic factors in aggression

Division C   Aggression as an adaptive response

Evolutionary explanations of human aggression
Explanations of group display in humans

Specification

Aggression	
Social psychological approaches to explaining aggression	• Social psychological theories of aggression, for example, social learning theory, deindividuation. • Institutional aggression.
Biological explanations of aggression	• Neural and hormonal mechanisms in aggression. • Genetic factors in aggression.
Evolution and human aggression	• Evolutionary explanations of human aggression, including infidelity and aggression. • Evolutionary explanations of group display in humans, for example, sport and warfare.

Chapter 4

Social psychological approaches to aggression	>	Social learning theory
Biological explanations of aggression		Deindividuation
Aggression	>	Aggression as an adaptive response		Institutional aggression

Social learning theory (SLT)

Observation

We learn aggressive behaviour through observation and imitation

People learn the specifics of aggressive behaviour and also its consequences by seeing others being rewarded or punished for their aggressive behaviour (vicarious reinforcement).

By observing the consequences of aggression, they learn when it is and isn't appropriate. For example, Bandura and Walters found that children who observed a model behaving aggressively later showed more aggression in their own play.

IDA Real-world application...

Studies of the effects of social learning are not restricted to lab studies of children. Philips found that murder and assault rates in the USA almost always increased in the week following a major televised boxing match, suggesting that viewers were imitating some of the aggressive behaviour they had observed in the boxing.

Explains cultural differences...

Aggression is rare among the !Kung San people because parents do not reward physical aggression in children (lack of direct reinforcement), nor do they model aggression, therefore there is no motivation for children to act aggressively.

The Bobo doll studies

Bandura et al. found that children who observed an adult behaving aggressively toward a Bobo doll were likely to reproduce those specific modelled behaviours.

This was particularly so if they observed the adult being rewarded for their aggression toward the doll.

The Bobo doll studies lack validity because...

Children in these studies may well have been aware of what was expected of them and responded accordingly (i.e. they responded to demand characteristics). Noble supports this claim with a report that at least one child reported that 'that's the doll we have to hit'.

Also...

The studies have also focused on aggression toward a doll rather than a real person; however, Bandura carried out a study using an adult beating up a live clown. Children who observed this behaviour later did imitate it.

Mental representation

For social learning to take place mental representations are required

The child must also represent possible rewards or punishments for their aggressive behaviour in terms of expectancies of future outcomes.

If opportunities for aggressive behaviour arise in the future, children display the learned behaviour, provided the expectation of reward is greater than the expectation of punishment.

SLT also explains adult aggressive behaviour...

Phillips found that SLT is not only restricted to the learning of aggressive behaviour in children. He found that daily homicide rates in the US almost always increased in the week following a major boxing match, suggesting that viewers were imitating behaviour they had watched.

Context-dependent aggression can be explained by SLT...

People behave differently in different situations because they have observed that aggression is rewarded in some situations and not in others, i.e. they learn behaviours that are appropriate to different contexts. This is a strength of this theory in that it can predict whether aggressive behaviour is likely in any specific situation dependent on previous experiences.

Production of behaviou

Maintenance through direct experience

An individual who is rewarded for their behaviour (e.g. is praised by others) is likely to repeat that action in similar situations in the future.

For example, a child who has a history of successfully bullying other children learns that aggression towards other children is likely to produce rewards.

A strength of social learning theory is...

Unlike operant conditioning theory, SLT can explain aggressive behaviour in the absence of direct reinforcement.

For example, in the Bobo doll studies, although participants behaved more aggressively after observing an aggressive model, at no point were these participants directly reinforced for their aggressive behaviour. The concept of vicarious reinforcement is necessary to explain these findings, i.e. that children have learnt by observing the actions of others, particularly where they see these actions rewarded.

Self-efficacy expectancies

Children must also develop confidence in their ability to successfully carry out the learned aggressive behaviours. Children who have been unsuccessful in their use of aggression in previous situations may develop less self-efficacy concerning their ability to use aggression and turn to other means of resolving conflict.

IDA Ethical issues make it difficult to test SLT experimentally...

Exposing children to aggressive behaviour (either in real life or on film) with the knowledge that they may reproduce it in their own behaviour raises ethical issues concerning protecting participants from psychological harm.

As a result, experimental studies such as the Bobo doll studies would no longer be allowed. This means that it is difficult to test experimental hypotheses about the social learning of aggressive behaviour in children, and consequently difficult to establish the scientific credibility of the theory by this means.

Chapter 4

Social psychological approaches to aggression	>	Social learning theory
Biological explanations of aggression		Deindividuation
Aggression	>	Aggression as an adaptive response		Institutional aggression

Deindividuation

The nature and process of deindividuation

Nature of deindividuation is a psychological state characterised by lowered self-evaluation and decreased concerns about evaluation by others.

This leads to an increase in behaviours that would normally be inhibited by personal or social norms.

The psychological state of deindividuation is aroused when individuals are in:

• crowds or large groups
• situations that increase anonymity
• a state of altered consciousness (e.g. through drugs or alcohol).

Process of deindividuation

People move from an individuated to a deindividuated state when inhibitions concerning aggressive behaviour are removed.

In a large group, the individual loses awareness of their individuality and feels faceless and anonymous.

As a result, inner restraints are reduced and inhibited behaviours (such as aggression) are increased.

Deindividuation does not necessarily lead to aggression...

Johnson and Downing showed that, rather than aggression being an automatic consequence of deindividuation, behaviour was more likely to be the product of local group norms.

They found that participants dressed in an anonymous mask and overalls (looking like Ku Klux Klansmen) delivered more shocks than a control group dressed normally. Participants dressed anonymously in nurses' uniforms delivered fewer shocks than the control group, suggesting that participants felt that aggression was more appropriate when dressed like Ku Klux Klansmen than as nurses.

There is a lack of research support...

Evidence for deindividuation theory is mixed. For example, a meta-analysis of 60 studies of deindividuation (Postmes and Spears) concluded that there was insufficient support for the major claims of deindividuation theory, particularly the claim that aggressive behaviour is more common in large groups and anonymous settings.

There are prosocial consequences of deindividuation...

Rather than engaging in behaviour based on primitive urges, people may be conforming to a local group norm. This need not necessarily be antisocial, and would account for the fact that some studies have found increased *prosocial* behaviour in large crowds.

Spivey and Prentice-Dunn found that deindividuation could lead to either prosocial or antisocial behaviour depending on situational factors. When prosocial cues were present (e.g. a prosocial model), deindividuated participants performed significantly more prosocial acts and significantly fewer antisocial acts compared to a control group.

Research on deindividuation

Anonymity in the lab

Anonymous conditions within a group means people lack awareness of who they are as individuals, which makes deindividuation more likely.

Zimbardo claimed that anonymity was also a cause of diminished concern for self-evaluation, which means individuals can act without regard for societal norms of behaviour.

Anonymity in real-life

Rehm *et al.* investigated whether wearing a uniform while playing sports (deindividuation through greater anonymity) increased aggression in group sports.

Children playing handball while wearing the same colour shirts were consistently more aggressive than children wearing their normal street clothes.

The faceless crowd

Mullen analysed newspaper cuttings of lynchings in the US between 1899 and 1946. He found that the more people there were in the mob (large crowds equal greater deindividuation of individuals within the crowd), the greater the savagery with which they killed their victims.

There is research support for anonymity...

Zimbardo divided undergraduates into two groups:

• One group was in a deindividuated condition (in lab coats and hoods).
• The other group was in an individuated state (wearing normal clothing and wearing a name tag).

Those in the deindividuated state shocked a 'learner' for twice as long as did those in an individuated state.

IDA There is a gender bias...

Aggression as a result of deindividuation may be more of a male characteristic than a female one. Cannavale *et al.* found that male and female groups responded differently under deindividuation conditions. An increase in aggression was obtained only in the all-male groups.

There are cultural differences...

Research by Watson found that tribes that significantly changed their appearance through war paint or body decoration (i.e. became deindividuated) when going to war were far more aggressive (e.g. torturing and mutilating their victims) than those who did not.

IDA Real-world application...

Mann used the concept of deindividuation to explain the behaviour of 'baiting crowds'. Suicide jumpers were encouraged to jump (verbal aggression) when crowds were under conditions of deindividuation (e.g. large crowd, night time, some distance from the potential jumper, etc.).

The concept of deindividuation can also be used to explain the behaviour of lynch mobs. Mullen found that the more people there were in the mob, the greater the savagery with which they killed their victims.

Deindividuation can also be a force for good...

Adolescents reported feeling significantly more comfortable seeking help with mental health problems under the deindividuated circumstances of Internet chatrooms compared to the individuated circumstances of a personal appointment with a health professional (Francis *et al.*).

Chapter 4

Social psychological approaches to aggression	>	Social learning theory
Biological explanations of aggression		Deindividuation
Aggression	>	Aggression as an adaptive response	Institutional aggression

Institutional aggression

Institutional aggression within groups

The importation model

Interpersonal factors – Irwin and Cressey claim that, in prisons, inmates bring with them (i.e. *import*) their own social histories and violent characteristics and this influences their behaviour in prison.

Gang membership – Pre-prison gang membership appears to be an important determinant of prison misconduct. Within prison, gang members disproportionately engage in acts of prison violence (Allender and Marcell).

There is research support for the importation model…

Harer and Steffensmeier, in a study of 58 US prisons, found that patterns of misconduct for particular groups *within* prisons tended to parallel differences observed *outside* prison.

They found that black inmates showed significantly higher rates of violent behaviour within prison and white inmates showed higher rates of drug- and alcohol-related misconduct, reflecting behaviour outside prison.

These differences reflect the statistical differences found in US society generally, thus suggesting that they were *imported* into the prison environment.

Research challenges the importance of pre-prison gang membership…

Evidence from DeLisi *et al.* challenges the claim that pre-prison gang membership predicts violence whilst in prison. Inmates with prior street-gang involvement were no more likely than other inmates to engage in prison violence, although this may be due to the fact that violent gang members tend to be isolated from the general inmate population.

The deprivation model

Situational factors – prisoner aggression or patient aggression (in mental institutions) is a consequence of stressful and oppressive conditions, including overcrowding, physical conditions of heat and noise, and a lack of any meaningful activity. Crowding, for example, is assumed to increase fear and frustration levels, which then leads to aggression.

The 'pains of imprisonment' – Sykes described the specific deprivations within prison which might be linked to an increase in violence, e.g. loss of liberty, loss of autonomy and loss of security. Inmates cope with pains of imprisonment in several ways, including violence against other prisoners or staff.

There is research support for the deprivation model…

McCorkle *et al.* found that overcrowding, lack of privacy and a lack of meaningful activity all significantly increased interpersonal violence in prisons, supporting the view that aggression was a direct consequence of situational factors that deprived prisoners of normal living standards.

The deprivation model is challenged by…

Poole and Regoli – The best indicator of violence among juvenile offenders was pre-institutional violence regardless of any situational factors in the institution.

IDA *Real-world application of the deprivation model…*

Most violence occurs in environments that are hot, noise polluted (e.g. shouting, banging cell doors) and overcrowded. Wilson showed that changes to such deprived environments (e.g. reducing levels of noise, heat and crowding) resulted in a dramatic decrease in violent conduct among inmates at HMP Woodhill.

However…

This application of the deprivation model does not work in all types of institution. Nijman *et al.* found that, in psychiatric institutions, increasing personal space failed to decrease violent behaviour among patients.

Institutional aggression between groups

Genocide

Acts committed with intent to destroy in whole or in part, a national, ethnical, racial or religious group.

Staub claims genocide is more likely if a less powerful group within society is scapegoated for the social problems experienced by others.

Dehumanisation

This can lead to dehumanisation of the target group. Minority group members (e.g. Jews in Nazi Germany) are seen as worthless animals and so not worthy of moral consideration due to fellow humans. This then leads to intergroup violence and mass killings.

Obedience to authority

Milgram believed that the Holocaust was primarily the result of situational pressures that forced Nazi soldiers to obey their leaders regardless of any personal moral objections.

Bystanders are important in preventing genocide…

Staub's model of genocide emphasises the importance of bystander intervention (e.g. by the UN) in preventing genocide. Doing nothing allows the killing to continue unabated, and may even escalate it by signalling apathy or consent.

There is support for this explanation…

There is historical evidence for the power of dehumanisation to influence mass violence against specific groups in society. For example, the actions of Nazis against Jews during the Holocaust, where Nazi propaganda referred to Jews as the 'Jewish disease'.

In the Rwandan genocide in 1994, the minority Tutsi were referred to as 'inyenzi' (cockroaches) by the majority Hutu, and their murder referred to as 'the work'.

Both of these examples of genocide show how killings were made easier by the dehumanising of victims.

IDA *Real-world application…*

Insights into dehumanisation can explain hostility towards foreign refugees and asylum seekers. Esses *et al.* found that people high in social dominance orientation (SDO) have a tendency to dehumanise outgroup members, e.g. foreign refugees and asylum seekers, who they believe deserve our hostility.

Mandel challenges the role of obedience…

Mandel rejects Milgram's claims that obedience to authority was sufficient to explain the behaviour of Nazis toward Jews during the Holocaust. He argues that Milgram's account ignores other and is not supported by real-life events.

Chapter 4

Social psychological approaches to aggression

Biological explanations of aggression >

Neural and hormonal mechanisms in aggression

Aggression >

Aggression as an adaptive response

Genetic factors in aggression

Neural mechanisms in aggression

Serotonin

Low levels of serotonin are associated with aggressive behaviour. Serotonin usually reduces aggression by inhibiting responses to stimuli that might otherwise lead to aggressive behaviour.

Low levels of serotonin have been associated with an increased susceptibility to impulsive and aggressive behaviour.

Drugs that deplete serotonin (e.g. dexfenfluramine) have been shown to increase aggression levels in participants (Mann et al.).

There is research support for the importance of serotonin…

A meta-analysis of studies published before 1992 (Scerbo and Raine) found lower levels of serotonin in individuals described as being aggressive. This supports the claim that serotonin depletion leads to impulsive behaviour, which in turn may lead to aggressive behaviour in various forms.

Evidence from studies using non-human animals…

Evidence for the importance of serotonin comes from studies of animals that have been specially bred for domestication and for increasingly docile temperaments. These animals have shown a corresponding increase, over generations, of levels of serotonin in the brain.

Evidence from the use of antidepressants…

If drugs that deplete serotonin activity lead to raised aggression levels, then drugs that raise it should lead to lower levels. This is what was found in clinical studies of antidepressant drugs, further supporting the link between serotonin and aggression.

Dopamine

Increases in dopamine **levels** have been shown to produce increases in aggressive behaviour.

Demonstrated in studies that used amphetamines (to increase dopamine activity in the brain) and found an associated increase in levels of aggressive behaviour (e.g. Lavine).

Studies that have reduced dopamine levels through the use of antipsychotic drugs have reported a reduction in aggressive behaviour (Buitelaar).

Evidence is inconclusive…

Evidence for the causal role played by dopamine in aggression is inconclusive, but a study by Couppis and Kennedy suggests that it may be a consequence rather than a cause. Some individuals may seek out aggressive encounters because dopamine is released as a positive reinforcer in the brain when they engage in aggressive behaviours.

There is research that challenges this…

A meta-analysis (Scerbo and Raine) examined neurotransmitter levels in antisocial children and adults. They found lower levels of serotonin in individuals described as aggressive, but found no significant rise or fall in dopamine levels for this group compared to 'normal' individuals.

Hormonal mechanisms in aggression

Testosterone

Testosterone is thought to increase aggression in adults due to its action on brain areas involved in controlling aggression.

Studies (e.g. Dabbs) have found that criminals with the highest levels of testosterone tended to have a history of mainly violent crimes, whereas those with the lowest levels had committed mainly non-violent crimes.

The challenge hypothesis proposes that testosterone would only rise above baseline level in response to social challenges (e.g. to status), with a resultant rise in aggressive behaviour.

Evidence is inconsistent for this link…

Although many studies show a link between testosterone and aggressive behaviour, many others do not. Most of the studies that do find a positive correlation between testosterone levels and aggression have used small samples of men within prisons relying on self-reports of aggressive behaviour.

IDA Gender bias…

Most studies of the links between testosterone and aggression have involved male participants, yet research suggests that the link between testosterone and aggression may be even stronger for females (Archer et al.). Studies suggest that successful career women have higher testosterone levels.

Aggression or dominance?…

Mazur claims that aggression is just one form of dominance behaviour. In humans, the influence of testosterone on dominance is likely to be expressed in more varied and subtle ways rather than only through aggressive behaviour.

Cortisol

High levels of cortisol inhibit testosterone levels and so inhibit aggression.

Low levels of cortisol have been reported in habitual violent offenders (Virkkunen) and violent schoolchildren (Tennes and Kreye).

This suggests that, although testosterone may be the main biochemical influence on aggressive behaviour, low cortisol levels increase the likelihood of aggressive behaviour.

There is support for this explanation…

The moderating effect of cortisol on aggressive behaviour is supported by research with boys with aggressive conduct disorder (McBurnett et al.). Boys with consistently low cortisol levels had three times the level of aggressive symptoms compared to boys with high or fluctuating levels of cortisol. This demonstrates that cortisol levels are strongly and inversely related to levels of aggression.

Why does this relationship exist?…

One possible reason is that boys who have low cortisol levels might be less afraid of punishment. As a result, such children may not experience anxiety at the threat of punishment and so do not avoid aggressive situations in the same way as do other children.

Chapter 4

Social psychological approaches to aggression

Neuronal and hormonal mechanisms

Biological explanations of aggression   >   in aggression

Aggression   >   Aggression as an adaptive response

Genetic factors in aggression

Genetic factors in aggression

Twin and adoption studies

Twin studies

MZ twins share all of their genes, while DZ twins share a maximum of 50%. If MZ twins are more alike than DZ twins in terms of their aggressive behaviour, then this suggests a strong genetic influence.

Studies of adult twins suggest that at least 50% of the variance in aggression can be explained in terms of genetic factors.

Adoption studies

If a positive correlation is found between an adopted child's aggressive behaviour and that of a biological parent, this implies a genetic effect.

If the correlation is stronger between the adopted child and their rearing (i.e. adoptive) family, then this suggests environmental influences are stronger.

A study (Miles and Carey) of adopted boys with criminal convictions found that a significant number had biological parents who also had criminal convictions, suggesting a strong genetic influence was at work.

There is research support for this...

A meta-analysis of 24 twin and adoption studies (Miles and Carey) found evidence of a strong genetic influence in the development of aggressive behaviour. In younger individuals, both genetic and environmental influences contributed to aggression, but in older individuals, environmental influences were less important and genetic influences more important in determining aggressive behaviour.

This finding was supported in a later meta-analysis (Rhee and Waldman) of 51 twin and adoption studies. They concluded that aggressive and antisocial behaviour was largely the product of genetic contributions.

However...

In both these studies, several variables moderated (i.e. contributed to the strength of) the genetic influence on aggression. These included the age of the participant and the method used to assess aggression.

This suggests that genetic factors are important in the development of aggression, but other factors determine the expression of aggressive behaviour.

There are problems in assessing aggression...

Most studies have relied on either parental or self-reports of aggressive behaviour. In the Miles and Carey study, those that found a stronger genetic influence on aggressive behaviour had used parental or self-reports, whereas those that had used observational techniques found significantly less genetic influence. This suggests that the method used to assess aggression is a significant influence on the findings of a study.

A gene for aggression?

The role of MAOA

One of the genes responsible for producing MAOA is associated with aggression. MAOA regulates the metabolism of serotonin in the brain, and low levels of serotonin are associated with aggression.

A study of a violent Dutch family found that many of the men had abnormally low levels of MAOA and also had a defective gene for the production of MAOA (Brunner et al.).

Gene–environment interactions

Caspi et al. discovered two variants of the gene for MAOA, one associated with high levels of MAOA and one with low levels. Those with low levels were significantly more likely to display aggressive behaviour, but only if maltreated as children. This suggests that it is the interaction between genes and environment that determines aggression, not genes alone.

There are problems of sampling...

Most studies have focused on individuals convicted of violent crime. There are two problems with this. First, these individuals represent a very small minority of those who regularly engage in aggressive behaviour. Second, a person who is imprisoned for a single violent offence (e.g. murder) is not necessarily a consistently violent individual. This means that the validity of conclusions drawn from these studies may be suspect.

There are difficulties in determining the role of genetic factors...

It is difficult to establish genetic contributions to aggression because:
- More than one gene contributes to a given behaviour.
- As well as genetic factors, there are many other influences on the manifestation of aggressive behaviour (e.g. social learning, environmental factors).
- These factors interact with each other.

IDA The value of animal research...

Studies of rodents (e.g. Young) have the advantage of allowing researchers to eliminate a single gene from an experimental group to see its effect.

Thus researchers can identify a genetic mutation that causes aggressive behaviour in mice. Although a counterpart to this gene exists in humans, its exact function is not yet known.

Genetics and violent crime

Research suggests that inherited temperament or personality characteristics make some people more likely to commit violent crimes. Adoption studies have shown that the highest rates of criminal violence occur when both biological and adoptive parents have a history of violent crime, clear evidence of a genetics/environment interaction.

IDA Real-life applications...

The possibility of a genetic influence in violent crime has led some to suggest using genetic engineering to prevent crime, or even using chemical castration to 'treat' potential violent offenders.

However...

This raises significant ethical concerns about the consequences of labelling someone as a threat to society on the basis of their genetic inheritance, particularly when the evidence for genetic influences in aggressive behaviour is far from conclusive.

Evolutionary explanations of human aggression

Jealousy

Cuckoldry and sexual jealousy

Cuckoldry refers to the reproductive cost that may be inflicted on a man as a result of his partner's infidelity.

The consequence of cuckoldry is that a man may unwittingly invest his resources in offspring that are not his own.

The adaptive functions of sexual jealousy, therefore, would have been to deter a mate from sexual infidelity, thus minimising the risk of cuckoldry.

Mate retention and violence

Males have a number of strategies that have evolved specifically for the purpose of keeping a mate. These include violence or the threat of violence (Buss).

Studies of battered women show that in the majority of cases, women cite jealousy as the key cause of violence toward them (Dobash and Dobash).

Sexual jealousy and extreme violence

Male sexual jealousy is claimed as the most common motivation for killings in domestic disputes in the US and the UK, with men being predominantly the perpetrators and the victims.

A summary of eight studies (Wilson and Daly) of same-sex killings involving 'love triangles' found that 92% were male–male murders and only 8% female–female.

IDA *Gender bias…*

Most studies of infidelity have focused on men's mate retention strategies and male violence against women. However, this view is gender biased because women also practice mate retention strategies and engage in violence against their partner. For example, Felson found that women were twice as likely to murder out of jealousy as were men.

There is research support for the relationship between sexual jealousy and violence…

Shackelford *et al.* found a clear relationship between sexual jealousy, the use of mate retention strategies and violence towards women. Buss and Shackelford found that men who suspected that their wives might be unfaithful over the next year used greater punishment for a known or suspected infidelity than did men who did not expect future infidelities.

IDA *Real-world applications…*

The use of mate retention tactics by males can be an early indicator of violence against the female partner. The findings from these studies suggest that awareness of the use of mate retention strategies by the male partner can be used to alert friends and family members to the danger signs that violence may follow. At this point, help can be sought (or offered) before inter-mate violence ever happens.

There is a physiological basis for jealousy-based aggression…

Takahashi *et al.* found that the neural response to imagined scenes depicting sexual infidelity and emotional jealousy were different for men and women. Men had greater activation in amygdala and hypothalamus when presented with scenes depicting sexual infidelity in their mate.

Research doesn't tell the whole story…

Edlund and Sagarin claim that our understanding of the relationship between sexual jealousy and aggression is limited as it doesn't tell us if the locus of responsibility (i.e. the female partner or the other male) influences the amount of jealousy experienced and therefore the degree of violence.

Infidelity

The detection or suspicion of infidelity is a key predictor of partner violence (Daly *et al.*).

Sexual coercion

A consequence of men's perceptions of infidelity in their partner is sexual coercion or partner rape (Goetz *et al.*).

Sexual assault of a female by her mate is directly linked to the perceived risk of her infidelity (Camilleri). Female victims of partner rape are likely to have engaged in extra-marital sex (Shields and Hanneke).

Violence toward pregnant partners

A man risks lowering his reproductive success if his partner becomes pregnant with another man's child.

The function of violence directed towards an unfaithful female may, therefore, be to terminate the pregnancy to eliminate the potential offspring of a male rival.

Uxoricide (wife-killing)

Men can guard against their partner's infidelity by either conferring benefits or inflicting costs (such as violence).

As not all men possess resources that might be used to provide benefits, some men are especially prone to the use of violence instead.

Daly and Wilson argue that death of the partner as a result of physical violence is an unintended consequence of an adaptation designed for control rather than death.

There is research support for the link between infidelity and partner violence…

Using a survey method, Camilleri found that the risk of a partner's infidelity predicts sexual coercion among males but not among females. This is significant as only males are at risk of cuckoldry. Camilleri and Quinsey also discovered that men convicted of raping their partners were more likely to have experienced cuckoldry risks prior to their offence compared to men convicted on non-sexual partner abuse.

There are problems with surveys…

Many of the studies in this area have made use of surveys, but these have their problems. Answers may not be truthful because of a social desirability bias. This takes the form of over-reporting desirable behaviour and under-reporting undesirable behaviour.

There is evidence of violence toward pregnant partners…

Burch and Gallup found that acts of violence toward pregnant mates was double that toward non-pregnant mates, with sexual jealousy cited as the main reason for this difference.

Taillieu and Brownridge found that women abused while pregnant were more likely to be carrying the child of someone who was not their mate.

Valladares *et al.* found that half the women abused while pregnant had blows directed at their abdomen, presumably designed to increase the probability of aborting the foetus.

There are limitations of evolutionary explanations…

An evolutionary perspective on violence cannot explain why people react in different ways when faced with the same adaptive problem. Buss and Shackelford suggest that although some men may react to infidelity with mate retention strategies or even murder, others will respond less violently or simply get drunk.

Explanations of group display in humans

Sport

Xenophobia

Natural selection favours genes that cause human beings to be altruistic towards members of their own group, yet intolerant towards outsiders. It would be adaptive to exaggerate negative stereotypes of outsiders, as the overperception of threat would be less costly than its underperception.

IDA *Real world application…*

The power of xenophobic group displays to invoke violence has motivated football clubs to take steps to minimise its influence. For example, in December 1992 all the teams in the German Bundesleague played in shirts displaying the slogan, 'My friend is a foreigner'. In Scotland, the Glasgow teams Celtic and Rangers have both introduced initiatives to end xenophobic sectarian displays by their supporters, and so end violence on the terraces.

Xenophobia on the terraces

Podaliri and Balestri analysed the behaviour of Italian football crowds, finding evidence of xenophobic tendencies. Group displays were characterised by racist chants and openly anti-Semitic banners.

There is research support for xenophobia in sports displays…

Foldesi found support for this view in a study of Hungarian football crowds, with violent incidents based on racist or xenophobic attitudes being observed at all stadia. Gypsies, Jews or Russians were the usual targets.

Territoriality threat displays

Non-human animals show threat displays towards outsiders and attack with greater vigour when defending a home territory (Huntingford and Turner). This has its human equivalent in the displays of sports teams prior to a match (e.g. the Samoan rugby team's *manu siva tau* war chant).

Aggressive displays would have been adaptive for our ancestors as they allowed groups to defend valuable resources associated with their territory.

Evidence for the power of territorial displays…

Lewis *et al.* found that, among football fans, crowd support was seen as the most significant factor contributing to a home advantage. Through their displays of support, home fans felt responsible for inspiring their team to victory and distracting opponents.

However…

The precise way in which crowd displays have an effect is not clear. Crowd size may not be as important as the effect has been shown to operate even with small crowd sizes (Pollard and Pollard). Likewise, it is not clear whether the primary function of crowd displays is to 'psych up' the home team or distracting the opposition.

Testosterone and territorial behaviour

Humans display more aggression when they have higher testosterone levels. Neave and Wolfson found higher testosterone levels among footballers when playing at home (an adaptation based on the need to defend home territory).

Does a home advantage really exist?…

A study by Moore and Brylinsky challenges the claim that home crowd displays provide a territorial advantage for sports teams. Two basketball teams forced to play home games without spectators because of a measles epidemic achieved higher points totals without spectators than they did when playing in front of their normal home crowd.

Warfare

The evolutionary explanation argues that aggressive group displays evolved because of the adaptive benefits for the individual and their offspring.

There is research support for the sexual selection explanation…

The claim that aggressive displays increase the sexual attractiveness of male warriors is supported by evidence from Palmer and Tilley, who found that male youth street gang members have more sexual partners than other males.

Leunissen and Van Vugt also found that military men have greater sex appeal, but only if they have been observed showing bravery in combat.

Benefits of aggressive displays

Sexual selection – In traditional societies men compete for mates; those who do well in battle are rewarded with access to females (Divale and Harris). Displays of aggression and bravery are attractive to females, and male warriors tend to have more sexual partners, which suggests reproductive benefit (Chagnon).

Acquisition of status – Displays of aggression and bravery in battle acquire status in the eyes of other group members. As a result, they are more likely to share the benefits associated with status, which in turn would increase their reproductive fitness.

War is not 'in the genes'…

War emerged when early humans shifted from a nomadic existence to a more settled one where they were tied to agriculture or fishing sites, giving them something to defend. It appears, therefore, that warfare emerged as a rational response to a changing lifestyle. Aggressive displays, therefore, are not likely to be a product of evolution, but a response to environment changes such as a rising population level and dwindling food supplies (LeBlanc and Register).

Costly displays signal commitment

Signals of commitment – By engaging in permanent displays (such as scars and mutilations), individual warriors can demonstrate their loyalty to the group and can benefit from the benefits of warfare against another group.

Limitations of an evolutionary explanation of warfare…

Explanations of aggressive displays based on mating success, status or commitment fail to explain the extreme cruelty that is found in many human conflicts yet is absent among non-human species. For example, it is not understood why humans torture or mutilate their opponents, even when they no longer pose a threat.

Minimising the likelihood of defection

In groups where warfare against other groups is relatively common, permanent displays also minimise the ability of males to abscond to another group and increase their commitment to their own group.

IDA *Explanations of aggressive displays are gender biased…*

Evolutionary explanations for aggressive displays in warfare are gender biased because they limited to the behaviour of males rather than females. Women would have considerably less to gain from fighting in near-certain death situations and considerably more to lose (loss of their reproductive capacity).

Eating behaviour

Division A Eating behaviour
Attitudes to food and eating behaviour
Explanations for the success and failure of dieting

Division B Biological explanations of eating behaviour
Neural mechanisms in eating behaviour
Evolutionary explanations of food preference

Division C Eating disorders
Psychological explanations for anorexia nervosa
Biological explanations for anorexia nervosa
Psychological explanations for bulimia nervosa
Biological explanations for bulimia nervosa

Specification

Eating behaviour	
Eating behaviour	• Factors influencing attitudes to food and eating behaviour, for example, cultural influences, mood, health concerns. • Explanations for the success and failure of dieting.
Biological explanations of eating behaviour	• Neural mechanisms involved in controlling eating and satiation. • Evolutionary explanations of food preference.
Eating disorders	• Psychological explanations in relation to either anorexia nervosa or bulimia nervosa or obesity. • Biological explanations, including neural and evolutionary explanations.

Chapter 5

Eating behaviour	>
Biological explanations of eating behaviour	Attitudes to food and eating behaviour
Eating behaviour > Eating disorders	Explanations for the success and failure of dieting

Attitudes to food and eating behaviour

Social learning

Impact of observing others

Parental modelling of attitudes to food affects children's own attitudes. Brown and Ogden found correlations between parents and their children in terms of snack food intake, eating motivation and body dissatisfaction.

There is research support for this…

Meyer and Gast surveyed 12 year olds and found a positive correlation between peer influence and disordered eating. 'Likeability' of peers was the most influential factor.

Birch and Fisher found that the best predictors of daughters' eating behaviours were their mothers' dietary restraint and their perception of the risk of their daughters becoming overweight

Media effects

MacIntyre *et al.* found the media has a major impact on what people eat and their attitudes to certain foods. However, many attitudes (e.g. healthy eating) are limited by personal circumstances (e.g. income and age). Therefore, people learn attitudes from the media, but then place these within the broader context of their lives.

Attitudes are about much more than just learning…

Social learning explanations focus exclusively on how children acquire attitudes towards eating from exposure to models (e.g. in the media).
However… Evolutionary explanations suggest that our preference for fatty and sweet foods is the direct result of an evolved adaptation.

IDA *There is a gender bias…*

Most studies have focused solely on women's attitudes to eating behaviour, yet research has shown that homosexual men are also at risk of developing disordered eating attitudes and behaviour, including body dissatisfaction and higher levels of dieting than heterosexual men.

Cultural influences

Ethnicity

Research suggests that body dissatisfaction and related eating concerns and disorders are more characteristic of white than black or Asian women (Powell and Khan).

Ball and Kenardy studied 14,000 Australian women of various ethnic origins. The longer they had spent in Australia, the more they reported eating attitudes similar to Australian-born women (the acculturation effect).

There is research that challenges this…

Mumford *et al.* found more evidence of body dissatisfaction and eating disorders among Asian schoolchildren than among their white counterparts.
Striegel-Moore *et al.* found more evidence of a 'drive for thinness' among black girls than among white girls.

There are cultural differences…

Rozin *et al.* explored the way food functions in the minds of people in four different cultures. Americans tended to associate food with health, whereas the French associated it with pleasure. Females of all four cultures had attitudes more similar to those of the Americans. Cultural background influences attitude to eating and therefore means the measurement of attitudes in one culture tells us little about attitudes in a different culture.

Social class

Body dissatisfaction and eating concerns are more common among middle and higher class individuals.

Dornbusch *et al.* surveyed 7000 American adolescents and found that higher class individuals had a greater desire to be thin and were more likely to be dieting to achieve this, than were lower class individuals.

There is research that challenges this…

The relationship between social class and attitudes to eating is not as straightforward as suggested by the Dornbusch *et al.* study. In a sample of American students, Story *et al.* found that higher social class was related to greater satisfaction with weight and *lower* rates of weight control behaviour.

There are problems of generalisability…

Some studies in this area are from clinical populations (e.g. people with bulimia nervosa), some sub-clinical (with certain disordered behaviours) and some non-clinical. This makes it difficult to generalise from one group to another and draw valid conclusions about the causal factors in attitudes toward eating.

Mood and eating behaviour

Binge-eating

Individuals with bulimia experience anxiety prior to bingeing. The same relationship between anxiety and binge-eating appears to hold for sub-clinical populations as well.

Wegner *et al.* found that people who binged had low mood before and after binge-eating. Although low mood may make binge-eating more likely, it does not alleviate the low-mood state.

The reinforcing qualities of binge-eating are not clear…

Although a number of studies have shown that low mood tends to precede a binge-eating episode, any reinforcement is fleeting and many studies report a drop in mood immediately after the binge. As a result, it is difficult to see what the reinforcing qualities of a binge-eating episode might be.

However, a recent article by Wedig and Nock identified four types of reinforcement that might explain why individuals engage in binge-eating behaviour. These include social negative reinforcement (to avoid interactions with others or escape their demands) and intrapersonal positive reinforcement (to increase the strength of a desired positive emotion).

Comfort-eating

Garg *et al.* observed food choices of participants as they either watched an upbeat movie or a depressing one. 'Happy' participants chose healthy food, but 'sad' participants went for the short-term pleasure of junk food.

Comfort-eating may not work…

Our attitude towards comfort foods such as chocolate is based largely on the belief that it can lift our mood. However, a study by Parker *et al.* found that chocolate, if used repeatedly, is more likely to prolong a negative mood than to alleviate it. This challenges the view that low mood causes comfort-eating, because comfort-eating may not be that effective in overcoming low mood.

Explanations for the success and failure of dieting

Restraint theory

Disinhibition

Restrained eating has become synonymous with dieting, but Herman and Mack's restraint theory suggests that attempting not to eat may actually increase the probability of overeating. It is the disinhibition (loss of control) of restraint that is the cause of overeating in restrained eaters.

Wardle and Beales randomly assigned obese women to one of three groups for 7 weeks: restrained eating, exercise or non-treatment. Women in the restrained eating group ate more than women in the other two groups.

The boundary model

This model explains the failure of dieting in terms of the greater distance between hunger and satiety in dieters. It takes dieters longer to feel hungry and therefore more food to reach a state of satiety.

In addition, dieters have a self-imposed desired intake. Unlike non-dieters, when they go over this threshold of desired intake, they experience a 'what the hell' effect, and continue to eat until they reach satiety, i.e. beyond the maximum level imposed as part of their diet.

Restraint theory has limited relevance...

Ogden argues that restraint theory may explain the overeating of some groups with disordered eating patterns (e.g. dieters, bulimics and some anorexics).

However...

The behaviour of restricting anorexics (where weight loss is achieved by restricting calories) cannot be explained in this way. If trying not to eat results in overeating, claims Ogden, then how do restricting anorexics manage to starve themselves?

Obesity treatments based on restraint may fail because...

Restraint theory suggests that restraint leads to overeating, yet the treatment of obesity typically recommends restraint as a way of losing weight. As a result, overeating may be a consequence of obesity treatment, leaving many obese individuals depressed, feeling a failure and unable to control their weight.

IDA *There is a cultural bias in obesity research because...*

Some cultural groups appear to find it harder to diet successfully because of a natural inclination to obesity. Asian adults are more prone to obesity than Europeans (Park *et al.*). Asian children and adolescents have a greater central fat mass compared to other ethnic groups (Misra *et al.*)

Psychology as science – the limitations of anecdotal evidence...

Many studies of dieting success or failure rely on personal accounts, and this evidence is then used to justify claims about particular dieting strategies. However, such anecdotal evidence has two problems that properly controlled scientific studies do not have:

• The main limitation is that memory is not 100% accurate.
• Assessment of the success or failure of dieting tends not to be objective.

Both these create problems for the reliability of anecdotal accounts.

The role of denial

The theory of ironic processes of mental control

Attempting to suppress a thought frequently has the opposite effect, making it even more prominent.

Central to any dieting strategy is the decision not to eat certain foods. This results in a state of denial as dieters attempt to suppress thoughts about foods 'forbidden' as part of their diet.

Wegner suggests any attempt to suppress thoughts of forbidden foods only increases the dieter's preoccupation with the very foods they are trying to deny themselves. As soon as food is denied, therefore, it becomes more attractive.

There is research support for this...

Soetens *et al.* found that participants who suppressed thoughts about food also showed a rebound effect, and were more likely to think about food after suppression. This might explain why denial of thoughts about food leads to greater rather than less preoccupation with it.

IDA *Free will or determinism – born to be fat?...*

Some people find dieting ineffective because they have high levels of *lipoprotein lipase* (LPL), which make the body more effective at storing calories. This would challenge the view that restraint or denial alone could be effective as a means of losing or maintaining weight.

There may be gender differences in LPL activity...

Research suggests that sex hormones play a part in LPL activity. For example, oestrogen inhibits LPL activity, which explains why women put on weight after menopause when oestrogen levels are lower.

A consequence of this is that dieting through restraint or denial may be more difficult for post-menopausal women for purely biological reasons.

Detail and dieting

Fending off boredom

Redden claims that people usually like experiences less when they have to repeat them constantly. When it comes to dieting, this makes it harder to stick to a particular regime. However, by focusing on the specific details of each meal, people get bored less easily and are better able to maintain their diet.

IDA *Real-world application...*

This has led to the development of anti-diet programmes aimed at replacing dieting with conventional eating. These emphasise regulation of eating by body hunger and satiety signals rather than the development of inappropriate attitudes to food (e.g. denial or restraint), which have been shown to be ineffective at weight control.

A meta-analysis of the effectiveness of anti-dieting programmes (Higgins and Gray) found that they could improve both eating behaviour and psychological wellbeing, and led to weight stability rather than weight change.

Neural mechanisms in eating behaviour

Homeostasis

Eating → Increase in blood glucose → Ventromedial hypothalamus activated → Satiety → Eating stops → Decrease in blood glucose → Lateral hypothalamus activated → Hunger

Homeostasis involves mechanisms that detect the state of the internal environment and also correct it to restore that environment to its optimal state.

The body has evolved two homeostatic mechanisms to regulate food intake, both dependent on glucose levels.

- Hunger increases as glucose levels decrease.
- A decline in glucose levels activates the lateral hypothalamus (LH) resulting in feelings of hunger.
- This causes the individual to search for and consume food, causing glucose levels to rise again.
- This activates the ventromedial hypothalamus (VMH), leading to feelings of satiation and a cessation of feeding.

There are limitations to a homeostatic explanation…

For a homeostatic hunger mechanism to have been truly adaptive, it must anticipate and prevent energy deficits, rather than just react to them. The claim that feelings of hunger and eating behaviour are only triggered when energy resources fall below their optimal level is inconsistent with the harsh environment in which this mechanism would have developed. A buffer against lack of future food availability would have been necessary in such circumstances.

IDA An evolutionary approach…

Evolutionary theorists offer an alternative explanation. They propose that the primary influence for hunger and eating is not homeostasis, but food's positive-incentive value, i.e. people eat because they develop a taste for foods that promote their survival.

Role of the hypothalamus

Lateral hypothalamus (LH)

Research discovered that damage to the LH in rats causes aphagia (absence of eating). Stimulation of the LH brings about feeding behaviour.

Neuropeptide Y (NPY) is important in turning on eating behaviour. When injected into LH of rats it causes them to immediately start feeding, even when satiated. Repeated injections of NPY cause obesity in just a few days.

There is a problem with this explanation…

Marie et al. genetically manipulated mice so that they did not make NPY, yet found no subsequent decrease in their feeding behaviour.

IDA Real-world application…

Yang et al. found that NPY is also produced by abdominal fat. This leads to a vicious cycle where NPY produced in the brain leads to more eating and the production of more fat cells, which in turn lead to the production of more NPY. By targeting individuals at risk of increased levels of NPY, it should, therefore, be possible to treat obesity.

Ventromedial hypothalamus (VMH)

Damage to VMH causes hyperphagia (overeating) in rats. Stimulation of this area inhibits feeding.

Damage to VMH also causes damage to the paraventricular nucleus (PVN). It is now believed that damage to PVN is what causes hyperphagia.

There is a problem with this explanation…

Gold claimed that lesions to the VMH alone did not produce overeating, but did so only when these lesions included the PVN; however, subsequent research studies failed to support Gold's findings.

As a result, it is now acknowledged that animals with VMH lesions eat substantially more and gain weight rapidly. However, in humans, the PVN has another function, i.e. to detect the specific foods that our body needs, which may account for many food 'cravings'.

Neural control of cognitive factors

Amygdala

The role of amygdala is to select foods on the basis of experience.

Rolls and Rolls surgically removed the amygdala in rats, which then consumed novel and familiar foods indiscriminately, whereas rats with an intact amygdala avoided novel (i.e. unfamiliar) foods.

IDA Real-world application…

Damage to these two areas could explain feeding abnormalities found in Klüver-Bucy patients. Research with these patients typically shows patterns of indiscriminate eating with individuals even trying to eat non-food items. The indiscriminate eating is caused by damage to the amygdala, and the 'eat anything' attitude observed in patients suggests that food cues (e.g. smell, taste) no longer represent their reward value to the individual.

Inferior frontal cortex

Receives messages from the olfactory bulb (responsible for smell). Damage to this area decreases eating because of diminished sensory information about the food, which in turn affects its taste (Kolb and Whishaw).

IDA Real-world application…

Recent research (Lutter et al.) suggests that hunger and eating may not be under purely neural control. The body produces extra quantities of the hormone ghrelin in response to stress. However, ghrelin also boosts appetite, leading to increased comfort-eating. This suggests that blocking the body's response to ghrelin may help people with a tendency to comfort-eat when stressed, to control their weight.

Evolutionary explanations of food preference

The environment of evolutionary adaptation (EEA)

EEA refers to the environment in which a species first evolved.

The adaptive problems faced by our ancestors in the EEA would have shaped early food preferences.

For most of human history, human beings would have lived in hunter-gatherer societies, which would have led to a preference for high-calorie (for energy) and easily available foods.

Evolutionary explanations can be tested…

By studying a related species that faces similar adaptive problems. After starving for much of the year, chimpanzees go straight for the fattiest parts of their kill (Stanford).

However…

Ultimate explanations of human behaviour (e.g. fatty foods because of the need for energy) may mask more proximate causes of the same behaviour (e.g. price, availability).

Not all food preferences can be traced back to the EEA…

Some modern preferences (e.g. low-cholesterol foods) could not have evolved during the EEA because they had no beneficial effects for our ancestors. Similarly, many things that were important to our distant ancestors (e.g. high-fat foods) are more likely to be avoided by modern humans because they are now known to be damaging to health.

Early diets

Preference for fatty foods was adaptive because harsh conditions in the EEA meant that for early humans energy resources were vital to stay alive.

Early humans evolved a preference for foods that were particularly rich in calories (fatty foods, sweet foods) because these promoted survival.

These preferences for calorie rich foods persist among modern humans, despite the fact that such foods are not particularly nutritious.

There is research that supports this…

Gibson and Wardle found the best way to predict which fruit and vegetables would be preferred by children was to measure how calorie-rich they were. Bananas and potatoes are rich in calories and were most preferred by 4–5-year-olds. This supports the claim that humans have an evolved preference for calorie-rich foods.

Preference for meat

Good for brain growth

A meat diet was full of densely packed nutrients and therefore provided a catalyst for the growth of the brain.

As a result, humans were able to evolve into the active and intelligent species that they became.

By supplying all the essential amino acids, minerals and nutrients needed to stay active and alive, this allowed early humans to supplement their diet with widely available, but less nutritious, plant-based foods.

However, early humans might have been vegetarian…

Cordain et al. claimed that early humans are more likely to have found most of their calories in sources other than saturated animal fats.

However…

Evidence (e.g. Abrams) has shown that all societies show a preference for animal fats, suggesting that this is a universal evolved preference. It is also unlikely that early humans could have found sufficient calories for an active lifestyle from a vegetarian diet.

Cultural factors are also important in food preferences…

It is likely that many food preferences (e.g. for spicy foods) developed because of cultural tastes and preferences.

However…

Although cultural differences do exist, they are usually a fine-tuning of evolved food preferences that are found in all cultures.

Taste aversion

Taste aversion was first demonstrated by Garcia et al. Rats, made ill through radiation after eating saccharin, developed an aversion to it because they formed an association between the illness and the taste of the saccharin.

Adaptive advantages

Taste aversion would have helped our distant ancestors to survive, because if they survived after ingesting poison then they could learn to avoid that food in the future.

Once learned, taste aversions are difficult to shift, an adaptation that would have helped survival.

The medicine effect describes a tendency for individuals to develop a preference for any food eaten just before recovery from an illness, which then becomes associated with feeling better.

Taste aversions can be explained by…

Biological preparedness. Differential learning abilities in different species means that each species has the ability to learn certain associations more easily than others, particularly associations that help them survive.

IDA *Real-world application…*

Research on the origins of taste aversion has been used to help understand the food avoidance that often occurs during chemotherapy in the treatment of cancer.

This claim was supported in a study by Bernstein and Webster, who gave patients a novel-tasting ice cream prior to their chemotherapy and the patients subsequently developed an aversion to that ice cream.

This has led to hospitals giving patients both a novel and a familiar food prior to their chemotherapy. Aversion then forms to the novel (i.e. unfamiliar) food and not to the familiar food.

This is consistent with our evolved avoidance of novel foodstuffs (*neophobia*), which is also consistent with our survival.

Chapter 5

Eating behaviour

Biological explanations of eating behaviour

Eating behaviour > Eating disorders >

Psychological explanations for anorexia nervosa

Biological explanations for anorexia nervosa

Psychological explanations for bulimia nervosa

Biological explanations for bulimia nervosa

Psychological explanations for anorexia nervosa (AN)

Cultural ideals and the media

Cultural ideals
Western standards of attractiveness are thought to contribute to body dissatisfaction, a distorted body image and AN.

Gregory et al. found that in the UK, 16% of girls aged 15–18 were dieting.

IDA Ethical issues in AN research...
Researchers are increasingly using anorexia chat rooms and newsgroups to gain qualitative data from those who actually have AN (or care for those with the disorder). This creates significant ethical issues for the researcher, particularly in relation to invasion of privacy, lack of informed consent and a breach of confidentiality.

Media influences
The portrayal of thin models on TV and in magazines is a significant contributory factor in body image concerns and the drive for thinness among Western adolescent girls.

Jones and Buckingham found people with low self-esteem are more likely to compare themselves to idealised images portrayed in the media.

There is research support...
A study of adolescent Fijian girls (Becker et al.) found that after the introduction of television to the island, these girls stated a desire to lose weight and to be like the women they saw on Western television.

However...
Other research has shown that instructional intervention prior to media exposure to idealised female images prevents the adverse effects of media influences (Yamamiya et al.). This suggests that the media can and does have an effect on the development of disordered eating and AN, but these effects can be avoided.

IDA Real-world application...
Because the media has such a powerful influence on eating behaviour in young people, the fashion industry in France has responded by pledging to use a diversity of body types and not to stereotype the 'thin ideal'.

Ethnicity and peer influences

Ethnicity
Other cultural groups place less emphasis on thinness in women, e.g. the incidence of AN in non-Western cultures and black populations in Western cultures is much lower.

In many non-Western cultures, there are more positive attitudes toward large body sizes, which are associated with attractiveness and fertility (Pollack).

Not all research supports ethnic differences in AN...
Cachelin and Regan found no significant differences in the incidence of disordered eating in African-American and Caucasian participants. Roberts et al. found that ethnic differences were only true for older adolescents.

Research shows that the view that white populations have a higher incidence of AN than black populations is only supported among older adolescents (Roberts et al.).

Peer influences
Eisenberg et al. found that dieting among friends was related to unhealthy weight control behaviours.

Teasing about overweight girls or underweight boys may serve to enforce gender-based ideals concerning weight.

Not all research supports the role of peer influences in AN...
Shroff and Thompson found no correlation among friends on measures of disordered eating in an adolescent sample.

Although...
Jones and Crawford did find support for the claim that overweight girls and overweight boys are more likely to be teased and so they develop disordered eating patterns. These gender differences did not emerge until adolescence.

Psychological factors and personality

Bruch's psychodynamic theory distinguished
between effective parents who respond to their child's needs, and ineffective parents who fail to respond appropriately.

Children of ineffective parents grow up confused about their internal needs and become overly reliant on their parents.

During adolescence these children strive for independence, but are unable to achieve this without taking excessive control over their body shape and developing abnormal eating habits.

There is support for this theory...
Steiner found that parents of adolescents with AN had a tendency to define their children's needs rather than letting them define their own needs. This supports the claim that children of ineffective parents become overly reliant on their parents to identify their needs.

Supporting the lack of control claim, Button and Warren examined a group of AN sufferers 7 years after they were diagnosed with the eating disorder. These individuals relied excessively on the opinions of others and felt a lack of control over their lives.

Personality
Two personality characteristics commonly associated with AN are perfectionism (Strober et al.) and impulsiveness (Butler and Montgomery).

Strober et al. found high levels of perfectionism in 73% of boys with AN and 50% of girls with AN. Butler and Montgomery found that patients with AN responded more rapidly and inaccurately on a task than did a control group.

There is support for the perfectionism claim...
Halmi et al. found that women with a history of AN scored higher on a scale of perfectionism, and the extent of perfectionism was directly related to the severity of AN experienced by these women.

A genetic explanation for the perfectionism/AN link...
Halmi et al. also studied the relatives of individuals with AN, and found that perfectionism as a trait appears to run in families. This suggests that perfectionism represents a genetic vulnerability (i.e. a diathesis) for the development of AN.

Chapter 5			
	Eating behaviour		Biological explanations for anorexia nervosa
	Biological explanations of eating behaviour		Psychological explanations for bulimia nervosa
Eating behaviour	>	Eating disorders >	Biological explanations for bulimia nervosa

Biological explanations for anorexia nervosa (AN)

Neural explanations

Serotonin
Disruption of serotonin levels leads to increased anxiety, which may then trigger AN. Bailer et al. found high levels of serotonin in women with binge-eating/purging AN, with highest levels in those with the most anxiety.

A problem for the serotonin explanation…
SSRIs, which alter levels of serotonin in the brain, are ineffective when used with AN patients. However, some studies (e.g. Tannenhaus) report that SSRIs may help to elevate mood and reduce some of the obsessive symptoms of anorexia.

Dopamine
Increased dopamine activity in the basal ganglia alters the way people interpret rewards, so individuals with AN find it difficult to associate good feelings with things that are usually pleasurable (e.g. food).

There is research support for this…
Castro-Fornieles et al. found that adolescent girls with AN had higher levels of HVA (waste product of dopamine). However, Wang et al. found that obese individuals had *lower* than normal levels of dopamine, suggesting an inverse relationship between levels of dopamine and body weight.

Season of birth
Individuals with AN are more likely to be born during spring months.
May be due to infections during pregnancy or temperature at time of conception.

There is research support for this…
Eagles et al. found that AN individuals tend to be later in birth order than healthy individuals. They may be at greater risk of being exposed to common infections from their siblings during the critical period of brain development in the second trimester of pregnancy.

Pregnancy and birth complications
Inadequate nutrition during pregnancy among mothers with an eating disorder may act as diathesis for the development of AN in the child.
Lindberg and Hjern found an association between birth complications and the development of AN.
Birth complications may lead to brain damage due to lack of oxygen, impairing neurodevelopment of a child.

There is research support for this…
Favaro et al. found that the perinatal complications associated with a risk of developing AN were: obstructed blood supply in the placenta, early eating difficulties and low birth weight.

Biological explanations can reduce parental feelings of guilt…
An advantage of these explanations of AN is that people realise they are dealing with a dysfunctional biology (which is treatable), rather than a dysfunctional family (which isn't). This reduces the guilt felt by many parents that *they* caused the development of AN in their child.

IDA *Biological determinism – a real-world application…*
Research in this area has implications for insurance payouts for psychiatric conditions which do not regard AN as 'biologically based' and therefore not liable for a payout.

Evolutionary explanations

Reproduction suppression
Females in the ancestral environment had a delayed onset of sexual maturation when conditions were not conducive to their offspring's survival.
AN may be a variation of this adaptation, causing females to alter the timing of their reproduction when they feel unable to cope with the biological, social and emotional responsibilities of womanhood.

There is research support for this…
This explanation is supported by the observation that the onset of puberty is delayed in prepubertal girls with AN. Additionally, because *amenorrhoea* is a typical characteristic of AN, this means that reproduction is suspended in AN females.

IDA *Gender bias…*
The reproduction suppression account of AN does not explain why AN would develop in men. According to recent statistics, 25% of adults with eating disorders are male, suggesting that AN is not solely a female disorder and therefore cannot be explained just in terms of the suppression of reproduction.

'Adapted to flee' famine hypothesis
Typical AN symptoms of food restriction, hyperactivity and denial of starvation reflect evolved adaptation in response to local famine conditions.
When individuals lose weight, adaptive mechanisms usually cause conservation of energy and an increase in desire for food.
This adaptation must be 'turned off' so that individuals increase their chances of survival by moving to a more favourable environment in terms of food resources.

There are limitations of evolutionary explanations of AN…
We might question how the symptoms of AN would have been passed on through generations by natural selection, particularly as AN decreases fertility and makes reproduction more difficult, and may even kill the individual with this condition.

Ultimate versus proximate factors…
In addition, although AN may have been an effective adaptation in the harsh conditions faced by our distant ancestors (an 'ultimate factors' explanation), outside these conditions the development of AN would not be favourable to the individual, suggesting that its development nowadays is a consequence of factors that have very little to do with evolution (i.e. caused by 'proximate factors', such as birth complications).

Chapter 5

Psychological explanations for anorexia nervosa
Eating behaviour
Biological explanations for anorexia nervosa
Biological explanations of eating behaviour
Psychological explanations for bulimia nervosa
Eating behaviour   >   Eating disorders   >   Biological explanations for bulimia nervosa

Psychological explanations for bulimia nervosa (BN)

Cognitive explanations

Cooper et al.'s cognitive model

People with BN are thought to have suffered early traumatic experiences that make them feel as though they are unlovable and worthless.

They may later experience criticisms about their shape and weight and so begin to diet in the belief that this will overcome thoughts of worthlessness.

BN maintained by 'circle of thoughts':

➔ Individual believes that binge-eating will make them feel better…

⬇ Triggers a binge until thought that 'I will get fat' takes over…

↖ Triggers purge to avoid harm of binge-eating episode…

Leads to feelings of worthlessness followed by binge-eating and the cycle starts again.

There is research support for this…

Leung et al. found that a lack of parental bonding was linked to the development of dysfunctional beliefs (e.g. feelings of worthlessness) among individuals with BN. Dysfunctional beliefs have been linked to bingeing and vomiting symptoms in a number of studies (e.g. Waller et al.).

Consistent with claims of Cooper et al.'s model, there is evidence that binge-eating in BN is preceded by feelings of distress, e.g. Abraham and Beaumont found that feelings of loneliness triggered bingeing.

Implications for treatment…

The use of CBT has been found to be reasonably successful in the treatment of BN.

However…

Not everybody gets better after cognitive treatment. A follow-up study of patients who had received CBT for their BN found that only half were symptom-free at the end of treatment and more than one-third still met the diagnostic criteria for BN (Fairburn et al.).

The functional model

People engage in binge-eating as a way of coping with problems associated with their self-image.

By overeating, an individual attributes the resulting distress to overeating rather than to low self-image.

Therefore the binge-eating associated with BN is functional for individuals trying to deal with life stressors.

Wheeler et al. propose that negative self-image and desire to escape from difficult life issues predict the onset of BN, the consequence of which is a 'diffuse-avoidant identity style'.

There is research support for this…

Polivy et al. found that, compared to ordinary dieters, stress-induced dieters consumed larger quantities of food regardless of its palatability. This lends support to the claim that the primary purpose of binge-eating is to alleviate identity-related stress, rather than because of the attractiveness of the food.

Implications for treatment…

Targeting the symptoms that lead to BN (such as self-consciousness) can both prevent the development of BN *and* prevent the development of the potentially harmful diffuse-avoidant identity style and its associated health problems.

IDA There is a cultural bias in bulimia research…

Most research on BN takes place in Western cultures, which means we know very little about how or whether BN develops in non-Western cultures. Research by Klump suggests that BN is a culture-bound syndrome, found mainly in Western cultures.

Explanations based on relationship processes

Insecure attachment

Women attempt to change their size and shape to meet some perceived idea of what men find attractive.

Insecure attachment in adult relationships is characterised by a strong desire for closeness and a fear of abandonment.

Evans and Wertheim found a relationship between insecure attachment and BN, as individuals try to lose weight to avoid rejection.

Bulimia or depression?

It is possible that the adverse relationship processes associated with BN may be part of a more general psychopathology that happens to accompany bulimic symptoms (e.g. depression and low self-esteem) rather than being specific characteristics of BN.

There is research support for this…

Schembri and Evans tested the link between relationship processes and bulimic symptoms. They found that self-consciousness during sexual activity was the strongest predictor of bulimic symptoms, followed by anxious attachment. These findings support the claim that adverse relationship processes are a significant risk factor for the development of BN.

However…

The findings of this study imply that adverse relationship processes have a causal relationship with the development of BN. This may not be the case as the study was a correlational design only, and so does not, for example, demonstrate a causal relationship between self-consciousness and BN.

Bodily self-consciousness

Cash suggested that women who are dissatisfied with their physical appearance become self-conscious about their bodies and worry about being accepted by their partners.

Allerdissen et al. found that women with BN reported more fear about meeting their partners' sexual expectations than did a sample of healthy volunteers.

IDA A heterosexual bias…

Most research has focused on risk factors for the development of BN in heterosexual women, although studies have shown that the incidence of eating disorders such as AN and BN among gay and bisexual men is much higher. Feldman and Meyer estimate that 15% of gay or bisexual men have suffered from an eating disorder, compared to just 8% of heterosexual women.

Chapter 5

Eating behaviour
Biological explanations of eating behaviour

Psychological explanations for anorexia nervosa
Biological explanations for anorexia nervosa
Psychological explanations for bulimia nervosa

Eating behaviour > Eating disorders > Biological explanations for bulimia nervosa

Biological explanations for bulimia nervosa (BN)

Neural explanations

Serotonin

The fact that depression and BN often occur together suggests they have a common cause.

A study by Kaye et al. of recovering bulimics and a control group of non-bulimics found that levels of dopamine and noradrenaline were the same in both groups, but the bulimic group showed elevated levels of serotonin.

Low levels of serotonin are associated with depression and high levels with anxiety.

Binge-eating relieves feelings of depression, but may raise levels of serotonin too high, leading to feelings of anxiety. To counter these feelings the person purges, reducing levels of serotonin too low, leading to depression once again.

There is research support for this…

If BN is a product of abnormal serotonin levels, then it should be possible to treat it with SSRIs, which raise levels of serotonin in the brain and should inhibit binge-eating episodes. Walsh et al. found that patients given SSRIs showed decreased binge-eating and purging, compared to a control group given placebo treatment.

Research can explain the serotonin–BN link…

Smith et al. found that, compared to a control group, women recovering from BN who were deprived of tryptophan (which makes serotonin) for 17 hours, showed greater dips in mood, were more concerned about their body image and feared losing control over their eating.

This shows that…

Lowered brain serotonin triggers some of the characteristic features of BN, even among recovered bulimics, who remain vulnerable to the disorder.

This has led to effective drug treatments for BN…

The success of drug therapies in the treatment of BN (e.g. Walsh et al.), compared to the limited success of similar drug therapies for AN, has made the case for a biological basis for bulimia more convincing.

Nitric oxide (NO)

NO is a neurotransmitter that is 'delivered' to receiving neurons by plasma nitrate.

This causes the production of cGMP.

Together, NO and cGMP regulate much of our eating behaviour. NO mediates the action of hormones involved in weight control (e.g. leptin and ghrelin).

IDA There is an age bias in research…

Research on the causes and development of BN has focused almost exclusively on adolescents and young women. Mangweth-Matzek et al. found that 3.8% of women between the ages of 60 and 70 met the diagnostic criteria for an eating disorder, yet this group is typically ignored.

This research concludes that although eating disorders and body dissatisfaction are typical for young women, they also occur in elderly females and should be considered when older women show excessive weight loss and vomiting.

Evolutionary explanations

The sexual competition hypothesis

Abed suggests that BN is a direct consequence of the evolved need to compete with other females in order to attract a mate.

Obsession with weight is an evolved adaptation to preserve a shape that is attractive to potential mates.

Evolution of nubility

Abed proposes that the traditional 'hourglass' female figure was designed by sexual selection, through the differential reproductive success of those who had this shape (i.e. nubile females).

Sexual competition

This adaptation enabled nubile females to differentiate themselves from lower reproductive value females, and allowed them to compete with other nubile females in the immediate vicinity.

Because of so many 'pseudo-nubile' older women, nubile females must set the desired shape much lower than it would have been in the ancestral environment to demonstrate their higher reproductive potential.

There is research support for this…

Sypeck et al. examined the covers of popular fashion magazines from 1959 to 1999 and found that they represented an increasing preoccupation with body size, particularly during the 1980s and 90s, reflecting the drive for thinness (as predicted by the sexual competition hypothesis) among their readers (mostly young women).

This explanation fits the statistics…

BN is an eating disorder where there is a particularly uneven sex ratio between males and females. A US study (Soundy et al.) found an incidence of BN in females 33 times greater than in males.

BN may be a universal syndrome…

Cross-cultural statistics suggest that BN is more a characteristic of Western rather than non-Western cultures (APA).

However…

Some studies suggest that BN symptoms are similar in both Western and non-Western cultures. This is important for the sexual competition hypothesis, because it suggests that BN arises because of a universal female concern for 'physical attractiveness'. If this were absent from some cultures it would pose a serious challenge to this explanation.

IDA The myth of genetic determinism…

The sexual competition hypothesis acknowledges the equally important influences of both genes (a male preference for nubile females and a female concern for attractiveness) and environment (e.g. competition with 'local' females and media influences in the development of eating disorders).

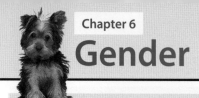

Gender

Division A Biological influences on gender

Note that this chapter does not follow the order given by the specification below, because it makes sense to start with biological influences.

The role of genes and hormones

Evolutionary explanations of gender roles

The biosocial approach to gender development

Gender dysphoria

Division B Psychological explanations of gender development

Kohlberg's cognitive developmental theory

Gender schema theory

Division C Social contexts of gender role

Social influences on gender role

Cultural influences on gender role

Specification

Gender	
Psychological explanations of gender development	• Cognitive developmental theory, including Kohlberg. • Gender schema theory.
Biological influences on gender	• The role of hormones and genes in gender development. • Evolutionary explanations of gender roles. • The biosocial approach to gender development, including gender dysphoria.
Social contexts of gender role	• Social influences on gender role, for example the influence of parents, peers, schools and media. • Cultural influences on gender role.

Chapter 6

Biological influences on gender >

The role of genes and hormones

Evolutionary explanations of gender roles

Psychological explanations of gender development

The biosocial approach to gender development

Gender > Social contexts of gender role

Gender dysphoria

The role of genes in gender development

Chromosomes

Humans have 23 pairs of chromosomes in each cell, each carrying hundreds of genes.

One pair of chromosomes determine an individual's sex:

XX is a female.

XY is a male.

The role of hormones

Chromosomal sex (XX or XY) determines what hormones are produced, e.g. more testosterone is produced in XY individuals. During prenatal development hormones cause changes to:

1. External genitalia.
2. The brain.

1. External genitalia

Initially male and female embryos have the same external genitalia, but at around 3 months' gestation, testosterone causes male external genitalia (penis, testicles) to develop.

This in turn affects later behaviour, because a baby is labelled as a boy or girl at birth based on their external genitalia, and this creates their gender identity.

2. Brain development

Exposure to male hormones creates a masculinised brain (Geschwind and Galaburda).

For example, girls are generally better at understanding what people think and feel (empathisers), whereas boys are better at categorising and understanding systems (systematisers) (Baron-Cohen).

Animal studies show that female monkeys deliberately exposed to testosterone during prenatal development are more masculine (more aggressive, more rough-and-tumble play) (Quadagno et al.).

Abnormal development

Male abnormal development, e.g. *androgen insensitivity syndrome* (AIS) is a condition where genetic males are insensitive to male hormones during prenatal development and born with no penis. One case study considered members of the Batista family, who were labelled as girls at birth, but later, during adolescence, high levels of testosterone led to the development of male external genitalia (Imperato-McGinley et al.).

Female abnormal development, e.g. female embryos whose mothers took drugs containing male hormones were born with swollen labia and some mistakenly sex-typed as boys. Those identified as girls appear to show an interest in male activities, which may be due to masculinisation of the brain.

There is evidence that biological sex is not the main factor…

Money and Ehrhardt claimed that sex of rearing is more important in determining gender identity than biology (as long as sex-typing is done before the age of three). Money used the case David/Bruce/Brenda Reimer to support this.

Bruce was born an XY male with a penis that was accidentally removed during surgery when he was an infant. Money advised that Bruce's parents raise him as Brenda and later claimed that this 'experiment' was successful, supporting his view that social not biological factors determined gender identity.

However…

Diamond and Sigmundson uncovered the true story and revealed Brenda's unhappiness as a girl and eventual decision in adolescence to become a boy (taking the name David). This suggests that genetic sex is important in the development of gender identity.

This is further supported…

Reiner and Gearhart studied 16 genetic males born with almost no penis; 14 were raised as females – eight had decided by adolescence to re-assign themselves as males, further supporting the importance of biological determinism.

IDA Is biological determinism correct?…

The evidence above suggests that gender identity is mainly determined by genetic sex (which determines production of hormones, external genitalia and brain development).

However… Socialisation matters too…

For example, *congenital adrenal hyperplasia* (CAH) is a condition where XX individuals have high levels of testosterone prenatally, causing varying degrees of external male genitalia at birth. Dessens et al. studied 250 cases where individuals were typed as females at birth and found that 95% were content with their role, despite prenatal exposure to male hormones. A further 33 patients were typed as males, of whom 12 experienced serious gender problems.

IDA Nature and nurture…

This research shows that biological factors (nature) are very important in determining gender identity, but socialisation and personal cognitive processes (nurture) also contribute.

IDA Real-world application…

Biological determinism is a real-world issue in sports because occasionally XY individuals have competed as females and had an unfair advantage (since males are more muscular). The Olympic Committee has tested all individuals since 1968, which meant that AIS individuals (XY genotype but raised as females) couldn't compete.

In 1991 a decision was made not to test genetic sex because of genetic abnormalities, and the only criteria that excludes anyone from female events is obvious male genitalia (Bown).

There are methodological issues with this research…

One problem with this research is the use of case studies of individuals with unique characteristics. Each individual has a special set of circumstances, e.g. the amount of testosterone they were exposed to prenatally, the availability of suitable gender role models, etc. This means it is impossible to generalise from such cases.

A second issue is that much of the research involves abnormal individuals – intersexes who are not clearly male or female (e.g. there is a mismatch between chromosomal sex and what hormones they were exposed to). Such individuals may be more vulnerable to social influences than 'normal' because their biological ambiguities mean they have to search for clues to their identity. This again threatens the extent to which the research findings can be generalised to all people.

Chapter 6

		The role of genes and hormones
Biological influences on gender	>	Evolutionary explanations of gender roles
Psychological explanations of gender development		The biosocial approach to gender development
Gender	>	Social contexts of gender role		Gender dysphoria

Evolutionary explanations of gender roles

Division of labour

Complementary division of labour was adaptive in the EEA because it enhanced reproductive success and also helped avoid starvation (by maximising food production).

- Men were hunters because, if women spent time hunting, this would reduce a group's reproductive success. Therefore men are physically and psychologically equipped to be hunters.
- Women contributed to the provision of food by growing vegetables, milling grain and producing clothing.

Lack of role division

Kuhn and Stiner propose that male and female Neanderthals both hunted (based on evidence of hunting injuries), which meant that when hunting failed the group starved because there was no backup. The evolution of a division of labour in humans (*homo sapiens*) enhanced their ultimate success over the rival Neanderthal species.

One consequence of men as hunters...

The meat-sharing hypothesis (Stanford) suggests that males use control of meat as a means of attracting female interest.

Studies of modern day hunter-gatherer societies support this (Hill and Kaplan), as do comparative studies of chimpanzees.

IDA *The evolutionary approach is speculative and lacks sound research support...*

This may be a fair criticism of some evolutionary accounts, e.g. the disappearance of Neanderthals being due to a lack of role division (an equally plausible suggestion relates to climate change).

It is not a fair criticism... of all evolutionary accounts, which are often supported by historical records, comparative studies and cross-cultural studies (see, for example, below).

IDA *The evolutionary approach is determinist...*

In terms of gender roles the evolutionary approach suggests that men and women are constrained to behave in predetermined ways in line with selective pressures that operated in the EEA.

However...

Evolutionary psychologists actually propose that our genes only predispose us to certain behaviours and that culture and personal experience are important influences (nature and nurture).

Mate choice

Gender role behaviours are related to adaptive reproductive strategies:

- Men increase their reproductive success by mating as frequently as possible and with those females who are most fertile. To ensure this, men look for indicators of youth and healthiness (e.g. smooth skin, glossy hair, thin waist – i.e. physical attractiveness) that indicate greater fertility.
- Women seek signs of fertility in a partner, but are also interested in the ability to provide resources (e.g. partner's wealth, power and possessions) because they need to be cared for during childbearing and rearing.

There is research support...

Buss questioned men and women in 37 cultures. He found that, as predicted:

- Men placed more importance on physical attractiveness in a mate, evidence of a woman's fertility and reproductive value.
- Women more than men desired mates who were good financial prospects (i.e. had resources or ambition).

Waynforth and Dunbar used personal ads to demonstrate that, as predicted:

- More men sought a physically attractive partner than did women (44% versus 22%).
- More women sought resources than did men (50% versus 34%).

One strength of this study is...

That the choices represented an individual's ideal bid in the process of mate selection.

Cognitive style

Empathising-systemising (E-S) theory

Baron-Cohen proposed that women are better at empathising (understanding what people think and feel) whereas men are better at systematising (understanding and building systems).

This may have evolved because of selective pressures – women make better mothers by being empathisers and men make better hunters by being systematisers.

There is research support...

Baron-Cohen has used his own *Systematising Quotient Questionnaire* (e.g. 'When I read a newspaper I am drawn to tables of information'), and found gender differences as expected. Only about 17% of men had a female empathising brain and 17% of women had a male systematising brain.

One implication of E-S theory...

Autism may be an example of the extreme male brain (Baron-Cohen). Autistic individuals lack the ability to empathise (poor Theory of Mind) and excel at systematising.

Stress responses

Another difference between men and women that would have been adaptive in the EEA is their complementary response to situations of threat:

- Men respond with fight or flight to deal with the threat.
- Women respond with tend and befriend to protect group members (Taylor *et al.*).

There is research support...

Ennis *et al.* tested levels of cortisol (stress hormone) just before and after taking exams (a 'threatening'/stressful situation). Cortisol levels increased in males but not females.

Taylor *et al.* showed that levels of oxytocin increase in females when stressed (not males); this hormone is associated with reduced anxiety and increased sociability.

Both studies show that there are gender differences in line with the predictions from evolutionary theory.

Chapter 6

Biological influences on gender >
Psychological explanations of gender development

Gender > Social contexts of gender role

The role of genes and hormones
Evolutionary explanations of gender roles
The biosocial approach to gender development
Gender dysphoria

The biosocial approach to gender development

Biosocial theory (Money and Ehrhardt)

Sex of rearing is the pivotal point in gender development.

What matters is what gender you are told you are, and this must happen before the age of three.

- Biology is likely to determine sex of rearing because babies are sexed at birth on the basis of external genitalia – which are usually in accord with genetic sex.
- In ambiguous cases, a child may be raised as a gender incongruent with genetic sex.

In both cases, gender identity will be determined by subsequent socialisation based on a person's gender assignment.

The research evidence is flawed…

Most of the evidence is derived from the study of abnormal individuals, e.g. the study of genetic females exposed to male hormones prenatally because of drugs taken by their mother.

Such evidence may not be relevant to understanding gender development, as it does not reflect experiences of normal individuals.

The research evidence supports biological determinism…

Initially, the case study of David Reimer (Brenda/Bruce) supported biosocial theory as he (Bruce) accepted his gender re-assignment until reaching adolescence. However, ultimately he rejected this, suggesting that biological sex is more important than socialisation.

Reiner and Gearhart studied 16 genetic males born with almost no penis; 14 were raised as females – eight had decided by adolescence to re-assign themselves as males.

Social role theory (Eagly and Wood)

An evolutionary approach

Traditional evolutionary theory proposes that both physical and psychological sex differences are naturally selected.

- Physical sex differences, e.g. men are stronger and faster, women bear children.
- Psychological sex differences e.g. men become more aggressive because they are hunters, women become more empathetic because they raise children.

The psychological differences lead to social role differences, e.g. men become hunters because they are stronger, women become homemakers because they have to be at home with children.

By contrast, Eagly and Wood suggested that only physical sex differences are naturally selected and these cause differential social roles, which in turn create psychological sex differences.

Division of labour

Social role theory predicts that:

- Physical sex differences can be related to social roles, e.g. men hunt because they don't have to stay at home for childcare.
- In societies where strength is not required for obtaining food or where childcare is shared, male/female social roles will be more similar and psychological differences will be reduced.

Mate choice

Traditional evolutionary theory: what men and women seek in a partner is related to the value of certain traits (e.g. red lips as a sign of youthfulness).

Social role theory: mate choice is related to social roles. Men and women maximise their reproductive success by seeking a mate who is a good homemaker or hunter (respectively).

Hormonal differences may be the outcome of social roles, rather than the cause.

For example, greater levels of testosterone in males occur because they engage in more athletic events and this creates higher levels of testosterone than in women.

IDA *It is also a social constructionist approach…*

Eagly and Wood's biosocial theory suggests that psychological sex differences are the outcome of social roles, which in turn are related to the behaviours of a particular society or culture. There is no objective reality, such as a real difference between men and women – or even if there is one, social factors tend to overshadow these differences. According to this approach, behaviours are best understood in terms of the social context in which they occur.

The findings from Buss' study of 37 cultures can be explained using social role theory…

Buss found that, in all cultures, men prefer younger, physically attractive women (because they are more fertile), whereas women seek men with resources (to make childrearing easier).

Eagly and Wood explain this as (1) men want younger women because they are more obedient, (2) women frequently earn less than men and therefore seek a partner with resources.

This is supported by…

Eagly and Wood who found, for example, that in situations where women have higher status Buss' sex differences were less pronounced. This supports the idea that social roles are the driving force in psychological sex differences.

However…

Gangestad et al. re-analysed Eagly and Wood's data, controlling for factors such as affluence and social structure. They concluded that gender equality was not related to sex differences, and therefore concluded that traditional evolutionary is adequate.

The traditional evolutionary approach may be better…

Luxen argues that traditional evolutionary theory is preferable for a number of reasons:

- It is simpler (Occam's razor).
- Selective pressure acts on behaviour as well as on physical characteristics and therefore psychological sex differences would be selected at the same time as physical ones.
- Research has shown that very young children and animals display sex differences – these must be biological rather than psychological because sex role socialisation is unlikely to have occurred.

IDA *Real-world application…*

The traditional evolutionary approach implies that sex differences are innate and cannot be changed by altering social context, whereas social role theory supports the feminist view that changes in social roles will lead to changes in psychological differences between men and women.

Chapter 6

Biological influences on gender   >   The role of genes and hormones
                                          Evolutionary explanations of gender roles
Psychological explanations of gender development   The biosocial approach to gender development

Gender   >   Social contexts of gender role   Gender dysphoria

Gender dysphoria

Psychological explanations

Mental illness

Gender dysphoria is a consequence of childhood trauma or maladaptive upbringing, leading to mental illness.

Coates et al. studied a boy with *gender identity disorder* (GID), suggesting this developed because of a defensive reaction to his mother's depression following an abortion. The trauma may have led to a cross-gender fantasy as a means of resolving the anxiety.

The research evidence is poor…

Cole et al. studied 435 individuals experiencing gender dysphoria and reported that the range of psychiatric conditions displayed were no greater than found in a 'normal' population.

This suggests that gender dysphoria is generally unrelated to trauma or to pathological families.

General psychological influences have been suggested…

However, Diamond claims that there is no evidence that, for example, persistently dressing a young boy in girl's clothing (or vice versa) causes transsexualism.

Mother–son relationships

Stoller found that individuals with GID had overly close mother–son relationships.

Some research support…

Zucker et al. studied boys with gender issues – 64% of those diagnosed with GID were also diagnosed with separation anxiety disorder, compared to only 38% of the boys whose symptoms were subclinical.

Biological explanations

Mismatch between hormones and genetic sex

Androgen insensitivity syndrome (AIS) and *congenital adrenal hyperplasia* (CAH) may result in an intersex condition when external genitalia do not match genetic sex, and so an individual may be assigned to the wrong sex at birth.

The research evidence challenges this…

In a sample of 250 genetic females with CAH who were raised as females, 95% were content with their female gender role despite prenatal brain exposure to male hormones (Dessens et al.).

IDA Real-world application…

Research on gender dysphoria is very important in providing information about the effects of erroneous assignations at birth. *The Organisation Intersex International* suggests that all infants born as intersexes (i.e. no clear sex) should have the right to determine their own sexual identity once they are old enough.

Transsexual gene

Hare et al. studied DNA of 112 MtF transsexuals. They were more likely to have a longer version of the *androgen receptor gene*, associated with reduced action of the male sex hormone testosterone, which might have an effect on gender development in the womb (e.g. under-masculinising the brain).

IDA Socially-sensitive research…

Research on gender dysphoria has potential social consequences for individuals represented by the research. If a biological cause is identified this may help other people to be more accepting about the needs of transsexuals (i.e. it is not their 'fault').

On the other hand, if a biological cause was identified this might harm individuals born with gender inconsistencies because people might assume certain outcomes, thus preventing individuals from making freer choices.

The brain–sex theory

Brain–sex theory proposes that the bed nucleus of the *stria terminalis* (BSTc) is abnormal in transsexuals.

Zhou et al. and Kruijver et al., found the number of neurons in the BSTc of MtF transsexuals was similar to that of the females. By contrast, the number of neurons in a FtM transsexual was found to be in the normal male range.

There are criticisms of brain-sex theory…

Chung et al. noted that the differences in BSTc volume between men and women do not develop until adulthood, whereas most transsexuals report that their feelings of gender dysphoria began in early childhood. BSTc differences may be an effect rather than a cause of dysphoria.

Hulshoff Pol et al. found that transgender hormone therapy influences the size of the BSTc and the individuals in the BSTc studies had been receiving hormone therapy.

However, there is some support for brain-sex theory…

Rametti et al. studied the brains of FtM transsexuals before they started transgender hormone therapy. In terms of amounts of white matter in their brains, the FtM individuals had a more similar pattern to individuals who share their gender identity (males) than those who share their biological sex (females).

Phantom limb

Ramachandran suggests that gender dysphoria is an innate form of phantom limb syndrome. FtM transsexuals are born with some cross-wiring which makes them feel they ought to have a penis.

Research support…

Two-thirds of FtM transsexuals report the sensation of a phantom penis from childhood onwards, including phantom erections. Nearly two-thirds of non-transsexual males who have a penis surgically removed experience the sensation of a phantom penis, whereas only one-third of MtF transsexuals do after sex reassignment surgery, i.e. there was something wrong with their original 'wiring'.

Environmental pollution

Insecticide DDT contains oestrogens, which may feminise male embryos.

There is research support…

A study in Holland found that boys born to mothers who were exposed to *dioxins* (which can promote oestrogen) displayed feminised play (Vreugdenhil et al.).

Kohlberg's cognitive developmental theory

Piaget's influence

Kohlberg drew on Piaget's ideas about cognitive development. Piaget suggested that the way we think changes (i.e. matures) as we get older, enabling qualitatively different thought.

The consequence of this is that cognitive development occurs in stages.

Stage 1: Gender labelling

Between 2 and 3 years of age.

Children select a gender label based on outward appearance, e.g. clothing. Gender label can change if, for example, clothing changes.

Piaget calls this pre-operational thinking, i.e. lacking internally consistent logic.

Stage 2: Gender stability

Around the age of 4, children realise that gender is consistent (stable) over time (e.g. boys grow into men).

However, they lack awareness that is consistent over situations, thus their understanding lacks true constancy.

Children are still swayed by outward appearances, an example of Piaget's concept of conservation (the understanding that things may appear to change but don't). Children under the age of 7 lack the ability to conserve.

McConaghy showed young children a drawing of a doll where the male genitals were visible through the doll's dress. Children under the age of 5 judged the doll to be female because of its external appearance despite the contrary evidence that it was a boy.

Stage 3: Gender consistency

Around the age of 6, children realise that gender is consistent across situations as well as across time. Therefore they have now developed full gender constancy.

It is only when a child has acquired gender constancy that they are ready to learn about gender-appropriate behaviour. Up until the stage of constancy, such information is not really relevant because the child believes that his/her gender may change.

There is research support…

• Gender *labelling* – Thompson found that 2-year-olds were less able to identify their sex than 3-year-olds (76% versus 90% correct).

• Gender *stability* – Slaby and Frey asked children 'Were you a little girl or a little boy when you were a baby?' There was no evidence of gender stability across time until they were 3 or 4 years old.

• Gender *consistency* – Slaby and Frey found that children high in gender constancy (stability+consistency) showed greatest interest in same-sex models, i.e. gender-appropriate models.

However, the studies may not be testing what they intend to test (i.e. they lack validity)…

Bem gave children aged 3–5 years a gender conservation task (they were shown photos of a nude child and then the same child dressed gender inappropriately). Those children who assigned gender on basis of clothing (i.e. no constancy) also tended to fail a genital knowledge test. This suggests that they were not failing to conserve gender because they lacked an understanding of consistency but they failed because there was nothing to conserve.

Bem also argued that the original task used to test gender conservation is nonsense – when children are asked to resolve a contradiction between genitals and clothing, the child goes for the cue that is most salient in our society, i.e. clothes.

Kohlberg may have underestimated children's capabilities…

Martin and Halverson (*gender schema theory*, see next page) suggest that children can acquire information about gender-appropriate behaviours before gender constancy is achieved.

Slaby and Frey did find that gender consistency appeared at a younger age than Kohlberg had suggested, as young as 5 years old.

However…

Slaby and Frey's methods have been criticised. Martin and Halverson analysed children's responses to the questions used by Slaby and Frey and judged that children were adopting a 'pretend' mode (i.e. pretending that they were in a particular situation) and answering the questions based on this rather than what they really thought.

There are gender differences…

Slaby and Frey also found that boys tended to exhibit gender consistency before girls. In general girls are more willing to take on masculine-type activities but the same cannot be said of boys.

This difference can be explained… in terms of social learning theory. The role models that boys identify with tend to be more powerful (males in our society have greater power). Therefore girls are less likely to identify with their role models because, even though the role models are gender appropriate they are less powerful.

Also boys are more likely to be punished for gender inappropriate behaviour than girls and therefore learn appropriate gender behaviour more rapidly (Langlois and Downs).

This means that Kohlberg's theory is incomplete because social learning theory principles are also involved.

IDA Approaches to explaining gender development…

The cognitive developmental approach suggests that the key to gender development is the way a child thinks about their gender.

There are many other approaches:

• The social learning approach suggests we learn about appropriate gender behaviour through direct and indirect reinforcement and punishment (e.g. boys are teased for wearing girls' clothes).

• The biological approach proposes that genes and hormones determine gender behaviours.

Gender schema theory (Martin and Halverson)

Two key factors distinguish *gender schema theory* (GST) from Kohlberg's cognitive-developmental theory:

1. According to GST children start to learn about gender-appropriate behaviour *before* gender constancy is achieved. Basic gender identity (gender labelling) is sufficient for a child to identify him/herself as boy/girl and to take an interest in what behaviours are appropriate.

2. GST includes an explanations of *how* cognitive development affects behaviour. The acquisition of stereotypes/schema affects memory and attention, and these affect behaviour.

Gender schema

A schema is a mental representation of an aspect of the world, a personal 'theory'. Gender schemas provide information about what behaviour is appropriate for boys and girls.

Children learn such schemas as a result of their interactions with people, e.g. learning what clothes to wear.

Ingroup and outgroup schemas

Children focus on ingroup schemas, e.g. if you are a girl you identify with feminine schemas.

This identification leads you to positively evaluate girls as a group.

Identification also leads to negative evaluation of outgroup (male) schemas, and a motivation to avoid male behaviours.

According to GST, from an early age, before gender constancy, children focus on ingroup schemas and avoid behaviours that belong to outgroup schemas.

Resilience of gender beliefs

Children hold very fixed gender attitudes because they ignore information that is inconsistent with ingroup information.

For example, if a boy sees a film with a male nurse this information (i.e. that nurses can be male) is ignored (because it's not consistent with the ingroup schema) and therefore the boy doesn't alter his existing schema.

Gender schema appear before constancy, as predicted by GST...

Martin and Little found that children under the age of 4 showed no signs of gender stability, but did display strong gender stereotypes.

However, GST may even appear before gender-typed preferences appear...

According to social learning theory, gender typed preferences appear even before gender identify (Bandura and Bussey), which challenges GST.

There is recent support for GST...

Zosuls *et al.* showed that children are able to label their gender group by the age of 19 months, earlier than indicated in previous studies. This means that earlier gender-typed preferences may still be due to gender schema.

Research shows that gender schemas do affect memory...

- *Greater attention to information consistent with gender schemas* – Martin and Halverson found that children under 6 recalled more gender-consistent pictures (e.g. male fire-fighter) than gender-inconsistent ones (e.g. female chemist), as we would expect.

- *Greater attention to ingroup schema* – Children aged 4–9 took a greater interest in toys labelled as belonging to the ingroup and one week later were better able to remember these (Bradbard *et al.*).

This may result in distortion of information...

Martin and Halverson showed children consistent or inconsistent (counter-stereotypical) pictures e.g. a boy holding a gun (consistent) or a boy holding a doll (inconsistent). The recalled information was distorted, e.g. when children were asked to describe the picture they insisted the doll was held by a girl.

IDA Real-world application...

Such distortion has important implications for efforts to reduce gender stereotypes because, even when children are exposed to counter-stereotypes, they don't remember them accurately. This suggests that the use of counter-stereotypes may not be the best way to reduce children's gender schema.

GST explains why children's stereotypes (schema) are so resilient...

GST claims that children actively seek to acquire gender-appropriate schema and this results in a resistance to any gender inappropriate information, e.g. attempts by parents to encourage boys to play with Barbie dolls.

However...

Gibbons *et al.* found that children whose mothers work outside the home have less conservative gender-role attitudes, suggesting that children are not entirely fixed in their views but are receptive to some gender inconsistent ideas.

IDA Contrast with the Freudian approach...

There are some similarities between Freud's theory and GST. Freud proposed that gender identity develops around the age of 3, an age that is closer to the predictions of GST than Kohlberg's gender constancy.

Freud also suggested that identification with the ingroup (same-sex parent) was important in taking on gender attitudes.

Gender constancy versus schema...

The key argument is whether gender knowledge is absorbed after gender constancy (Kohlberg) or before (Martin and Halverson).

Stangor and Ruble proposed a compromise, and supported this with a study, finding that:

- Preference (motivation) for same-sex toys increased with gender constancy (supporting gender constancy theory).
- Memory (organisation) for gender-consistent pictures increased with age (supporting gender schema theory).

Social influences on gender role

Social cognitive theory

Bandura renamed social learning theory to emphasise the role of cognitive factors in learning. Bandura proposed that gender role development is the result of learning from social agents who model and reinforce gender role behaviours:

- **Indirect reinforcement** – The experiences of others are observed and the consequences of this behaviour stored as *expectancies of future outcomes*, which later results in modelling.
- **Direct reinforcement** – Boys and girls are only reinforced when performing gender appropriate behaviours even if they model gender inappropriate ones.
- **Direct tuition** – Direct instructions affect behaviour as soon as children acquire linguistic skills and can be told what gender behaviours are appropriate or inappropriate.

There is research support...

Bandura's Bobo doll studies (see page 32) demonstrated the effects of an adult model on aggression, thus demonstrating imitative behaviour. This has also been established for gender by Perry and Bussey.

However, the effects of modeling are limited...

Perry and Bussey found that children only imitated same-sex models if the behaviour was not counter to existing stereotypes.

Direct tuition may be more important...

Martin *et al.* found that preschool boys played with toys labelled 'boys' toys' (a form of 'direct tuition') even after seeing girls playing with them, but did not play with toys labelled 'girls' toys' even when they saw boys playing with them (i.e. they did not model same-sex behaviour when it was counter to direct tuition).

However... The impact of 'tuition' is weakened when what is being taught is contradicted by what is being modelled (Hildebrandt *et al.*).

IDA *The biological approach...*

The social learning approach is not in opposition to the biological approach. Bandura suggested that the starting point for a behaviour is often biological – it is the means of expressing it that is learned.

Sources of social influence

The influence of parents

Reinforcement is differential, e.g. Smith and Lloyd found that mothers selected gender-appropriate toys for an infant presented as a boy or girl.

Fagot *et al.* found that parents who differentially reinforce gender behaviour have children who are quickest to develop strong gender preferences.

There are gender differences...

Fathers are more openly disapproving about son's gender inappropriate behaviour. Mothers ignore gender-inappropriate play and just reinforce gender-appropriate play (Langlois and Downs).

This may be explained...

Female behaviour has a lower value and therefore gender-inappropriate behaviour in females is more acceptable than gender inappropriate behaviour in boys (e.g. dressing like a girl).

The influence of peers

Peers provide gender specific models and also reinforce gender appropriate behaviour.

Perry and Bussey showed that boys and girls selected items they previously saw same-gender children selecting.

Peers 'punish' gender inappropriate behaviour, including the use of direct tuition (e.g. 'Don't be a cissy') (Lamb *et al.*).

There is research support...

Peer behaviour probably doesn't create gender role stereotypes but simply reinforces existing ones,.

For example, Lamb and Roopnarine found that when male-typed behaviour was reinforced in girls, the behaviour continued for a shorter time than when male-typed behaviour was reinforced in boys. This suggests that peer reinforcement mainly acts as a reminder of what is gender-appropriate behaviour.

The influence of the media

The media communicate cultural stereotypes, e.g. males are portrayed as independent and directive, females as unambitious and emotional (Bussey and Bandura).

Men are shown as more in control (Hodges *et al.*).

Individuals who watch more TV tend to display more gender stereotypic role conceptions than do light viewers (McGhee and Frueh).

The media provide role models and also enhance self-efficacy, leading males to have increased self-confidence.

There is research support...

Rare cases of communities that have no TV allow us to observe the effects of exposure to media stereotypes, e.g. Williams found that children with no TV had weaker gender stereotypes (especially girls). After exposure to TV their views became more gender stereotyped.

However... A similar study (Charlton *et al.*) found no changes in levels of aggression before and after TV was introduced, suggesting that simply exposing children to stereotypes is not sufficient to lead to behaviour change.

This is further supported by Signorelli and Bacue who concluded that TV programming had done little to change gender stereotypes.

IDA *Real-world application...*

Such research leads to pressure on programme makers to try to use this media to alter gender stereotypes. Pingree found that stereotyping was reduced when children were shown commercials with women in non-traditional roles. However, pre-adolescent boys displayed *stronger* stereotypes after exposure to the non-traditional models.

However... Martin and Halverson found that gender inconsistent messages are mis-remembered and therefore have no effect on changing stereotypes (schema).

Cultural influences on gender role

Cultural similarities

Division of labour

In almost all societies women prepare food and care for children. Even when such activities are shared, it tends not to be a major male responsibility.

Girls are raised to be compliant and responsible, and males to be more assertive and independent.

The existence of cultural similarities suggests that…

Biology underlies gender role development – which could be a direct consequence of biological differences (the evolutionary approach) or an indirect outcome (as proposed by Eagly and Wood, see page 51).

Labour divisions are not the same in all cultures…

There are some exceptions, for example Japanese men reject the American 'macho' male stereotype and prefer to be well rounded in the arts (Sugihara and Katsurada).

Aggressive behaviour

Mead studied three groups in Papua New Guinea (the *Arapesh*, the *Mundugumor*, and the *Tchambuli*).

She eventually concluded that there were cultural similarities – in all societies men were more aggressive.

There are methodological criticisms of Mead's study…

Freeman also worked with native Samoans who reported that they had provided Mead with the information she wanted to hear.

However…

Appell later criticised Freeman for being inaccurate in the claims he made.

Sex stereotypes

Williams and Best studied people in 30 countries, using a 300-item adjective checklist.

• Men were seen as more dominant, aggressive and autonomous.

• Women were seen as more nurturant, deferent and interested in affiliation.

There are methodological criticisms of this study…

The task was a forced choice one so divisions between gender stereotypes may be exaggerated.

The task was related to stereotypes and not to actual behaviours.

Participants were university students who may share a high level of consensus across cultures.

Characteristics desirable in a partner

Buss questioned people in 37 cultures about what they look for in a partner. He found that gender role behaviours were related to strategies that ensure the greatest reproductive success, for example:

• Women valued good financial prospects, ambition and industriousness in a partner more highly than did men.

• Men preferred physically attractive mates and those who were younger; both are signs of good genes and youthfulness (indicators of fertility).

IDA *Cultural bias…*

Western research investigating non-Western cultural practices is likely to be biased even when indigenous researchers are used (as in Buss' study), e.g. because it tends to use questionnaires, methods and concepts developed in the West (imposed etics) (Berry *et al.*).

IDA *Genetic determinism and relativism…*

Initially Mead found evidence for *cultural determinism* (gender roles varied in the different groups, e.g. sometimes women were more aggressive than men or vice versa).

Subsequently she decided the evidence pointed towards *cultural relativism* (there were cultural differences but in all cultures men were more aggressive). The fact that there are cultural similarities in gender role behaviour suggests that these behaviours are genetically determined, but the question is whether this is a direct or indirect effect of inherited factors.

Cultural differences

Spatial perception

Berry *et al.*'s study of 17 societies found male superiority on spatial perceptual tasks only in relatively tightly knit, sedentary societies but absent or even reversed in 'looser' nomadic societies.

This shows that sex differences on spatial perceptual tasks interact with ecological and cultural factors.

IDA *Social versus biological approach…*

The social approach: In sedentary societies men are the hunters and women stay at home, whereas in nomadic groups both men and women hunt and both therefore develop spatial perceptual abilities (Van Leeuwen).

The biological approach: In hunting societies those with poor spatial abilities die. Therefore the men who remain in such societies have better spatial abilities then the women (where no selection has taken place). This doesn't happen in nomadic groups (Kimura).

Conformity

Women are generally more conformist than men, but this difference varies with culture. Berry *et al.* report that conformity is highest in tight, sedentary societies.

This may happen because…

In nomadic societies women contribute to food accumulation and thus are more highly valued, less regarded as objects for reproduction and have more power and so less need to conform (Schlegel and Barry).

Historical differences

In the UK, women continue to perform more domestic duties than men and continue to occupy less powerful positions, but this gender gap has been decreasing.

On the other hand…

Increased wealth leads to higher status for working women and thus greater role equality not difference (Eagly and Wood).

IDA *Culture or biology?…*

The existence of universal gender differences supports biology, but the decrease in these differences (such as women gaining greater power in wealthier societies) supports the role of social factors.

Intelligence and learning

Division A Theories of intelligence
Psychometric theories
Information-processing theories

Division B Animal learning and intelligence
Classical conditioning
Operant conditioning
Conditioning and the behaviour of animals
Intelligence in non-human animals

Division C Human intelligence
Evolutionary factors in human intelligence
Genetic factors in intelligence-test performance
Environmental factors in intelligence-test performance

Specification

Intelligence and Learning	
Theories of intelligence	• Psychometric theories, for example Spearman, Cattell, Thurstone.
	• Information-processing theories, for example Sternberg, Gardner.
Animal learning and intelligence	• Simple learning (classical and operant conditioning) and its role in the behaviour of non-human animals.
	• Intelligence in non-human animals, for example, self-recognition, social learning, Machiavellian intelligence.
Human intelligence	• Evolutionary factors in the development of human intelligence, for example, ecological demands, social complexity, brain size.
	• Influence of genetic and environmental factors associated with intelligence-test performance, including the role of culture.

Chapter 7

Theories of intelligence	>	Psychometric theories
Animal learning and intelligence		Information-processing theories
Intelligence and learning	>	Human intelligence

Psychometric theories

General intelligence

General intelligence (g) is considered a general factor underlying performance in different types of intelligence test.

Intelligent behaviour is therefore derived from an underlying 'mental energy' (g).

Spearman's two-factor theory

Using factor analysis, Spearman found that individuals who performed well on one IQ test also performed well on other types of test. This was explained by:

- *Specific abilities* (s) – Individuals tend to perform consistently well on specific aspects of intelligence such as vocabulary and mathematics.
- *General intelligence* (g) – The positive correlation between individuals' performance on different tests is explained by general intelligence (g), something that is almost entirely inherited.

There is neurophysiological evidence for general intelligence...

Duncan *et al.* used PET scans and presented participants with tasks that required general intelligence or did not. Regardless of the type of task, the same areas of the frontal lobes 'lit up' during 'g' tasks' but not during 'non-g' tasks.

Spearman committed the logical error of reification...

Gould claimed that Spearman gave an abstract thing (g) a 'concrete' status. This leads to circular reasoning where the explanation for a positive correlation between test performances is an underlying general intelligence, but its proof of existence is solely that correlation.

> **IDA** *Cultural bias in intelligence testing...*
>
> In 1921, the US army tested 1.75 million men using psychometric IQ tests. The tests showed that white Americans scored significantly higher than European immigrants and black Americans.
>
> However, the poor scores found in the immigrant and black groups were a result of the cultural bias of the test items used to test them; these included questions relating to US sports, food and customs. Black Americans and immigrants could not answer questions relating to white, middle-class experiences.

Multifactor theories

Theories that focus on multiple factors in intelligence rather than one underlying 'g' are known as multifactor theories.

Cattell's Gf-Gc theory

Cattell proposed that intelligence was comprised of two distinct components:

- *Crystallised intelligence* (Gc) – Acquired knowledge and skills (e.g. vocabulary and general knowledge), which are the result of cultural and educational experiences.
- *Fluid intelligence* (Gf) – Reasoning and problem solving ability, which is not dependent on experience. This provides the 'raw material' for development of Gc.

Relationship between Gc and Gf – People with high capacity for Gf acquire Gc at faster rates and develop a greater level of Gc.

There are advantages in Cattell's explanation of intelligence...

It appears better able to explain what typically happens over an individual's lifespan. Gc tends to rise over the lifespan, whereas Gf usually falls (McArdle *et al.*). This cannot be explained in terms of one unchanging general intelligence, which underestimates the complexity of cognitive changes throughout the lifespan.

Distinction between Gc and Gf is supported by the Flynn effect...

Flynn provided evidence that IQ scores have been increasing steadily over the past 50 years. However, the 'Flynn effect' appears only to hold for measures of fluid intelligence, and has ignored measures of crystallised intelligence. Raven confirmed Flynn's findings, but also found much smaller increases in adults (and in some cases *decreases*) in vocabulary and other measures of crystallised intelligence over the same period.

Psychometric tests may not be a fair measure of ability...

Bunting and Mooney found that pupils who were coached in how to do well in IQ tests tended to improve their 11-plus scores by 40%, giving an inaccurate measure of their true abilities. The consequence was that many then struggle to keep up with the academic demands in selective post-11 education.

Thurstone's primary mental abilities

Thurstone believed that rather than intelligence being based on one general factor, it was made up from a group of mental abilities, referred to as 'primary abilities', each of which could be measured separately. These include:

- Verbal comprehension – The ability to understand and define words.
- Number – The ability to solve arithmetic problems.
- Spatial ability – The ability to visualise relationships between objects.
- Inductive reasoning – The ability to draws inferences from observations in order to make rules.

Thurstone's theory is not universally supported...

Although Thurstone's theory of intelligence was well supported when tests were given to university undergraduates, he failed to find evidence for his proposed seven distinct primary abilities in a group of intellectually diverse schoolchildren. Instead he found more evidence of g, with the children differing not so much in terms of their primary mental abilities but in terms of their general underlying intelligence. This led to a compromise to his original theory that accounted for the presence of both the seven primary abilities and a general factor.

> **IDA** *Real-world application...*
>
> Thurstone's view of intelligence as a series of differing abilities was shown to have some importance when used in the selection and classification of pilots, navigators and other aircrew during World War II (Flanagan, 1948).

Chapter 7

Theories of intelligence	>	Psychometric theories
Animal learning and intelligence		Information-processing theories
Intelligence and learning	>	Human intelligence

Information-processing theories

The triarchic theory

Sternberg identified three distinct aspects of intelligence: analytical, practical and creative intelligence.

Analytical (componential) intelligence

The ability to combine most appropriate mental mechanisms (components) when applying intelligence to a problem. Sternberg believed these to be universal.

- *Metacomponents* determine the exact nature of a problem, develop strategies and allocate resources.
- *Performance components* are cognitive processes used in solving a problem.
- *Knowledge-acquisition components* are used to acquire and learn new material.

Practical (contextual) intelligence

The ability to make a considered response that is dependent on the context in which the problem occurs.

This involves selecting a response that is most likely to bring success.

Creative (experiential) intelligence

Helps an individual identify when a problem is a new one, and so requires intelligent behaviour to solve it (*novelty*).

Automisation refers to the performance of an action that requires little thought.

There is evidence for Sternberg's theory…

Grigorenko *et al.* taught reading either triarchically or through the regular curriculum to middle- and high-school students. In all settings, students who were taught triarchically substantially outperformed students who were taught in standard ways, supporting the importance of identifying three aspects of intelligence.

Berg and Sternberg supported the main predictions of Sternberg's theory *and* the predicted decline in cognitive abilities associated with ageing. They found that younger adults were superior in the metacomponents and performance components associated with analytical intelligence.

However…

Cunningham and Tomer suggest that not all aspects of analytical intelligence decline with age. Knowledge-acquisition components based on experience may stay relatively stable in old age.

IDA *Real-world application…*

Sternberg's theory has been successfully applied to education at both school and university levels. Williams *et al.* assessed the impact of the *Practical Intelligence for School* (PIFS) intervention, in which all three types of intelligence are emphasised. When PIFS was used as a major part of the curriculum, significant improvements in practical intelligence were obtained.

There are criticisms of this theory…

Gottfredson claims that Sternberg has failed to provide sufficient evidence to support his claim that practical intelligence is distinct from general intelligence and that it is superior to *g* in predicting academic success.

IDA *There may be a cultural bias in triarchic theory…*

Sternberg tested the triarchic model on a sample of Kenyan schoolchildren. From this study, he concluded that we cannot assume that the cognitive skills we value or label as intelligence in one culture are those valued or labelled in another culture.

Gardner's theory of multiple intelligences (MI)

Gardner believed that many different abilities could count as 'intelligence' if they resolve genuine problems within a particular cultural setting.

Criteria for inclusion as an 'intelligence'

- *Neuropsychological evidence* – People have multiple intelligences because they have distinct neural modules.
- *Existence of individuals with exceptional talent*, e.g. autistic savants who have exceptional talent in one particular area.
- *Distinct developmental history* – Some skills are acquired by most people, others by very few.
- *Research evidence* – People are less able to carry out tasks concurrently if they require the same type of intelligence.

Gardner's eight intelligences

- Linguistic intelligence
- Numerical skills
- Spatial intelligence
- Bodily-kinaesthetic intelligence
- Musical intelligence
- Interpersonal intelligence
- Intrapersonal intelligence
- Natural intelligence

There isn't a great deal of empirical support for MI…

There have been very few studies that offer empirical support for the validity of MI as an explanation of intelligence.

However…

Some research support is starting to appear, e.g. Douglas *et al.* found that, compared to direct instruction, teaching methods that concentrated on fostering multiple intelligences produced significant increases in students' academic, social and emotional wellbeing.

There are positive implications from MI theory…

MI theory suggests how children might succeed both educationally and in life generally. By assuming that there are many different ways to approach a problem, educators can help children to improve their skills and feel good about themselves in the process.

There are implications for assessment…

Gardner claimed that the assessment of intelligence should involve multiple measures rather than relying on one single measure of IQ. A single measure provides too little information for educational intervention. As such, Gardner believes that the primary purpose of assessment in education is to help children rather than rank them.

IDA *There is a cultural bias in this theory…*

It is clear from research that some intelligences are more highly valued than others in different cultures. For example, in China, mathematical intelligence is very highly valued, whereas bodily-kinaesthetic and natural intelligence are less highly valued.

A consequence of this is that…

Individuals in some countries (e.g. China) are considered 'intelligent' if they possess particular, more highly valued, forms of intelligence. This undermines the importance of other types of intelligence proposed by Gardner in those cultures.

Chapter 7			Classical conditioning
Theories of intelligence		Operant conditioning
	Animal learning and intelligence	>	Conditioning and the behaviour of animals
Intelligence and learning	>	Human intelligence	Intelligence in non-human animals

Classical conditioning

The nature of classical conditioning

Classical conditioning explains learning thus:
A reflex consists of an unconditioned (i.e. unlearned) stimulus and its naturally associated response. By repeatedly associating a neutral stimulus (NS) with this unconditioned stimulus (UCS), it is possible to produce the same response even in the absence of the unconditioned stimulus.

IDA *Real-world application…*

In advertising, humans can be conditioned to associate neutral stimuli (such as cars, coffee or perfume) with stimuli that already make them feel good (e.g. lifestyle, celebrity, humour, etc.).

Advertisers must deal with the problem of stimulus generalisation. An advertisement may lead a consumer to buy a similar product, because the association has generalised to 'similar' stimuli. Therefore, advertisers may use stimulus discrimination techniques where they urge consumers not to buy 'cheap imitations' as results will not be what they expect..

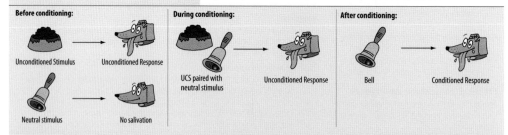

Before conditioning:

Unconditioned Stimulus — Unconditioned Response

Neutral stimulus — No salivation

During conditioning:

UCS paired with neutral stimulus — Unconditioned Response

After conditioning:

Bell — Conditioned Response

Characteristics of classical conditioning

Acquisition

Prior to conditioning, the NS doesn't bring about a response, but after many pairings of the UCS and NS, this changes.

If the NS is able to produce the same response *in the absence* of the UCS, it becomes a conditioned stimulus (CS) and produces a conditioned response (CR).

Timing

Precise timing of NS–UCS pairing is important in determining whether the NS becomes a reliable CS.

- NS precedes UCS = strong conditioning.
- The longer the delay after NS before onset of UCS = weaker conditioning.
- NS at same time as UCS = weak conditioning as cannot *predict* UCS.
- NS after UCS = ineffective conditioning.

Extinction and spontaneous recovery

Extinction – CS–CR link does not last very long after the removal of the UCS because CS no longer predicts the coming of the UCS.

Spontaneous recovery – If CS and UCS are paired together again in the future, a link between them is made more rapidly, suggesting that it has merely been inhibited.

Generalisation and discrimination

Stimulus generalisation – If a stimulus is presented that is similar to the CS but isn't the CS, then it still produces the CR.

Stimulus discrimination – If one NS is presented with a UCS and other NS are presented that are not associated with it, eventually only the former develops into a CS.

The neutral stimulus may not be truly neutral…

Domjan suggests that the NS cannot be totally unrelated to the UCS in the natural environment. For one to predict the other, they must occur together frequently in an animal's environment. It they didn't, there would be no predictive value in the NS and conditioning would not take place.

There will be many occasions when a stimulus appears without being followed by the UCS. It is unlikely, therefore, that conditioning would occur simply because some totally random stimulus happens to appear prior to a natural reflex.

Taste aversion learning…

Doesn't require NS and UCS to occur closely together in time nor require many repetitions of NS–UCS association for conditioning to take place. Very resistant to extinction and persists long after withdrawal of UCS. This challenges traditional classical conditioning theory which requires:

- That the NS and UCS should be paired together many times before conditioning can take place.
- That delay between NS and UCS is critical, yet in taste aversion learning this can be several hours and still lead to strong conditioning.
- That the withdrawal of UCS means extinction sets in rapidly, yet in taste aversion this time period is far beyond what we might expect.

Is classical conditioning universal?…

Species differ in terms of their motives, cognitive capacities and the degree to which their lives depend on learning. Each species' genetic make-up would place limitations on its learning abilities, which therefore means that the principles of classical conditioning cannot be applied in the same way across all species or even all situations.

IDA *An evolutionary perspective – biological 'preparedness'…*

Relationships between CS and UCS are more difficult to establish for some species than others because different species typically face different challenges, and therefore must learn some things more rapidly than others in order to survive. Animals are *prepared* to learn associations that are significant in terms of their survival needs; *unprepared* to learn associations that are not significant in this respect; *contraprepared* if, after many associations of NS and UCS, no learning occurs.

Chapter 7

Theories of intelligence

Animal learning and intelligence >

Intelligence and learning >   Human intelligence

Classical conditioning

Operant conditioning

Conditioning and the behaviour of animals

Intelligence in non-human animals

Operant conditioning

Operant conditioning theory explains learning thus:

Spontaneous behaviours (operants) produce reactions in other animals or in the environment, i.e. they have *consequences*.

Whether or not a particular behaviour reappears depends on these consequences, desirable consequences leading to greater frequency of response and undesirable consequences to lower frequency.

Reinforcement

A reinforcer is something in the animal's environment that is a consequence of a particular behaviour and makes that behaviour more likely to recur.

- *Positive reinforcement* – Behaviour produces a consequence that is satisfying or pleasant to the animal.
- *Negative reinforcement* – Behaviour terminates something that the animal finds unpleasant. Negative reinforcers strengthen a behaviour because they remove an aversive stimulus.
- An animal may learn to avoid an aversive stimulus completely by responding to a stimulus that precedes it (*avoidance conditioning*).

Schedules of reinforcement

Reinforcement can either be *continuous* (i.e. full) or *partial*. Partial reinforcement schedules are more effective at maintaining a behaviour.

- *Fixed-ratio* – Animal receives reinforcement for a fixed proportion of responses (e.g. every 10th response).
- *Variable-ratio* – Animal receives reinforcement for fixed percentage of responses (e.g. 60%), although the number of responses required before each reinforcement is unpredictable.
- *Fixed-interval* – Animal reinforced after fixed period (e.g. every 10 minutes) provided it performs the behaviour.
- *Variable-interval* – Animal receives reinforcement at certain time intervals (e.g. four per hour) but at varying intervals between each reinforcement.

Punishment

Reinforcement increases the likelihood of a behaviour recurring, whereas punishment *decreases* it.

- *Positive punishment* means adding an unpleasant consequence (e.g. an electric shock) after a behaviour.
- *Negative punishment* means taking away something pleasant (e.g. removing a dog's food after it has growled at someone).

A longitudinal study (Hemphill and Sanson) found that children were more likely to develop behavioural problems if their parents used punishment rather than positive reinforcement to control their behaviour.

There is the problem of instinctive drift…

Not only are some behaviours easier to learn because the animal is biologically prepared to learn them, but they can also override more artificial conditioned behaviours.

For example, Breland and Breland trained animals to perform cute, human-like behaviours using operant conditioning techniques. Over time, however, their conditioned behaviours deteriorated as the animals' more natural behaviours intruded on their performance. Breland and Breland called this '*instinctive drift*'.

IDA *Real-world application…*

The power of operant conditioning has been demonstrated in behaviour modification (replacing undesirable with desirable behaviours). Research has shown that operant conditioning techniques have been used successfully to help people avoid obesity, give up smoking and in toilet training (e.g. Azrin and Foxx).

A meta-analysis of 34 studies comparing the Azrin and Foxx method with conventional methods of toilet training found the use of operant conditioning techniques particularly effective for children with learning difficulties (Kiddoo).

IDA *Problems with the use of non-human animals…*

Skinner's reliance on rats and pigeons for his experiments on operant conditioning has led some critics to suggest that such studies can neither confirm nor refute hypotheses about *human* behaviour. They can, at best, only suggest new hypotheses that might be relevant to humans.

However…

Skinner's reliance on the experimental method allowed him to establish a cause and effect relationship between the consequences of a behaviour and its future frequency of occurrence.

IDA *The illusion of free will…*

Skinner believed that all behaviour was the result of either positive or negative reinforcement, and therefore any perception of free will was an illusion. What we may think of as behaviours chosen by free will are really behaviours that are determined by external influences (e.g. parents, educators) within our culture.

There are cultural differences in reliance on conditioning…

These reflect the dangers that confront a particular society, e.g. the Gusii of Kenya have a history of tribal warfare and face constant threats from wild animals. As a result, Gusii parents make more frequent use of punishment than reward to shape appropriate behaviour in their children.

Caning (positive punishment) and withdrawing food and shelter (negative punishment) are common ways of bringing about compliance in such a dangerous environment.

There are problems with punishment…

Because reinforcement cannot, by itself, eliminate undesirable behaviours, punishment becomes necessary. However, it is often used in ways that render it ineffective.

For example, the individual may come to fear the person doing the punishing, rather than the action that led to the punishment.

If children are punished physically for their transgressions, they may learn that problems can be solved with violence, which legitimises it for them and so more likely to use it in their own behaviour.

Chapter 7

Theories of intelligence | Classical conditioning
Operant conditioning
Animal learning and intelligence | > | Conditioning and the behaviour of animals
Intelligence and learning | > | Human intelligence | Intelligence in non-human animals

Conditioning and the behaviour of animals

Classical conditioning

Training animals for release

Animals are sometimes held in captivity prior to release. This creates a problem because they become dependent on humans, e.g. learning that feeding is associated with human presence.

- *Simple conditioning* – Among captive dolphins, food (the UCS) always appears in the presence of humans (NS) and never when they are absent. This means that dolphins learn a strong association between humans and food, which puts them in danger when back in the wild.
- *Compound conditioning* – The learned association between human and food can be prevented by combining the human presence with a more appropriate stimulus (e.g. an auditory stimulus). For captive dolphins an auditory stimulus is a more reliable predictor because it *always* precedes food, whereas humans do not (i.e. they sometimes appear without food).

There is a problem with the use of compound conditioning…

It would be difficult and even undesirable to totally isolate many species completely from humans. Goldblatt, in a review of research on captive animal stress, concluded that understimulating environments, including those totally devoid of human contact, were more likely to be associated with stress responses in a wide range of species, including marine mammals.

Training animals for release is a necessity because…

A critical objective in caring for animals in captivity is to ensure that they do not learn responses that they will transfer to the wild and that will endanger them there. This means that the researcher cannot rely on learned associations between humans and food extinguishing naturally; they must prevent them from being learned in the first place.

IDA *There are ethical issues with using animals for research…*

The use of conditioning techniques in the training of animals while in captivity may both create and alleviate problems for these animals. Reliance on humans for food may create learned patterns of behaviour that prevent their post-release adjustment. However, the use of compound conditioning techniques may go some way to alleviating this.

Reproductive success

Researchers have puzzled over why the CR has developed. One possibility is increased reproductive success.

For example, a CS that occurs before mating (e.g. a signal from the female) serves to predict mating opportunities and therefore would increase an animal's reproductive success if they can respond appropriately to the CS.

There is evidence to support this…

The importance of classical conditioning in reproductive success is demonstrated in a laboratory study using quail. Matthews *et al.* found that male birds that received a CS signal prior to mating fertilised more than double the number of eggs compared to males who received no CS.

An arbitrary CS–UCS association is not adaptive in the natural environment…

This is because the CS–UCS pairing must occur regularly in the natural environment. If it does not, this would undermine any learned association as such accidental pairings of CS and UCS would be rare.

Operant conditioning

Foraging

Animals are subject to the principles of operant conditioning as they try to find food in their environment.

For example, woodpeckers are reinforced for pecking a certain tree if they find insects there. They return to that spot frequently because of that reinforcement. When the supply of insects becomes exhausted, the pecking response is gradually extinguished.

There is evidence to support this…

The role of operant conditioning in foraging strategies among non-human animals is supported by a study of foraging behaviour in monkeys. Agetsuma manipulated the quality of food patches frequented by monkeys by making the probability of food higher in one patch than another. Consistent with an operant conditioning prediction, subsequent visits were more frequent to the high-quality patch than the low-quality patch.

Positive reinforcement training (PRT)

Desensitisation – Pairing positive rewards with objects or procedures that cause fear so that they become less frightening and less stressful.

Cooperative feeding – Dominant animals are rewarded for allowing subordinate animals to feed and subordinate animals for being 'brave' enough to accept food in the presence of dominant animals.

The use of PRT events has been associated with enhanced psychological wellbeing of animals used in research.

There is supporting evidence for PRT…

Bloomsmith *et al.* used PRT to train dominant chimpanzees not to chase and steal subordinate's food by reinforcing behaviours incompatible with chasing and stealing (e.g. sitting in one spot while feeding). This had the desired effect of decreasing aggression from dominants and submission from subordinates during feeding periods.

Clay *et al.* used PRT with macaques to desensitise them from feeling fearful in the presence of humans. A group who received positive reinforcement whenever they were in the laboratory environment subsequently showed less fearful behaviour than a control group who were simply exposed to the same environment without reinforcement.

IDA *PRT deals with ethical issues in animal research…*

PRT has alleviated many of the stressors associated with research participation, and has satisfied both the requirements of the Animal Welfare Act, and the needs of the different species used in research.

Chapter 7

Theories of intelligence

Classical conditioning

Operant conditioning

Animal learning and intelligence >

Conditioning and the behaviour of animals

Intelligence and learning >

Human intelligence

Intelligence in non-human animals

Intelligence in non-human animals

Machiavellian intelligence

Social problem solving

Intelligence may be an adaptation to social problem solving in large groups.

Individual animals that are able to manipulate others in their group without causing aggression are at an advantage and possess Machiavellian intelligence.

Manipulation and deception

Social-living animals can use behavioural tactics to manipulate and deceive others for their own ends. This ability is restricted to the great apes.

Manipulative tricks include:

• *Management of attention* – Target's attention is diverted to or away from something so as to profit the deceiver.

• *Creating an image* – Deception changes the way the target views the individual (e.g. grooming prior to snatching food).

Forming alliances

Power in social groups is often determined more by having the right allies than by physical strength.

Many apes form alliances based on an individual's ability to provide useful help in the future. For example, males may form alliances with more powerful individuals.

A female ape may behave in Machiavellian ways by having sex with a dominant male to increase the likelihood that he will protect her and her offspring.

There is support for the existence of Machiavellian intelligence…

Studies of agonistic buffering (Deag and Crook) showed that subordinate Barbary macaque monkeys would sometimes carry an infant monkey when approaching a high-ranking male to reduce the likelihood of being attacked by the dominant male.

Machiavellian intelligence may not be restricted to primates…

The idea that intelligence and social complexity are linked is supported by research which suggests an important role of the neocortex in the rise of Machiavellian intelligence in primates.

Burish *et al.* have also provided evidence for this relationship in birds where the degree of social complexity is positively related to the size of the *telencephalon* (equivalent to cortex) in the brain.

A consequence of Machiavellian intelligence…

More highly developed social intellect in some individuals will exert selection pressures on others, so that over evolutionary time, there will be an 'arms race' of social intelligence within a particular species.

Machiavellian intelligence alone may not be enough…

Maestripieri found evidence for many of the behaviours associated with Machiavellian intelligence (e.g. forming alliances, strategic sexual alliances with dominant males) in a colony of rhesus macaques.

However… The macaques failed on another criterion of intelligence – self-recognition. Rhesus macaques will viciously attack their own image in a mirror, suggesting that they do not recognise it as their own image.

> **IDA** *A biological approach to Machiavellian intelligence…*
>
> Byrne and Corp found a positive correlation between the amount of tactical deception used by a species and their typical neocortex volume. Among primate species, neocortex volume varies much more than the volume of other brain areas. Neocortical enlargement appears necessary to give individuals sufficient memory to develop the extensive social knowledge necessary for Machiavellian intelligence.

Self-recognition

Research into self-recognition

The ability of an animal to recognise itself in a mirror is usually accepted as indicating a form of intelligence.

• *Chimpanzees* – Gallup found that chimpanzees used their image in a mirror to touch a red mark placed on their forehead and ears.

• *Dolphins* – Reiss and Marino used either a black ink marker or a 'sham marker' that was just water. They found that those marked with black ink spent longer in front of reflective surfaces.

• *Killer whales* – A similar study using killer whales (Delfour and Marten) found that they also appear to possess the cognitive abilities necessary for self-recognition.

Why species differ

Self-recognition may result from large brains and advanced cognitive ability rather than species-specific characteristics.

For example, dolphins and primates have a very different evolutionary history, but both possess large brains and self-recognition.

Self-recognition may be evident in other species also…

Research by Plotnik *et al.* suggests that elephants are also able to recognise themselves in a mirror, a key criterion for 'intelligence'. The researchers found that the elephants used the mirror to guide them, touching a mark on the side of their head.

However… There remains the possibility that the elephants simply touched the mark because they felt it on their skin, therefore did not possess self-recognition. The researchers overcame this possibility by also using a transparent mark, which would have felt the same yet was largely ignored by the animals.

There is a general lack of research support for this…

Heyes argues that there is little reliable evidence that self-recognition is present in all primate species. First of all, the fact that chimpanzees may use a mirror to explore parts of their body is unconvincing as a demonstration of self-recogniton. Second, not all chimpanzees pass the mark test. Thus, Heyes claims that the evidence does not indicate the possession of a self-concept or other aspect of self-recognition that might be equivalent to the cognitive abilities of human beings.

> **IDA** *There are ethical issues associated with this research…*
>
> The rarity of self-recognition among non-human species and the fact that it is more common in species that help other individuals in need indicates a certain level of consciousness in these animals.
>
> This emphasises the need to extend many of the ethical issues currently associated with humans to these species and to protect species such as the Asian elephant, which is currently on the endangered species list.

Chapter 7

Theories of intelligence | Evolutionary factors in human intelligence
Animal learning and intelligence | Genetic factors in intelligence-test performance
Intelligence and learning > Human intelligence > Environmental factors in intelligence-test performance

Evolutionary factors in human intelligence

Heritable characteristics such as intelligence are changeable rather than fixed, and likely to be caused by natural or sexual selection.

The measure of evolutionary success is reproductive fitness.

Ecological (foraging) demands

These are aspects of the environment that must be adapted to in order to survive. Two such demands are:

- *Finding food* – Intelligence evolved because of an increased cognitive demand on frugivores to monitor a food supply that was only available at certain times and locations.
- *Extracting food* – Tool use is an indication of intelligence in non-human and human species. A study of chimpanzees by Mercader *et al.* found evidence of tool use. Successful hunter-gatherer groups (e.g. *!Kung San*) use elaborate tools, whereas less successful groups use simple tools.

Social complexity

Individuals who best dealt with the demands of group living increased their reproductive fitness. This involves:

- *Machiavellian intelligence* – Whiten and Byrne suggest the evolution of human intellect was primarily driven by the need to deal with problems posed by group members. This selective pressure led to Machiavellian intelligence (see page 63).
- *The meat-sharing hypothesis* – Meat was an important source of saturated fat for early humans. Meat could be used to forge alliances and to persuade females to mate. Strategic meat sharing requires considerable cognitive abilities to keep a running score of debts and credits.

Brain size and intelligence

Broman found that measures of head size at birth and at age seven significantly predicted later IQ.

The use of MRI allows researchers to measure brain size more directly. Studies (e.g. Andreasen *et al.*) have found significant correlations of around +.40 using this method.

Evolutionary factors in the development of large brains

- *Innovation, social learning and tool use* provide a measure of behavioural flexibility of a species. Reader and Laland found the frequency of all three was positively correlated with brain size in 116 primate species.
- *Sexual selection* – Miller suggests that large brains evolved in humans because they enhanced reproductive success, with intelligence attractive to the opposite sex.

Foraging versus social theories of intelligence…

Dunbar found that only social complexity correlated with neocortex volume, suggesting that the social demands of group living shaped human intelligence more than the demands of the physical environment.

However…

Byrne claims that group size alone cannot explain why apes are more intelligent than monkeys, as both species live in groups of similar size and complexity.

IDA *Cultural bias in the brain size and intelligence relationship…*

Beals *et al.* found significant differences in cranial volume between East Asians, Europeans and Africans. Rushton explains this in terms of the 'Out of Africa' hypothesis, in that early humans left Africa and encountered more cognitive demanding problems to stay alive. This led to larger brain sizes in East Asians.

However…

Higher levels of intelligence found in East Asians (Jensen and Rushton) may also be due to the fact that intelligence is more highly valued in East Asian cultures.

IDA *Gender bias in the brain size and intelligence relationship…*

Ankney found male brains were consistently heavier than female brains, yet there is no difference in IQ levels in men and women (Peters).

This may be explained by the possibility that brain organisation is more important than brain size and female brains are better organised.

There is evidence to support the Machiavellian intelligence hypothesis…

Mitani and Watts provide support for the importance of alliances (a key aspect of Machiavellian intelligence) and the role of meat sharing among primates. They found that male chimpanzees were more likely to share meat with other males than with females. This is important in forging alliances because hunting is more successful when carried out in groups.

Consequently, it may be 'meat for alliance' rather than 'meat for sex' that explains the strategic importance of meat sharing.

There is evidence to support the meat-sharing hypothesis…

Hill and Kaplan found that among the *Ache* people of Paraguay, meat is frequently shared outside of the family. Skilled hunters are rewarded with disproportionate sexual favours from women in the group.

However…

Wrangham suggests a simpler explanation for this. Males must expend considerable energy defending a kill or deterring scavengers. By sharing with others, they can eat without interruption.

Brain size does not correlate with all types of intelligence…

Witelson *et al.* studied the brains of 100 adults. Before their death the adults had completed a full IQ test as part of the study. Researchers found that performance on the test correlated with brain volume, but the relationship depended on the type of intelligence studied, with only verbal intelligence having a significant relationship with brain volume.

There are problems associated with large brain size…

Large brains are extremely demanding in terms of energy, and must compete with other body organs for resources. A large brain takes longer to mature, which means that infants are heavily dependent on their parents for much longer, which in turn limits how quickly they reach reproductive age. Given these factors, we might expect there would be considerable selective pressure *against* the evolution of large brains.

Large brains are not only found in humans…

Despite the costs associated with large brains, progressively larger brains have evolved in all primates, not just in humans. Reader and Laland's research challenges the view that large brains arose in human beings because of the development of uniquely human characteristics such as language. Many other primates have brains of a similar relative size (in terms of body/brain size), yet lack language.

Chapter 7

Theories of intelligence	Evolutionary factors in human intelligence
Animal learning and intelligence	**Genetic factors in intelligence-test performance**
Intelligence and learning >	Human intelligence >	Environmental factors in intelligence-test performance

Genetic factors in intelligence-test performance

Twin and adoption studies

Twin studies

Dizygotic twins (DZ) share 50% of their genes, monozygotic (MZ) share 100%.

Because it is difficult to disentangle the effects of genes and environment, the real value of twin studies comes from twins who are raised apart.

Bouchard and McGue found that the concordance rate (the degree to which IQ is the same for two related individuals) was 60% for DZ twins reared together, but this was higher (72%) for MZ twins reared apart, suggesting a stronger genetic component for IQ.

Malouff et al. carried out a meta-analysis that covered more than 400 twin studies. The overall finding was that approximately half of the variation in IQ test scores could be attributed to genetics.

Adoption studies compare the IQ of
adopted children with other members of their adoptive and biological families.

If genetic factors influence intelligence, research should find a greater similarity between IQ scores of adopted children and their biological families than with their adoptive families.

The Texas Adoption Project (Horn
et al.) studied adopted children on two occasions, 10 years apart. When first assessed, IQs correlated more strongly with the IQs of their adoptive parents than their biological mothers. However, 10 years later, correlations were higher with their biological mothers.

This suggests that the impact of family influences decreases with age, while the impact of genetic influences increases.

There are problems with twin studies…

Kamin and Goldberger claim that the result of twin studies may overestimate the heritability of intelligence. They argue that MZ twins share a more similar environment than DZ twins because they are identical. Therefore, some of the estimated similarity that is attributed to genetic influences may be the product of a shared environment instead.

Twins may not be a representative sample…

Voracek and Haubner carried out a meta-analysis of studies that had compared more than 30,000 twins and nearly 1.6 million singletons (non-twins). On average, twins score more than 4 IQ points lower than singletons. Consequently, this may lead to a biased estimation of the heritability of intelligence.

IDA Real-world application: Genetic engineering…

If genetic factors are important in intelligence, then genetic engineering might be used to raise the intelligence of children, provided a candidate gene can be identified. If such a gene can be found, it may be possible to alter human DNA to include that gene. Researchers have already genetically modified mice to be better at learning and remembering (Tang et al.), so the possibility of boosting human intelligence in the same way may also be possible.

IDA A sub-cultural bias in the study of genetic factors…

Turkheimer et al. have identified a potential bias in the reporting of studies in this area, i.e. that the same gene can have different effects in different environments. They found that in children from affluent families, about 60% of the variance in IQ scores could be accounted for by genes. However, for children from poorer backgrounds, genes accounted for almost none of the variance in their IQ scores.

Genetic 'influences' may be due to selective placement…

Children are often adopted into environments similar to the ones they came from, which would explain why correlations for IQ between adopted children and their biological family remain high.

Genes can also mould the environment…

Genes may also influence behaviour in terms of how intelligence develops, by moulding the intellectual environment in particular ways. For example, genes may cause us to seek out some experiences rather than others, which in turn affects our intelligence for better or worse.

A gene for intelligence

IGF2R gene

Hill et al. divided children into 'super-bright' and 'average' groups. Twice as many of the children in the super-bright group had a particular variant of the IGF2R gene than in the average group. They concluded that this form of the gene contributes to high intelligence test performance.

Genetic markers for intelligence

Curtis et al. studied the DNA of more than 7000 children. They found six genetic markers that showed any sign of influencing IQ test scores. However, after subjecting the data to more stringent statistical tests, only one gene passed, and this accounted for just 0.4% of the variation in IQ scores.

The IGF2R gene cannot cause high IQ on its own…

More than half of the children in the 'super-bright' group did not have this variant of the gene. Similarly, some of the children in the 'average' group did have this variant of the IGF2R gene. This clearly indicates that many other factors, some genetic, some environmental, must contribute to the overall level of intelligence possessed by any one individual.

IDA Research into genetic markers is socially sensitive…

The discovery of any genes associated with high IQ could divide society by marginalising and discriminating against those individuals who did not possess these 'IQ genes'. This also highlights the importance of the peer review process, which aims to ensure that only properly controlled studies with appropriate conclusions are allowed to be published.

Breastfeeding may influence IQ…

Caspi et al. found that children with one version of the FADS2 gene scored 7 points higher in IQ tests if they were breastfed, whereas children with another variant of this gene showed no such benefits. This is significant because it suggests that genes can alter the effect that a particular environmental influence has on intelligence.

Chapter 7

Theories of intelligence | Evolutionary factors in human intelligence
Animal learning and intelligence | Genetic factors in intelligence-test performance
Intelligence and learning > Human intelligence > Environmental factors in intelligence-test performance

Environmental factors in intelligence-test performance

Family environment

Socioeconomic status (SES)

In the UK, SES is determined by parental occupation from Class I (professional) to Class V (unskilled).

Mackintosh found that even after factors such as financial hardship and area of residence were taken into account, children of Class I fathers scored, on average, 10 IQ points higher than children of Class V fathers.

Why does SES influence intelligence?

Families with high SES are better able to prepare their children for school because they have better access to resources (e.g. the Internet) and information (e.g. from better educated parents) that is essential to children's cognitive and intellectual development.

IDA Real-world application…

If SES has such a strong effect on intelligence, then improvements in SES should produce a corresponding increase in IQ. Adoption studies where low SES children have been adopted into high SES families (e.g. Schiff et al.) have demonstrated substantial IQ gains in those children.

Birth order and family size

Belmont and Marolla studied family size, birth order and IQ in a sample of 386 19-year-old Dutch men. They found that, when SES was controlled, children from larger families had a lower IQ than children from small families, and first-born children typically had higher IQ than later-born children.

There is research evidence to support these effects…

Bjerkedal et al. confirmed the importance of birth order in a Norwegian sample. They found that first-born children had higher IQs than later-born children and also found that when a first-born child had died, the second-born scored closer to the IQ score of an average first-born child.

Birth order effects on IQ may be short-lived…

A study (Blake) of more than 100,000 people found that in small- and medium-sized families, birth order had no effect on how far adults progressed in education, suggesting that birth order effects do not persist.

Culture

Group socialisation theory

Harris claims that experiences outside the home may be more important in developing a child's intelligence than experiences within it. As children grow older, they are less influenced by their family life, and more influenced by life outside the home (e.g. peer groups).

The group socialisation explanation is rejected…

Pinker argues that the interaction between genes and peer group influence is a possible explanation for some behaviours (e.g. smoking), but there is little, if any, evidence for an influence on intelligence.

IDA A physiological explanation for the influence of poverty on IQ…

Kishiyama et al. found that children from low SES backgrounds showed a lower prefrontal cortex response to novel stimuli; possibly a consequence of a stressful and impoverished environment that is often associated with low SES.

Ethnicity and IQ

Herrnstein and Murray found that immigrants to the US had IQ levels that were significantly lower than US residents. They argued that immigration into the US created a downward pressure on intelligence levels, and an increase in the social problems typically associated with people with low IQ.

IDA IQ tests are culturally biased…

Greenfield argues that assessing the IQ of people from cultures other than the one in which the test was developed represents a cultural bias (an imposed etic). This inevitably influences any results when such tests are used and leads to invalid conclusions about the measure of IQ in such groups.

School effects

Ceci carried out a meta-analysis to see if school boosts intelligence. He found that children who attended school regularly scored higher in tests of IQ than those who attended less regularly, and that IQ scores decreased over the long summer holidays. IQ scores were also found to rise by an average of 2.7 points for each year of formal education completed.

Not everybody agrees that education has such an effect…

Herrnstein and Murray claim that intelligence is mostly genetically heritable, and that no one has been able to manipulate IQ to a significant degree through changes in environmental factors such as improved education.

As a result, they argue that attempts to raise IQ through compensatory education are doomed to failure.

Explaining contradictory viewpoints…

These contradictory claims (i.e. Ceci versus Herrnstein and Murray) can be explained as follows:

- There is a failure to define what constitutes 'an improvement'. Both would accept that education has an effect, but disagree on the size of that effect and how it might be measured.

Compensatory education

Head Start, which began in the1960s, was an attempt to provide compensatory education for disadvantaged children in the US.

There were some initial gains in IQ, but longer-term examination questioned its effectiveness, with some studies showing positive gains from participation but others reporting no significant gains.

Compensatory education projects can work…

The Perry Preschool Project provided high-quality preschool education to African-American children living in poverty and considered at high risk of school failure. When the children started school, 67% of those in the programme group had IQs greater than 90, whereas only 28% of those not involved in the programme scored above 90.

Chapter 8

Cognition and development

Division A   Development of thinking
Piaget's theory of cognitive development
Vygotsky's theory of cognitive development
Applications of cognitive development theories to education

Division B   Development of moral understanding
Kohlberg's theory of moral understanding

Division C   Development of social cognition
Development of a child's sense of self
Development of a child's understanding of others
Biological explanations of social cognition

Specification

Cognition and development	
Development of thinking	• Theories of cognitive development, including Piaget and Vygotsky. • Applications of cognitive development theories to education.
Development of moral understanding	• Kohlberg's theory of moral understanding
Development of social cognition	• Development of the child's sense of self, including Theory of Mind. • Development of children's understanding of others, including perspective-taking, for example Selman. • Biological explanations of social cognition, including the role of the mirror neuron system.

Chapter 8

Development of thinking > Piaget's theory of cognitive development
Development of moral understanding   Vygotsky's theory of cognitive development
Cognition and development   >   Development of social cognition   Applications of these theories to education

Piaget's theory of cognitive development

Mechanisms of cognitive development

Maturation and the environment

As a child gets older (maturation), certain mental operations become possible and at the same time, through interactions with the environment, their understanding of the world becomes more complex.

There is little direct research support…

Inhelder *et al.* found that children's learning was helped when there was a mild conflict between what they expected to happen and what did happen, but Bryant claims that this wasn't really the sort of conflict that Piaget was talking about.

Key mechanisms

Schema are self-constructed mental structures for dealing with the world. Some are innate but most are learned as a consequence of the child's interaction with the environment.

Assimilation occurs when an existing schema (such as sucking) is used on a new object (such as a toy car). It involves the incorporation of new information into an existing schema.

Accommodation occurs when a child adapts existing schema in order to understand new information that doesn't appear to fit.

Equilibration drives cognitive development. An imbalance between existing thinking and what is encountered in the child is dealt with using assimilation or accommodation until equilibrium is restored.

Operations are logical mental rules such as the rules of arithmetic.

Limitations of Piaget's theory…

The research evidence given below (e.g. Samuel and Bryant) suggests that Piaget underestimated children's abilities at younger ages, and may have overestimated the ability to use abstract logic at older ages.

His theory focuses too much on logic and generally ignores social factors, such as the benefit of cooperative group work.

The research methods he used were flawed…

• He used a biased sample of middle-class Western children who value logical thinking.
• The research designs may have confused younger children, e.g. the three mountains task was unrealistic (Hughes), younger children were confused by two questions in the conservation task (Samuel and Bryant), the conservation transformation acted as a demand characteristic (McGarrigle and Donaldson).

Strengths of Piaget's theory…

Subsequent evidence from critics (see below) still supports qualitative changes in cognitive development as a child matures.

Piaget's main contribution was in increasing our understanding of the qualitative differences between child and adult thinking.

Stages in cognitive development

Stage 1: Sensorimotor (0–2 years)

Children learn to coordinate sensory input (e.g. what they see) with motor actions (e.g. hand movements) through circular reactions.

They lack an understanding of object permanence.

Nativists claim that infants have more knowledge…

Baillargeon and DeVos showed that infants as young as 3–4 months did display object permanence, using a carrot rolled on a toy train set behind a screen with a large window. A large carrot should be visible as it passes behind the window, whereas a small carrot (not as broad) should remain hidden. The infants looked longer for the large carrot when it didn't appear, presumably expecting the top half to be visible.

Stage 2: Pre-operational (2–7)

Children's thought becomes symbolic but they are not capable of *reversibility of thought* because they rely on perceptual rather than internally consistent logical reasoning (appearance–reality distinction). Children are also egocentric.

There is research evidence…

Piaget illustrated pre-operational thinking using the three mountains task. Children 3–4 years old chose their own perspective when asked for the dolls' perspective.

However…

Hughes showed that younger children could cope with the task if it was more realistic, for example, using a naughty boy doll that was hiding from a toy policeman.

Stage 3: Concrete operational (7–11)

Children acquire the rudiments of *logical reasoning*, and display skills of *reversibility* and decentration (no longer focusing on just one aspect of a task). This means that they are capable of *conservation* (e.g. recognising quantities don't change even if they look different).

There is research evidence…

Children younger than seven weren't able to conserve when tested using rows of counters, cylinders of plasticine, or beakers of water. Each display was transformed so the quantity *appeared* to have increased (e.g. the counters were spread out) i.e. if it looked bigger, it was bigger.

However…

Younger children can conserve if not confused by questions and only asked one question (after the transformation) (Samuel and Bryant).

Stage 4: Formal operational (11+)

Children can now solve abstract problems using hypothetico-deductive reasoning (e.g. testing hypotheses) and idealistic thinking (they are no longer tied to how things are, but can imagine how things might be).

There is research evidence…

Piaget and Inhelder demonstrated that younger children do not use logical thinking using the *beaker problem* (children asked to work out how to turn a liquid yellow by combining various liquids).

However…

Wason and Shapiro found that only 10% of university students could cope when given an abstract test of logical reasoning.

Dasen claims that only one-third of adults ever reach this stage.

IDA *Real-world application… to education* (see page 70)

Chapter 8

Development of thinking	>	Piaget's theory of cognitive development
Development of moral understanding		Vygotsky's theory of cognitive development
Cognition and development	>	Development of social cognition		Applications of these theories to education

Vygotsky's theory of cognitive development

Mental processes

The importance of culture

The main theme of Vygotsky's theory is that social interaction plays a fundamental role in cognitive development.

Elementary and higher mental functions

Children are born with *elementary mental functions*, such as perception.

These are transformed into *higher mental functions* (such as use of mathematical systems) by the influence of culture. Higher mental functions are exclusively human.

What to think and how to think

Through culture, children acquire:
- The *content* of their thinking, i.e. their knowledge.
- The *processes* of their thinking, i.e. the tools of intellectual adaptation.

Importance of culture supported by research...

Gredler cited the primitive counting system used in Papua New Guinea as an example of how culture can limit cognitive development, because using body parts alone makes it very difficult to deal with large numbers.

There is challenging research evidence...

Attempts to teach chimpanzees to use language (e.g. Savage-Rumbaugh) suggest that they can acquire higher mental functions.

Limitations of Vygotsky's theory...

This theory does not lend itself as readily to experimentation as Piaget's because the concepts are more difficult to operationalise.

Whereas Piaget underplayed social influences, Vygotsky may have overplayed the importance of the social environment – if social influence was all that was needed to advance cognitive development then learning would be a lot faster than it is.

Vygotsky's theory may lack detail because he died at such a young age and did not have time to fully develop it (Lindblom and Ziemke).

Strengths of Vygotsky's theory...

The Vygotskian approach provides a bridge between social and cognitive domains.

It is a more positive approach than Piaget's because it offers ways that others can be actively involved in assisting a learner.

In this way, Vygotsky's theory may potentially have more educational applications than Piaget's theory.

Process of cultural influence

The role of others: experts

A child learns through problem-solving experiences shared with an 'expert' (i.e. parent, teacher or more competent peer).

The expert guides problem solving activity, but gradually this ability to guide learning transfers to the child.

Semiotics and the role of language

Culture is transmitted by experts using *semiotics* (cultural signs and symbols such as language and mathematics).

- Language begins as shared dialogues (*preintellectual speech*).
- Around 2–3 years children use language to solve problems, often out loud (*egocentric speech*).
- About age 7, this gives way to silent or *inner speech*, which continues to be used as a way of reflecting upon and solving problems.

Zone of proximal development (ZPD)

The ZPD is the distance between what a child actually can do (determined by independent problem solving) and their potential (determined through problem solving under expert guidance).

The ZPD is the region where cognitive development is taking place. Learning between people (social) later becomes internalised (individual), i.e. 'internalisation'.

The social and individual levels

Every aspect of a child's cognitive development appears first at a social level (i.e. between the child and others), and later, at an individual level (i.e. inside the mind of the child).

There is research evidence for the role of language in cognitive development...

The acquisition of a new word is the beginning of the development of a concept, illustrated in a study by Carmichael *et al.* where participants' recall of a drawing was influenced by the label given to it (e.g. a kidney shape labelled as a kidney bean or a canoe).

However...

Sinclair-de-Zwart tried to teach non-conserving children to use comparative terms such as bigger and shorter. She found very little improvement in their ability to conserve, a finding that does not support Vygotsky because his theory suggests that cultural tools (such as language) should lead to cognitive development.

There is research evidence...

McNaughton and Leyland observed young children working with their mothers or alone on jigsaw puzzles of increasing difficulty. The children could do more when working with their mothers than individually.

- When children were doing easy puzzles (below the child's ZPD) the mothers were mainly concerned with keeping them on task.
- When they were working within their ZPD, mothers focused on helping the children solve the puzzle themselves.
- At the third level (beyond the child's ZPD) the emphasis was on completing the puzzle by whatever means.

IDA *Comparing Piaget's approach with Vygotsky's...*

The two theories represent different styles of learning and different kinds of learner. Vygotsky was a communist believing in the power of society in the development of the individual; Piaget was a product of individualist European society. Piaget's child is an introvert, whereas Vygotsky's child is an extravert (Miller).

The theories have similarities; both emphasise the interactionist character of development, the importance of scientific thought and the learner as active rather than passive (Glassman).

IDA *Real-world application... to education* (see page 70)

Applications of cognitive development theories to education

Applying Piaget's theory to education

Readiness

Piaget proposed that cognitive development is due to the process of ageing, therefore you can't teach a child to perform certain activities before they are biologically 'ready'.

Stages of development

Educational programmes should follow Piaget's stages of development.

Motivation to learn

Cognitive growth comes from the desire to resolve the disequilibrium caused by cognitive conflict. The teacher's role is to create an environment where the learner is challenged, so knowledge develops through discovery learning.

Logical thinking

Logical thinking is the spur to cognitive development and needs to be taught through maths and science.

Practice may be more important than readiness...

Bryant and Trabasso showed that pre-operational children could be trained to solve logical tasks (by practicing simple tasks first) and suggested that failure was due to memory restrictions rather than a lack of operational (logical) thinking (readiness).

However...

Danner and Day found that students aged 10–13 showed no improvements when tutored on three formal operational tasks, whereas 17 year olds (who were 'ready') did show significant improvements, i.e. they had to be 'ready' in order for practice to improve performance.

However...

Even when practice does improve performance, this doesn't mean a child can transfer the understanding to a novel situation.

Limitations of the Piagetian approach...

Piagetian discovery activities are often at the expense of content knowledge and may lead to backwardness in reading and writing, because children spend too little time practising these skills (Modgil *et al.*).

IDA *Culture bias...*

The Piagetian view may be culture biased. It suggests that the child is the sole agent of his learning, which is an individualist approach.

Applying Vygotsky's theory to education

Collaborative learning

Students at various abilities work together in groups towards a common goal and shared understanding.

Peer tutoring

The *more knowledgeable other* (MKO) is someone with better knowledge.

Experts guide learners through the *zone of proximal development* (ZPD). Experts can be a child's teacher or older adult, or a peer with more knowledge (peer tutoring).

Scaffolding

The process of offering assistance to a learner to assist progress through the ZPD (Wood *et al*).

Scaffolding involves:
- Recruitment – engage interest.
- Reduction in degrees of freedom – simplify the task.
- Direction maintenance – keep up motivation.
- Marking critical features – highlight relevant features of task.
- Frustration control – reduce frustration.
- Demonstration – model solutions.

Motivation to learn

The learner is motivated to move through their ZPD by MKOs using the process of scaffolding.

There is research support for the value of collaborative learning...

Students who participated in collaborative learning later performed better on an individual critical-thinking test than students who studied individually (Gokhale).

There is research support for the value of peer tutoring...

Peer tutoring leads to improvements in tutees' performance (Cohen *et al.*); however, it is most effective for peer tutors (Cloward).

However, one confounding variable is...

That experimental groups often receive peer tutoring in addition to normal lessons, thus receiving more instruction overall (Slavin).

There is research support...

Wood and Middleton observed mothers (the MKO) helping their 3–4-year-old children assembling a 3D pyramid puzzle, a task beyond the ZPD. There was a positive association between children's independent task mastery and contingent regulations – when a mother responds to her child's failure by providing more explicit instructions and responds to success by providing less explicit instructions.

IDA *Culture bias...*

Vygotsky's approach may be more appropriate in collectivist settings because true sharing is the basis of such cultures, whereas in individualist settings children are encouraged to be more competitive and self-reliant.

This is supported by...

Stigler and Perry who found group work was more effective in Asian schools (collective culture) but not in American ones (individualist culture).

General methodological issues...

It is difficult to assess and compare approaches because outcome measures depend on the aims of the technique and because teachers may adapt methods and thus not be comparable.

IDA *Comparing and contrasting the two approaches...*

- Both approaches place importance on discovery (active) learning.
- Both approaches have influenced education practice, however they may just provide 'after the fact' justifications (Walkerdine).
- More traditional, teacher-oriented approaches lead to higher achievement than active learning (Bennett), possibly because 'formal' teachers spend more time on core topics and because active learning requires more sensitivity from teachers.
- Both approaches are more concerned with problem-solving abilities and ignore the importance of emotion in learning.

Kohlberg's theory of moral understanding

General principles

Moral decisions

Kohlberg focused particularly on the way that children think about moral decisions rather than on their moral behaviour.

Stage theory

The theory was based on extensive interviews with boys aged 10–16. The boys were given moral dilemmas (e.g. the Heinz dilemma) and asked what should be done and why.

Each stage:

- Is invariant and universal.
- Represents a more equilibrated form of moral understanding, resulting in a more logically consistent and morally mature form of understanding.
- Forms an organised whole – a qualitatively different pattern of moral understanding applied across all situations.
- Moral maturity is achieved through (1) biological maturation, (2) disequilibrium (noticing weaknesses in existing style of thinking) and (3) gains in perspective-taking (understanding another's point of view).

Stages of moral development

I Preconventional level

Children accept the rules of authority figures and judge actions by their consequences. Actions that result in punishments are judged as bad, those that bring rewards are judged as good.

Stage 1   Punishment and obedience orientation

Stage 2   Instrumental purpose orientation

II Conventional level

Individuals continue to believe that conformity to social rules is desirable, but not out of self-interest. Maintaining the current social system ensures positive human relationships and social order.

Stage 3   Interpersonal cooperation

Stage 4   Social order maintaining orientation

III Post-conventional level

The post-conventional individual moves beyond unquestioning compliance with the norms of their own social system. They now define morality in terms of abstract moral principles that apply to all societies and situations.

Stage 5   Social-contract orientation

Stage 6   Universal ethical principles orientation

Do moral *principles* explain *moral behaviour?*...

When students could cheat on a test, only 15% at the post-conventional stage did so, whereas 70% at the pre-conventional stage did, showing that moral principles are related to moral behaviour (Kohlberg).

However...

Burton found that people only behave consistently with their moral principles on some *kinds* of moral behaviour, such as cheating. Likelihood of punishment or the nature of the situation may be critical in determining whether or not someone behaves morally, rather than moral principles.

Krebs and Denton found, when analysing real-life moral decisions, that moral principles were used to justify behaviour *after* it had been performed – therefore moral behaviour isn't based on principles.

Research support for the stage theory...

Colby et al. re-interviewed Kohlberg's original participants regularly over 20 years, confirming that stage 1 and 2 reasoning decreases with age, while stage 4 and 5 reasoning increases.

Walker et al. interviewed 80 children (boys and girls). Six-year-olds were at stages 1 or 2, whereas by age 15 most children had reached stage 3.

A further sample of adults (average age 40) were tested and were mainly between stages 3 and 4, with only 3% between stages 4 and 5.

Stage 6 may be an unrealistic ideal, which is rarely achieved.

Moral dilemmas lack realism...

Kohlberg's evidence is not based on real-life decisions and the moral dilemmas may have made little sense to young children. Gilligan conducted research interviewing people about their own moral decisions.

IDA Gender bias...

Kohlberg's dilemmas are based on a male morality of justice and ignore female concerns with relationships (a morality of care), making women appear morally inferior.

Gilligan's stage theory is based on principles of care, intended as an expansion of Kohlberg's theory rather than an alternative (Jorgensen).

IDA Culture bias...

Kohlberg's moral dilemmas are rooted in Western moral principles, nevertheless evidence from Mexico, Turkey, India and Kenya, using the dilemmas, found the stages and sequence are universal (Colby and Kohlberg).

Snarey found the same using the dilemmas in 27 countries.

However...

Snarey and Keljo found cultural differences – post-conventional understanding occurs mainly in more developed, industrialised societies.

This may occur because diverse communities (found in industrialised societies) pose more conflicts, which promotes moral development because individuals have to question moral standards (Kohlberg).

Ignores emotional factors...

Eisenberg criticised Kohlberg's restricted view of morality because it ignored emotional factors.

IDA Real-world application...

Kohlberg set up democratic groups (*Cluster Schools*) in schools and prisons where people had the power to define and resolve disputes within their group, encouraging moral development.

Strengths of Kohlberg's approach...

The core concepts put forward by Kohlberg remain unchallenged, such as the invariant sequence of development and the importance of social interactions.

Chapter 8

Development of thinking | Development of a child's sense of self
Development of moral understanding | Development of a child's understanding of others
Cognition and development > Development of social cognition > Biological explanations of social cognition

Development of a child's sense of self

Subjective self-awareness

At birth, an infant is aware of basic sensations, e.g. fullness.

Age 2 months – Shows a sense of 'personal agency' (responsibility for the movement of their limbs). Bahrick and Watson showed that 5-month-olds responded differently to a real-time video of their leg movements and one taken at an earlier time.

Age 5 months – They can recognise their own face. Legerstee et al. found that 5–8-month-old infants looked longer at pictures of other children than pictures of themselves (which were less novel).

Not all psychologists agree…

Freudians such as Mahler et al. argue that, at birth, an infant has no sense of separateness from his/her mother. Individuation (the infant's recognition of self as distinct from others) is something that develops over the first few months of life.

Research with infants is difficult…

Understanding children's sense of self involves inferring what is going on in their mind on the basis of outward behaviours.

Psychologists have devised some ingenious ways of doing this, such as the mirror test and the false-belief task, but such measures are not perfect and may possibly underestimate what children can actually do.

Objective self-awareness

Subjective self-awareness (ability to perceive oneself as distinct) is different to objective self-awareness (the ability to reflect upon oneself) (Lewis).

Recognising your own face (subjective) is different to self-recognition (being conscious of your own existence).

The mirror test (red mark placed on face) is used to demonstrate self-recognition (Amsterdam, Gallop). Lewis and Brooks-Gunn found that 19% of babies touched their nose by 15 months and 66% did it by 24 months.

Around the same age, babies start to use personal pronouns such as 'me' and 'mine' (Slater and Lewis).

One consequence of objective self-awareness…

One consequence is the ability to display emotions. Very young children display the basic emotions of pleasure, sadness, fear and surprise, but the development of the conscious awareness of self is an important step in emotional development and leads to self-conscious emotions such as empathy, jealousy and embarrassment.

Individual differences…

Children who are securely attached develop self-recognition earlier than those who are not (Pipp et al.).

The same has been found to be true for children whose fathers encourage independence (Borke et al.).

IDA Link to intelligence in non-human animals…

Psychologists have sought to establish self-awareness in other species by using the mirror test (see page 64). Such self-awareness is evidence of intelligence, consciousness, emotions and the experience of pain – which creates ethical issues about using such animals in research.

Psychological self

Children aged 4–5 years describe themselves in terms of physical features e.g. 'I've got black hair' or 'I can ride my bike' (Damon and Hart).

Older children use psychological concepts, e.g. 'I like to play by myself.'

Children also start comparing themselves to others, e.g. 'I can run faster than my sister.'

Self-esteem begins to appear around the age of four.

IDA Cultural bias…

Descriptions of the development of a child's sense of self assume that children all over the world follow a similar sequence, whereas research shows that this is a culturally biased perspective, e.g. Van den Heuvel et al. compared Dutch, Turkish and Moroccan children aged 10–11 years. As predicted, Western (individualist culture) children used many more psychological statements than the non-Western (collectivist) children, whereas the non-Western children used more references to the social aspects of self.

Individual differences…

Verschueren and Marcoen found that securely attached children rated themselves more favourably (higher self-esteem) than did insecurely attached children and this was stable over time (Verschueren et al.).

Theory of Mind (ToM)

Newborns can distinguish between humans and other objects, therefore displaying a knowledge of others (Legerstee).

By the age of 2 years, children display some understanding of the mental state of others, e.g. they comfort others (Dunn).

However, a distinction is made between knowing about someone else's internal state and knowing about how they feel.

At about 4 years of age children develop ToM, as demonstrated by false-belief tasks (e.g. the Sally Anne test, where a child with ToM should recognise that Anne can hold a belief that isn't true). ToM is important in conducting social relationships and distinguishing self from others.

Link with autism…

Children with autism find social interaction difficult, which may be due to a ToM deficit. Baron-Cohen et al. found that autistic children failed the Sally Anne test, whereas children with Down's syndrome (genetic condition associated with low IQ) coped normally.

This shows that social abnormalities typical of autism are not linked to low IQ, but to a specific ToM deficit.

IDA Nature and nurture…

Baron-Cohen has proposed a ToM module (ToMM) that matures in the brain around the age of 4.

ToM is not solely determined by biology. Research has shown that discussion about motives and other mental states promotes the development of ToM (Sabbagh and Callanan).

Cross-cultural research also reveals the effect of experiential factors. Liu et al. compared more than 300 Chinese and North American children in terms of ToM. They found a similar sequence of development in both groups, but the timing differed by as much as 2 years in different locales supporting the role of biological and experiential factors.

Chapter 8

| Development of thinking | Development of a child's sense of self |
| Development of moral understanding | **Development of a child's understanding of others** |

Cognition and development > **Development of social cognition** > Biological explanations of social cognition

Development of a child's understanding of others

Early development

Imitation

Meltzoff and Moore showed that newborns less than 72 hours old will imitate facial gestures (e.g. mouth opening, tongue protrusion) and manual gestures (e.g. opening of the hand).

Intentions

This is a 'lower' mental ability than understanding the thoughts of others.

Infants of 3 months follow a person's gaze to nearby objects, showing an understanding of intention (D'Entrement et al.).

At 1 year, infants reliably follow gaze and pointing gestures to more distant objects (Carpenter et al.).

Autistic children aged 2½–5 years are the same as normal children, suggesting that understanding intentions is separate to Theory of Mind (ToM) (Carpenter et al.).

Are these abilities separate or interdependent?...

Does the development of ToM depend on earlier abilities (e.g. imitation)?

Evidence for separate biological mental modules...

Neurophysiological evidence exists for a unique, innate ToM module that is activated around 3 years of age (see facing page).

Behavioural evidence comes from the fact that autistic children can understand the intentions of others, but do not develop ToM. Hobson found that autistic children performed 'normally' on the three mountains task (perceptual perspective-taking), but ultimately do not develop conceptual perspective-taking.

Evidence for interdependence...

Children with sensory impairments (such as hearing or visual difficulties) usually experience significant delays in the development of ToM (Eide and Eide). It is possible that their restricted sensory experiences slow down the development of perceptual perspective-taking and this, in turn, slows down the normal development of ToM.

Perspective-taking

Egocentricity

Piaget described the pre-operational child as 'egocentric' (see page 68).

This egocentricity concerns perceptual perspective-taking ability (tested in Piaget's three mountains task) as distinct from conceptual perspective-taking ability (tested by the Sally Anne test used to assess ToM).

IDA Nature and nurture...

The key feature of stage theories is that they describe an invariant developmental sequence, i.e. all children go through the stages in the same order. Each stage is an outcome of the previous stage, such that the behaviours associated with later stages build on behaviours developed in earlier stages.

The invariant nature of the stages implies some underlying biological mechanism. Biological maturation sets the bottom limits so that children below a certain age, for example, cannot develop ToM or abstract logical thinking.

However, nurture as well as nature is important. The speed of development is related to experience (nurture), for example, deaf children are slower to develop ToM.

Role-taking

Role-taking (conceptual perspective-taking) involves a child's comprehension about other people's internal experiences, leading to true ToM.

Selman used dilemmas to explore children's reasoning when faced with conflicting feelings. He constructed a stage model of the development of perspective-taking:

- Stage 0: Undifferentiated (3–6 years)
- Stage 1: Social-informational (6–8)
- Stage 2: Self-reflective (8–10)
- Stage 3: Mutual (10–12)
- Stage 4: Societal (12+)

As children grow older they develop the ability to analyse the perspectives of several people.

Role-taking and social behaviour

This enables a child to understand the perspective and feelings of another person. Ultimately this leads to prosocial behaviour.

Role-taking and deception

Aged 3, children can plant a false belief in someone else's mind, e.g. hiding disappointment when filmed with another person but not when filmed on their own (Cole).

IDA Evolutionary approach...

Role-taking skills produce adaptive advantages:

- They are a critical component of all social behaviour, e.g. popular children have better role-taking skills (Schaffer).
- The ability to deceive or manipulate others (sometimes called Machiavellian intelligence) is naturally selected. Anyone capable of deceiving their conspecifics (members of the same species) has an evolutionary advantage, because they can manipulate others for their own advantage.

IDA Real-world applications...

The fact that perspective- or role-taking skills can be fostered by experience has important implications for schools, therapy, the treatment of criminals, and parenting.

Such training can be done with younger children through play, as it is the natural way in which role-taking skills are learned (Smith and Pellegrini).

Social skills training (SST) programmes are used with older children and in therapeutic settings with people with mental disorders.

Criminals may lack empathy and role-taking skills, which explains their 'willingness' to harm others. SST programmes teach prisoners role-taking skills to increase their empathic concern for others.

Parents may be interested in research by Sommerville et al. They used 'sticky mittens' to enable very young infants to manipulate objects (the mittens had Velcro on them so that infants were able to pick objects up). These infants then showed earlier-than-usual abilities to understand the intentions of others, suggesting that if you give infants earlier-than-normal experiences, this may speed up the development of understanding intentions and ultimately may speed up the development of perspective-taking.

Chapter 8

Development of thinking | Development of a child's sense of self
Development of moral understanding | Development of a child's understanding of others

Cognition and development > Development of social cognition > Biological explanations of social cognition

Biological explanations of social cognition

The role of the mirror neuron

Mirror neurons (MNs) in macaque monkeys

Rizzolatti *et al.* discovered neurons in the F5 premotor cortex that were active either when the monkey observed another monkey/experimenter performing a task (e.g. tearing up paper) or if the monkey repeated the action themselves.

MNs in humans

Brain imaging studies have revealed areas of the human brain rich in MNs:

- The *inferior frontal lobe* is linked to emotional MNs (Wicker *et al.*) and Broca's area (see below).
- Areas in the *temporal lobe* may be related to auditory MNs (Gazzola *et al.*) and in the occipital, parietal and temporal lobe to visual input.
- The *frontopolar cortex* (in the frontal lobe) and the right inferior parietal lobule are key areas (Decety).

Imitation

MNs explain imitation.

MNs are important in the acquisition of skilled behaviours (observer watches someone else perform an action and models that behaviour).

Imitation is also the beginning of the development of social cognition.

Behavioural regulation – MN response is generally 'off-line'. However, individuals who have damage to their frontal cortex (the part of the brain involved in inhibitory control) do display compulsive imitation (Lhermitte *et al.*).

Understanding intention

MNs may also encode another person's intentions. Iacoboni *et al.* recorded neural activity (using fMRI) while participants watched clips of a 'tea party' – context (tea cups), action (hand grasping a cup) and intention (context plus action). Highest MN activity was recorded in the *inferior frontal cortex* for the intention clip.

Perspective-taking and ToM

Gallese and Goldman suggest that MNs are a precursor to perspective-taking and Theory of Mind (ToM), because they enable us to experience someone else's actions and intentions as if they are our own.

This may lead to empathy because MNs enable us to experience not just the same actions of another person but also the same emotions.

Language acquisition

Binkofski *et al.* demonstrated MNs in Broca's area (for speech production).

MNs may assist in the imitation of speech sounds, important in language acquisition (Rizzolatti and Arbib).

MNs support simulation theory...

The discovery of MNs provided a neurological basis for simulation theory (ST) which proposes that we read other people's minds by experiencing what they are experiencing and use this to predict the other's actions and feelings.

There are alternative views...

'Theory' theory (TT) suggests that we infer mental states from observations, and construct a 'theory' about what the other person is thinking on the basis of all available information. ToM is essentially a 'theory' theory.

Borg argues that there is a difference between experiencing the actions of another person and reading their mind. Borg likens the MN approach to behaviourism where it is assumed that, for example, crying (a behaviour) is all there is to being sad (a mental state).

Research support...

Iacoboni recently recorded the activity of almost 300 individual neurons in the frontal lobes of epileptic patients (wired up to investigate their seizures). The patients were asked to perform simple actions and to observe short films of others executing the same actions, which enabled the researchers to identify 34 mirror neurons activated by both performance and observation. They also found some MNs that suppress imitation (important for inhibitory control).

Gazzola *et al.* have produced evidence that people high in empathy (as measured by self-report) show greater activity in the MN brain regions.

However, research support has generally been weak...

It isn't easy to gain direct evidence of human neural activity because such research requires placing electrodes inside the brain. Almost all of the human evidence so far is based on imaging studies, which can only tell us about hundreds of thousands of neurons, not individual ones.

Is it all a myth?...

Gopnik suggests that MNs have taken on the status of a scientific myth, claiming to offer explanations of many different behaviours, e.g. ToM, empathy, altruism and moral behaviour. There are two main objections:

- The only real evidence is derived from non-human animal studies. These studies may not generalise to humans since non-human animals, arguably, do not have ToM.
- Systems as complex as moral behaviour or ToM are unlikely to be explained by the rather simple idea of MNs. They may form the basis of such systems but more is likely to be involved.

IDA *Nature and nurture...*

The original suggestion is that MNs are an innate system, since MNs enable imitation and, as we have seen on the facing page, imitation is an ability that is present from birth.

Gopnik suggests instead that MNs might arise as a result of experience because neurons learn by association – when two events are associated the neurons for each event form a connection. An infant's first experience is to see a hand moving (its own) and at the same time experience that hand moving. This creates a mirror connection.

IDA *Real-world application...*

Williams *et al.* suggest that MN abnormalities may well underlie the fact that people with autism frequently have difficulty copying actions.

Dapretto *et al.* compared brain activity in autistic and non-autistic children as they watched faces that showed emotion or no emotion. Autistic children showed reduced activity in a part of the *inferior frontal gyrus*, a section of the brain identified as forming part of the mirror neuron system.

It might be possible to help autistic individuals by strengthening their MNs through activities that require the imitation of others (Slack).

Chapter 9

Schizophrenia

Division A   Overview
Classification and diagnosis of schizophrenia

Division B   Explanations of schizophrenia
Biological explanations of schizophrenia
Psychological explanations of schizophrenia

Division C   Therapies for schizophrenia
Biological therapies for schizophrenia
Psychological therapies for schizophrenia

Issues, debates and approaches
In the Psychopathology section (Section A) of the Unit 4 exam there is no explicit credit given to issues, debates and approaches. This doesn't mean that such material would not be creditworthy (it would) but it means it is not required. So, in this chapter we have not specifically identified IDA.

Specification

Schizophrenia	
Overview	• Clinical characteristics of schizophrenia.
	• Issues surrounding the classification and diagnosis of schizophrenia, including reliability and validity.
Explanations	• Biological explanations of schizophrenia, for example genetics, biochemistry.
	• Psychological explanations of schizophrenia, for example behavioural, cognitive, psychodynamic and socio-cultural.
Therapy	• Biological therapies for schizophrenia, including their evaluation in terms of appropriateness and effectiveness.
	• Psychological therapies for schizophrenia, for example behavioural, psychodynamic and cognitive-behavioural, including their evaluation in terms of appropriateness and effectiveness.

Chapter 9

Overview   >
Explanations of schizophrenia
Schizophrenia   >   Therapies for schizophrenia   Classification and diagnosis of schizophrenia

Classification and diagnosis of schizophrenia

Clinical characteristics

Positive symptoms

Symptoms that appear to reflect an excess or distortion of normal functions. Under DSM-IVR, the diagnosis of schizophrenia requires at least a 1-month duration of two or more positive symptoms.

- *Delusions* – Bizarre beliefs that seem real to the person with schizophrenia, but they are not real, e.g. inflated beliefs about the person's power or importance.
- *Experiences of control* – The person may believe that they are under the control of an alien force that has invaded their mind or body.
- *Hallucinations* – Bizarre, unreal perceptions that are usually visual (e.g. seeing lights, objects or faces that aren't there), but may also be olfactory or tactile.
- *Disordered thinking* – The feeling that thoughts have been inserted or withdrawn from the mind or that thoughts are being broadcast so that others can hear them.

Negative symptoms

Symptoms that appear to reflect a diminution or loss of normal functioning and which persist even in the absence of positive symptoms.

- *Affective flattening* – A reduction in the range and intensity of emotional expression (e.g. lack of eye contact).
- *Alogia* – Poverty of speech, characterised by the lessening of speech fluency and productivity.
- *Avolition* – The reduction of, or inability to initiate and persist in, goal-directed behaviour.

Reliability

Reliability refers to the consistency of a measuring instrument, such as a questionnaire or scale to assess the severity of schizophrenic symptoms or the extent of cognitive dysfunction.

Inter-rater reliability

Whether two independent assessors give similar diagnoses.

Publication of DSM-III in 1980 was specifically designed to provide a more reliable way of classifying mental disorders.

Carson claimed that later editions of DSM would mean much greater agreement over who did or did not have schizophrenia.

Test–retest reliability

Whether tests used to determine diagnoses give the same results across a time interval.

Cognitive screening tests such as RBANS are important in the diagnosis of schizophrenia as they measure the degree of neuropsychological impairment.

Wilks et al. administered two versions of RBANS over intervals ranging from 1–134 days. Test–retest reliability was high at .84.

Claims of good inter-rater reliability may be exaggerated...

More recent studies (e.g. Whaley) have found inter-rater reliability correlations for the diagnosis of schizophrenia as low as .11.

Rosenhan highlighted the unreliability of diagnosis when 'normal' people presented themselves to psychiatric hospitals claiming they were hearing voices. They were diagnosed as schizophrenic despite the subsequent complete absence of symptoms.

Cultural differences in reliability...

The inter-rater reliability of diagnosis in schizophrenia is further challenged by the finding that there is a massive variation between countries. Copeland found that 69% of US psychiatrists and only 2% of UK psychiatrists gave a diagnosis of schizophrenia when given the same description of a patient.

Comparing DSM and ICD...

Cheniaux et al. found that, although the inter-rater reliability of both DSM-IV and ICD-10 was above .50, schizophrenia was more frequently diagnosed when using ICD criteria than DSM criteria.

Test–retest reliability is generally good...

Prescott et al. analysed the test–retest reliability of several measures of cognitive functioning used in the diagnosis of schizophrenia in 14 schizophrenics. Performance on these measures was stable over a 6-month period.

Validity

Validity refers to the extent that a diagnosis represents something that is real and distinct. A classification system such as DSM or ICD should also measure what they aim to measure.

Comorbidity refers to the extent to which two or more conditions co-occur. Comorbidities are common among patients with schizophrenia and create difficulties in its diagnosis, e.g. depression occurs in 50% of people with schizophrenia (Buckley et al.).

Positive or negative symptoms?

Klosterkötter et al. found that positive symptoms were more useful for a diagnosis of schizophrenia than negative symptoms.

Prognosis

People diagnosed as schizophrenic rarely share the same symptoms nor the same outcomes, suggesting poor predictive validity (Bentall et al.)

The problem of comorbid medical complications...

The poor level of functioning found in many schizophrenics may in part be the result of their comorbid medical problems, such as hypertension and diabetes. Weber et al. discovered that many patients with schizophrenia receive a lower standard of medical care because of their comorbid medical conditions, which in turn affects their prognosis.

Ethnicity may lead to misdiagnosis...

Research (e.g. Harrison et al.) suggests that rates of schizophrenia among African–Caribbeans are much higher than among white populations. Part of any misdiagnosis may result from factors such as cultural differences in language and mannerisms, and difficulties in relating between black patients and white clinicians.

The symptoms of schizophrenia are also found in other disorders...

Despite the belief that identification of the symptoms of schizophrenia would make for more valid diagnoses, many of these symptoms are also found in other disorders, such as depression and bipolar disorder. Ellason and Ross claim that people with dissociative identity disorder actually have more schizophrenic symptoms than people diagnosed with schizophrenia.

Chapter 9

Overview

Explanations of schizophrenia	>	Biological explanations of schizophrenia
Schizophrenia	>	Therapies for schizophrenia	Psychological explanations of schizophrenia

Biological explanations of schizophrenia

Genetic factors

Family studies (e.g. Gottesman) show that schizophrenia is more common among biological relatives of a person with schizophrenia than in the general population. The greater the degree of genetic relatedness, the greater the risk.

Children with two schizophrenic parents have a 46% risk of developing the disorder, with one schizophrenic parent a 13% risk and with a schizophrenic sibling 9% risk.

A problem for genetic explanations of schizophrenia is…

Heritable traits that are maladaptive would be selected out during the process of natural selection, and so schizophrenia would no longer exist. However, Stevens and Price suggest that, among our distant ancestors, the presence of charismatic leaders with schizophrenic-type symptoms (e.g. auditory hallucinations and delusions of grandeur) could have influenced other group members to follow them and form a new group (advantageous when the size of the existing group was greater than dwindling resources could sustain). Thus, the *'group-splitting hypothesis'* argues that schizophrenia is an extreme expression of an adaptive trait.

Twin studies

If MZ twins are more similar in terms of schizophrenia than DZ twins, this suggests a strong genetic influence for the disorder.

A meta-analysis of twin studies prior to 2001 (Joseph) found a concordance rate of just over 40% for MZ twins and just over 7% for DZ twins, but recent studies found lower concordance rates for MZ twins.

Concordance rates may only reflect environmental differences…

It is assumed that the greater concordance rate between MZ twins compared to DZ twins is a consequence of a greater genetic similarity, rather than a greater environmental similarity for MZ twins.

However, Joseph points out that MZ twins tend to be treated more similarly, and experience more 'identity confusion'.

As a result, there is reason to believe that differences in concordance rates for MZ and DZ twins reflect nothing more than the environmental differences that distinguish the two types of twin.

Adoption studies

Such studies are valuable because it is difficult to disentangle genetic and environmental influences for those who share genes *and* environment.

Tienari *et al.* found that for adoptees whose biological mothers had been diagnosed with schizophrenia, 6.7% of these individuals also developed the disorder, compared to just 2% of adoptees born to non-schizophrenic mothers.

The problem of selective placement…

An assumption is that parents who adopt a child with a schizophrenic biological parent are no different from other adoptive parents. This is unlikely, as adoptive parents are usually informed of the genetic background of potential adoptees prior to making a decision whether to adopt.

There are methodological problems with adoption studies…

Most adoption studies have only found differences between children born to schizophrenic and non-schizophrenic biological parents by broadening the definition to include the non-psychotic *'schizophrenia spectrum disorder'* rather than restricting it to full-blown schizophrenia.

The dopamine hypothesis

Neurons that transmit dopamine fire too easily or too often, leading to the symptoms of schizophrenia.

Schizophrenics have abnormally high numbers of D_2 dopamine receptors, resulting in more dopamine neurons firing. Dopamine neurons play a key role in guiding attention, so disturbances in this process might lead to the problems of perception and thought found in schizophrenia.

Dopamine alone does not cause schizophrenia…

Psychological factors (e.g. expressed emotion) influence the development of or recovery from the disorder. This suggests that for those with a biological vulnerability (e.g. high levels of dopamine), schizophrenia only develops in the presence of significant stressors.

High levels of dopamine may be consequence rather than cause…

A review of post-mortem studies (Haracz) found that most who showed elevated dopamine levels received antipsychotic drugs shortly before death. This suggests that high dopamine levels may just be a consequence of its treatment.

Evidence for the dopamine hypothesis

Amphetamines are dopamine agonists, stimulating nerve cells containing dopamine, causing the synapse to be flooded with dopamine. Large doses cause hallucinations and delusions.

Antipsychotic drugs are dopamine antagonists, blocking the activity of dopamine in the brain, and so reducing the symptoms of schizophrenia.

The dopamine hypothesis is reductionist…

If schizophrenia was caused solely by excess dopamine activity, then antipsychotic drugs should be effective for *all* schizophrenics. This is not the case, suggesting that the dopamine explanation alone cannot explain the development of schizophrenia.

Evidence from neuroimaging research is inconclusive…

The development of PET scans has led to more accurate measurement, but has failed to provide evidence of altered dopamine activity in brains of individuals with schizophrenia (Copolov and Crook).

Parkinson's disease

Low levels of dopamine activity are found in people who suffer from Parkinson's disease. It was found that some people who were taking the drug *L-dopa* to raise their levels of dopamine were developing schizophrenic-type symptoms (Grilly).

Evidence from the success of antipsychotics…

The dopamine hypothesis is supported by the fact that drugs that change levels of dopamine in the brain also reduce the symptoms of schizophrenia. Davis *et al.* carried out a meta-analysis that analysed the effectiveness of antipsychotic treatment compared with a placebo. Relapse occurred in 55% of the patients whose drugs were replaced by a placebo, but only 19% of those who remained on the drug.

Psychological explanations of schizophrenia

Psychological theories

Psychodynamic explanation

- *Regression to a pre-ego state* – If parents are cold and uncaring, a person regresses to an earlier stage before the development of the ego or a realistic awareness of the world.
- *Attempts to re-establish ego control* from this infantile state fail and can lead to symptoms of schizophrenia (e.g. delusions and narcissism), the product of a weak and confused ego.

There is little evidence to support the psychodynamic view…

Studies have shown that parents of schizophrenics do behave differently from parents of other kinds of patient, particularly in the presence of their disturbed offspring. However, this is likely to be the consequence rather than the cause of their illness.

If psychodynamic treatment is effective, this would lend support…

Although some critics have argued that it is impossible to draw definite conclusions about the effectiveness of psychodynamic therapy as a treatment of schizophrenia, a meta-analysis of 37 studies (Gottdiener) concluded that it was an effective treatment. This lends support to the claim that schizophrenia itself may have psychodynamic origins.

Cognitive explanation

This explanation acknowledges the role of biological factors in schizophrenia but claims that further features emerge as people try to understand their condition.

When schizophrenics first hear voices and have other sensory symptoms, they turn to others to validate these experiences. If others fail to confirm their validity, the person believes the others are hiding the truth and so the schizophrenic develops delusional beliefs.

There is physiological evidence to support this…

Meyer-Lindenberg *et al.* found a link between excess dopamine in the prefrontal cortex and working memory. Working memory dysfunction is associated with the cognitive disorganisation typically found in schizophrenics. Meyer-Linderberg *et al.* also found that treatment with antipsychotics significantly improved cognitive functioning.

There are implications for treatment…

Yellowlees *et al.* have trialled a machine that can deliver 'virtual' auditory and visual hallucinations. The intentions of this are to show schizophrenics that their hallucinations aren't real.

Socio-cultural factors

Life events

Discrete stressors, such as the death of a close relative, have been associated with a higher risk of schizophrenic episodes.

Brown and Birley found that prior to a schizophrenic episode, patients reported twice as many stressful life events compared to a healthy control group, who reported a low and unchanging level of stressful life events over the same period.

Prospective studies (e.g. Hirsch *et al.*) found that life events have a cumulative effect preceding relapse rather than a concentrated effect just before a schizophrenic episode.

Not all evidence supports the importance of life stressors…

Van Os *et al.* reported no link between life events and the onset of schizophrenia. In the retrospective part of this study, patients were not more likely to have experienced a major life event in the 3 months prior to an episode of schizophrenia. In the prospective part of study, patients who had experienced a major life event went on to have a *lower* incidence of relapse rather than an increased risk as predicted.

Research on the link is only correlational…

Therefore we cannot infer a causal relationship between stressful life events and schizophrenia. It could be that the early symptoms of the disorder (e.g. erratic behaviour) were the cause of the major life events (e.g. divorce, loss of a job). As a result, it is possible that the stressful major life events that are evident in the lives of some schizophrenics might be the consequence rather than the cause of the disorder.

Family relationships

Double-bind theory – Bateson *et al.* suggest that children who frequently receive contradictory messages (e.g. of affection *and* animosity) from their parents are more likely to develop schizophrenia.

This prevents the development of an internally consistent construction of reality, which can manifest itself as schizophrenic symptoms (e.g. withdrawal).

Expressed emotion (EE) is a family style of communication that involves criticism and emotional over-involvement. High levels of EE are likely to influence relapse rates. The negative emotional climate in these families leads to stress beyond the person's impaired ability to cope and triggers a relapse into schizophrenia.

Evidence supports the importance of family relationships…

Tienari *et al.* found that adopted children who had schizophrenic biological parents were more likely to develop schizophrenia than children of normal biological parents, but only when the adopted family was rated as disturbed, in other words, the illness only manifested itself under appropriate environmental conditions, genetics alone were not enough.

Double-bind theory has mixed support…

Berger found that schizophrenics reported a higher recall of double-bind statements by their mothers than did non-schizophrenics (although the accuracy of their recall may be affected by their schizophrenia). Other research (e.g. Liem) found no difference in patterns of parental communication in families of schizophrenics and non-schizophrenics.

Expressed emotion has led to successful therapy…

High EE relatives are taught how to reduce levels of expressed emotion. Hogarty *et al.* found that such therapy can significantly reduce relapse rates among schizophrenics.

Labelling theory

If a person displays unusual behaviours associated with schizophrenia, they are considered deviant by society. Once this diagnostic label is applied, it becomes self-fulfilling, leading to further symptoms.

There is evidence to support this…

In a review of the evidence, Scheff evaluated 18 studies explicitly related to labelling theory. He judged 13 to be consistent with the theory and five to be inconsistent. On balance, therefore, Scheff concluded that labelling theory was supported by the available evidence.

Chapter 9

Overview
Explanations of schizophrenia | Biological therapies for schizophrenia
Schizophrenia > Therapies for schizophrenia > Psychological therapies for schizophrenia

Biological therapies for schizophrenia

Antipsychotic medication

Antipsychotic drugs block the action of neurotransmitters that bring about the symptoms of schizophrenia and consequently help the person with schizophrenia function more effectively.

Conventional antipsychotics

Conventional antipsychotics are used primarily to combat the positive symptoms of schizophrenia – such as hallucinations and thought disturbances – products of an overactive dopamine system. The atypical antipsychotic drugs also combat the positive symptoms of schizophrenia, but there are claims that they have some beneficial effects on negative symptoms as well.

These drugs reduce the effects of dopamine and so reduce the symptoms of schizophrenia. They bind to dopamine receptors but do not stimulate them, thus blocking their action.

By reducing stimulation of the dopamine system in the brain, conventional antipsychotics can eliminate the hallucinations and delusions experienced by people with schizophrenia.

Atypical antipsychotics

These also act on the dopamine pathway but only temporarily occupy the D_2 dopamine receptors and then rapidly dissociate to allow normal dopamine transmission. It is this characteristic which is thought to be responsible for the lower levels of side effects associated with atypical antipsychotics (e.g. tardive dyskinesia).

Effectiveness of conventional antipsychotics…

Most studies on the effectiveness of conventional antipsychotics have compared the relapse rates of those on medication with those on a placebo. Davis *et al.* reviewed 29 studies and found that relapse occurred in 55% of those whose drugs were replaced by a placebo, and 19% of those who remained on the drug.

However…

Ross and Read argue that placebo studies are not a fair test of the effectiveness of an antipsychotic, as under a placebo condition, the patient is in a drug withdrawal state and is overwhelmed by dopamine.

Effectiveness of atypical antipsychotics…

A meta-analysis of studies found that the superiority of atypical antipsychotics compared to conventional antipsychotics was only moderate (Leucht *et al.*). Two of the atypical antipsychotics tested were only 'slightly' more effective and the other two were no more effective.

The claim that atypical antipsychotics are effective with the negative symptoms of schizophrenia was also challenged. Two of the atypical drugs were 'slightly' more effective than conventional antipsychotics, one was 'as effective' and one 'slightly worse'.

Appropriateness of antipsychotics…

About 30% of people taking conventional antipsychotics develop tardive dyskinesia, which is irreversible in 75% of cases. Jeste *et al.* found that 5% of those treated with atypical antipsychotics developed this. The fact there are fewer side effects with atypical antipsychotics means patients are more motivated to continue with their medication.

Ross and Read argue that being prescribed medication reinforces the view that there is 'something wrong with them', which reduces their motivation to look for other possible causes (e.g. life stressors) and then take steps to deal with these to reduce their suffering.

Electroconvulsive therapy (ECT)

ECT in practice

Using ECT in the treatment of schizophrenia is usually restricted to certain forms of the disorder (e.g. *catatonic schizophrenia*) that do not respond to other kinds of treatment. Although relatively rare today, catatonic schizophrenia is responsive to ECT, which can bring about a rapid alleviation of its symptoms.

- In unilateral ECT, an electrode is placed on the non-dominant side of the brain and another on the forehead.
- The patient is injected with a barbiturate to make them unconscious during ECT. They are then given a nerve-blocking agent to prevent fractures during the seizure.
- A small amount of current is passed through the brain for half a second.
- This creates a seizure, which affects the whole brain.
- A patient usually requires between 3 and 15 treatments.

Effectiveness of ECT…

A meta-analysis of studies that used ECT in the treatment of schizophrenia (Greenhalgh *et al.*) found that ECT (either combined with antipsychotic medication or as a therapy on its own) is no more effective than antipsychotic medication.

An Indian study (Sarita *et al.*) found no difference in the reduction of symptoms between 36 schizophrenia patients given either ECT or simulated ECT.

Tharyan and Adams carried out a review of 26 studies in order to assess whether ECT resulted in any meaningful benefit for schizophrenic patients. They found:

- When 'real' ECT was compared with 'simulated' ECT, more people improved with 'real' ECT.
- When ECT was compared with antipsychotic medication, results favoured patients who received the antipsychotic medication.
- There was some evidence that ECT *plus* medication produced a superior outcome to either used alone.

Appropriateness of ECT…

Because there are significant risks associated with ECT, including cognitive dysfunction, brain damage and even death, the use of this technique as a treatment for schizophrenia has declined. In the UK, the decline between 1979 to 1999 was 59% (Read) and it is no longer recommended in the general management of schizophrenia by NICE (National Institute for Health and Clinical Excellence).

Chapter 9

Overview
Explanations of schizophrenia
Biological therapies for schizophrenia
Schizophrenia > Therapies for schizophrenia > Psychological therapies for schizophrenia

Psychological therapies for schizophrenia

Cognitive behavioural therapy (CBT)

Distorted beliefs alter the person's behaviour in maladaptive ways.

In schizophrenia, the person may believe that their behaviour is being controlled by somebody or something else.

Delusions are thought to result from faulty interpretations of events. CBT is used to help the patient identify and correct these.

CBT techniques

Patients are encouraged to:

- Trace the origins of their symptoms to see how they might have developed.
- Evaluate the content of any delusions or voices and consider ways in which they might test validity of their faulty beliefs.
- Develop their own alternatives to previous maladaptive beliefs and develop appropriate coping strategies.

Outcome studies

Outcome studies of CBT suggest that patients who receive cognitive therapy experience fewer hallucinations and delusions and recover their functioning to a greater extent than those who receive antipsychotic medication alone.

Effectiveness of CBT...

Research has shown that CBT has a significant effect on improving the symptoms of schizophrenia, e.g. Gould *et al.* found that all seven studies in their meta-analysis reported a significant decrease in the positive symptoms of schizophrenia after treatment.

Kuipers *et al.* found a significant reduction in positive symptoms following CBT combined with antipsychotic drugs, and also found that there was a lower rate of patient drop-out and greater patient satisfaction when these two types of treatment were combined.

However...

Most of the studies of the effectiveness of CBT have combined CBT with antipsychotic medication. As a result, it is difficult to assess the effectiveness of CBT independently of antipsychotic medication.

Appropriateness of CBT... For negative symptoms...

CBT for schizophrenia works by generating less distressing explanations for negative experiences rather than trying to eliminate them completely. Negative symptoms may well serve a useful function for the individual, so may be understood as 'safety behaviours'.

Who benefits from CBT?...

It is commonly believed within psychiatry that not everybody with schizophrenia would benefit from CBT. For example, in a study of schizophrenic patients in the UK (Kingdon and Kirschen), it was found that many patients were not deemed suitable for CBT (e.g. older patients) because they 'would not engage fully with the therapy'.

Psychodynamic therapy: Psychoanalysis

Psychoanalytic therapy is based on the assumption that individuals are often unaware of the influence of unconscious conflicts on their psychological state.

The psychoanalytic approach to schizophrenia assumes that all symptoms are meaningful and reflect unconscious conflicts that must be brought into the conscious mind to be resolved.

Other psychodynamic therapies

What these have in common with Freudian psychoanalysis is the belief that the first task of psychodynamic therapy is to win the trust of the patient and to build a relationship with them.

The therapist achieves this by replacing the harsh and punishing conscience (based on patient's parents) with one that is less destructive and more supportive.

As the patient gets healthier, they take a more active role (and the therapist a less active role) in their own recovery.

Psychodynamic therapy takes a long time to complete, therefore many patients withdraw without completing their therapy.

Outcome studies

Gottdiener reviewed 37 studies where psychological therapies had been used in the treatment of schizophrenia.

Results showed that psychodynamic and cognitive-behavioural therapies produced similar levels of therapeutic benefit.

There was no difference in improvement when psychological therapy was accompanied by antipsychotic medication.

Effectiveness of psychodynamic therapy...

Gottdiener's meta-analysis of psychological treatment for schizophrenia concluded that psychodynamic therapy was effective for schizophrenia.

However...

The relatively small number of studies used meant it was difficult to assess the impact of variables such as therapist training on the outcome for patients. Also, half the studies in this analysis did not randomly allocate patients to treatment conditions, thus introducing a treatment bias that may have affected the results.

Contrary evidence...

Malmberg and Fenton argue that it is impossible to draw definite conclusions for or against the effectiveness of psychodynamic therapy in the treatment of schizophrenia. In fact, research (*Schizophrenia Patient Outcome Research Team*) has even suggested that some forms of psychodynamic therapy are harmful for schizophrenics (many find the experience of psychodynamic therapy traumatic).

There are also contradictory findings...

May found that patients treated with psychodynamic therapy plus antipsychotic medication had better outcomes than those treated with therapy alone. Antipsychotic medication alone was better than therapy alone. Other research (e.g. Karon and VandenBos) found the opposite, with patients receiving therapy alone improving more than those receiving medication alone.

Appropriateness of psychodynamic therapy...

Despite the uncertain nature of the effectiveness of psychodynamic therapy in the treatment of schizophrenia, the APA recommends 'supportive interventions' such as psychodynamic therapy when used in conjunction with antipsychotic medication.

A costly therapy?...

One argument against the use of psychodynamic therapy is the expense involved (therapy takes a long time). As it is no more effective than antipsychotic medication, the extra expense is not justified.

However...

A counter-argument is that the extra expense is worth it because the overall cost of treatment decreases with time as patients are less likely to seek inpatient treatment and are more likely to gain employment (Karon and VandenBos).

Depression

Division A Overview
Classification and diagnosis of depression

Division B Explanations of depression
Biological explanations of depression
Psychological explanations of depression

Division C Therapies for depression
Biological therapies for depression
Psychological therapies for depression

Issues, debates and approaches

In the Psychopathology section (Section A) of the Unit 4 exam there is no explicit credit given to issues, debates and approaches. This doesn't mean that such material would not be creditworthy (it would) but it means it is not required. So, in this chapter we have not specifically identified IDA.

Specification

Depression	
Overview	• Clinical characteristics of depression.
	• Issues surrounding the classification and diagnosis of depression, including reliability and validity.
Explanations	• Biological explanations of depression, for example genetics, biochemistry.
	• Psychological explanations of depression, for example behavioural, cognitive, psychodynamic and socio-cultural.
Therapy	• Biological therapies for depression, including their evaluation in terms of appropriateness and effectiveness.
	• Psychological therapies for depression, for example behavioural, psychodynamic and cognitive-behavioural, including their evaluation in terms of appropriateness and effectiveness.

Classification and diagnosis of depression

Clinical characteristics

Diagnosis

The formal diagnosis of 'major depressive disorder' requires the presence of five of the following symptoms, including either depressed mood or loss of interest and pleasure. The symptoms must also cause significant distress or impairment in general functioning and should be present all or most of the time, persisting for longer than 2 weeks.

- *Sad depressed mood* – as indicated by either subjective report or observation made by others.
- *Loss of interest and pleasure in usual activities* – as indicated by either subjective report or observation made by others.
- *Difficulties in sleeping (insomnia)* – or a desire to sleep all the time (hypersomnia).
- *Shift in activity level, becoming either lethargic or agitated* – observable by others, not merely subjective feelings or being slowed down.
- *Poor appetite and weight loss or increased appetite and weight gain* – significant weight loss when not dieting or a significant decrease (or increase) in appetite.
- *Loss of energy and great fatigue.*
- *Negative self-concept, feelings of worthlessness and guilt* – feelings of worthlessness or excessive or inappropriate guilt (which may be delusional).
- *Difficulty in concentrating* – such as slowed thinking and indecisiveness.
- *Recurrent thoughts of death or suicide.*

Reliability

Reliability refers to the consistency of a measuring instrument, such as a questionnaire or scale, to assess the severity of depressive symptoms.

Inter-rater reliability

Whether two independent assessors give similar diagnoses.

Low levels of inter-rater reliability may lead to faulty diagnosis and inappropriate treatment for depression.

Lobbestael *et al.* assessed the inter-rater reliability of the Structured Clinical Interview for major depressive disorder and found moderate agreement with an inter-rater coefficient of .66.

Test–retest reliability

Whether tests used to determine diagnoses give the same results across a time interval.

Current measurement scales such as the Beck Depression Inventory (BDI) have been assessed for their test-retest reliability.

Beck *et al.* assessed 26 patients at two therapy sessions one week apart using the BDI. Test–retest reliability was high at .93.

There is research evidence for the reliability of diagnosis using DSM…

Research (e.g. Keller *et al.*) has established that inter-rater coefficients for the diagnosis of depression using DSM-IV are 'fair to good' although test–retest reliability is only 'fair' at best.

Zanarini *et al.* also established a high inter-rater reliability of .80, but test–rest reliability was only .61 with 1 week between diagnostic sessions.

Reasons for low reliability…

Keller *et al.* point out that for major depression to be diagnosed, a minimum of five out of nine symptoms must be present. When the severity of the disorder is such that it is just at the diagnostic threshold, a one item disagreement (e.g. in determining whether an individual is sufficiently lethargic to satisfy the symptom of 'shift in activity levels') makes the difference between diagnosis of major depressive disorder or a less serious illness.

Diagnosis could be simplified…

Zimmerman *et al.* claim that the DSM-IV criteria are unnecessarily lengthy and that doctors have difficulty recalling all symptoms. Their briefer diagnostic system had 95% agreement with DSM-IV diagnoses for depression and is free from somatic symptoms that are difficult to apply in patients with medical conditions.

Validity

Validity refers to the extent that a diagnosis represents something that is real and distinct. Also a classification system such as DSM or ICD should measure what it aims to measure.

Comorbidity refers to the extent to which two or more conditions co-occur.

Research has shown that the presence of an anxiety disorder is the single biggest clinical risk for the development of major depression.

Content validity

The BDI is considered to be high in content validity as it was constructed as the result of a consensus of clinicians regarding the symptoms found in depressive patients.

Concurrent validity

Research (e.g. Beck *et al.*) has consistently demonstrated concurrent validity between BDI and other measures of depression.

GP diagnoses may be less valid…

Van Weel-Baumgarten *et al.* suggest that diagnoses made by GPs (rather than secondary care specialists) are made against a background of previous patient knowledge, therefore could be biased and less valid as a result.

There are cultural differences in the diagnosis of depression…

Karasz found that members of ethnic minority groups are less likely than middle-class white people to seek professional help for depression. This may be because they see the 'problem' as a 'social' problem, requiring non-professional help, rather than a biological problem requiring medical help.

DSM and ICD are equally accurate in the diagnosis of depression…

The symptoms required for a diagnosis of depression in these two systems are very similar, with a concordance between the two of 75%. Andrews *et al.* found that the two classification systems do not produce a high number of discrepant diagnoses, and therefore one system relative to the other cannot be considered as being more valid in the diagnosis of depression.

Biological explanations of depression

Genetic factors

Family studies

Having a first-degree relative with depression appears to be a risk factor for depression. Research has found that around 20% of first-degree relatives of a proband with depression also have depression compared to 10% of general population (Harrington et al.).

Twin and adoption studies

McGuffin et al. studied 177 probands with depression and their same-sex twins. They found 46% concordance rates for MZ twins and 20% for DZ twins, suggesting that depression has a substantial heritable component.

Wender et al. found a much higher incidence of severe depression in the biological relatives of adopted individuals hospitalised for severe depression, compared to biological relatives of a non-depressed group.

Genes as diatheses

Genetic factors are thought to act as diatheses (predispositions), which interact with environmental stressors (diathesis-stress) to produce a depressive reaction.

There is research to support a genetic explanation…

A mutant gene that starves the brain of serotonin has been found to be ten times more common in depressed patients than in normal individuals (Zhang et al.), resulting in an 80% reduction of normal serotonin levels in the brain.

Caron et al. found this mutant gene in nine out of 87 depressed patients but only three out of 219 healthy controls. Patients with this mutation failed to respond to SSRI medications, which work by increasing serotonin levels in the brain.

Low concordance rates explained in terms of comorbidity…

It is possible that people inherit a vulnerability for a wider range of disorders than depression alone, which would explain the relatively low concordance rates for depression alone.

For example, Kendler et al. found a higher incidence of mental disorders in twins of depressed probands when looking at depression and generalised anxiety disorder than when looking at just depression.

Depression may have an evolutionary significance…

The fact that depression is so widespread suggests that it may have some adaptive significance. As depression is costly for the individual, it serves as an 'honest' signal of need, so that others in the social network respond by providing much-needed help and support for the individual.

Depression and adolescents…

Our understanding of the genetics of depression among adolescents is limited as most research has focused on adults only. Glowinski et al. found that, among adolescents, the proportion of risk for major depression due to genetic factors was approximately 40%. This is very close to findings from adult samples.

Neurotransmitter dysfunction

Noradrenaline

Depression can be caused by a deficiency of noradrenaline in the brain.

Evidence for this link comes from research that shows waste products associated with noradrenaline are low in depressed individuals (Bunney et al.).

Post-mortem studies show increased densities of noradrenaline receptors in brains of depressed suicide victims (caused by process of up-regulation).

There is research support for the role of noradrenaline…

Leonard showed that drugs that lowered noradrenaline levels bring about depressive states, while those that increase noradrenaline levels show antidepressant effects.

Successful treatments with SNRIs support this link…

Kraft et al. treated patients with major depression for 6 weeks with a dual serotonin-noradrenaline re-uptake inhibitor (SNRI). The patients showed a significantly more positive response than those treated with a placebo, thus strengthening the link between the depletion of these neurotransmitters and the development of depressive symptoms.

Serotonin

Depression can be caused by a deficiency of serotonin in the brain.

Evidence comes from the discovery that SSRIs, which selectively block the reuptake of serotonin from the synaptic gap, reduce the symptoms of depression.

Delgado et al. gave depressed patients a diet that lowered tryptophan (precursor of serotonin) levels – the majority experienced a return of their symptoms.

There is evidence to support the importance of serotonin…

Amr et al. found an association between high-level exposure to pesticides and an increased risk of depression. Animal studies have shown that exposure to pesticides leads to serotonin disturbances in the brain and therefore depression.

A problem for the serotonin explanation is…

That tryptophan depletion studies have used patients who are in remission from depression. Individuals who have no history of depression tend not to show any mood changes following tryptophan depletion, despite the fact that it alters the same mood regulating areas of the brain.

Cortisol hypersecretion

Cortisol

Levels of cortisol rise in depressed individuals, but reduce to normal once depression disappears.

Cortisol levels reduce brain serotonin levels, which in turn leads to depression.

Dexamethasone suppresses cortisol secretion in normal people, but in depressed people this suppression is not maintained.

There is conflicting research evidence…

Strickland et al. found no evidence of increased cortisol levels in a large group of women with depression or in the majority of those who were vulnerable to depression through adverse life stressors.

However…

They did find elevated cortisol levels in some individuals who had experienced recent severe life events, yet were not depressed. It appears that stressful life events can result in elevated cortisol levels, but this does not necessarily lead to the development of depression.

Chapter 10

Overview	
Explanations of depression	> Biological explanations of depression
Depression > Therapies for depression	Psychological explanations of depression

Psychological explanations of depression

Psychodynamic explanations

Mourning and melancholia

Freud claimed melancholia (depression) was a pathological reaction to the loss of a loved one (or loss of their affection).

Following a loss, there is a mourning period after which life returns to normal.

In some people, this mourning never ends.

The pathology of depression

Freud believed that we unconsciously harbour some negative feelings towards those that we love.

When we lose a loved one, these feelings are turned inwards and we continue a pattern of self-abuse and self-blame.

Depression is 'anger turned upon oneself'.

There is research support for this explanation…

Barnes and Prosen found men whose fathers died when they were boys scored higher on depression than those who had not lost their fathers.

Bifulco *et al.* found that individuals who lost their mothers during childhood were more likely to experience depression later in life.

Shah and Waller found that many depressed people described their parents as 'affectionless' supporting Freud's claim of 'loss of affection'.

However…

Paykel and Cooper argue that 'loss' only explains a relatively small percentage of cases of depression. Possibly only 10% of those who experience an early loss of this sort go on to become depressed.

Psychodynamic therapies don't work with depression…

Psychoanalysis is not particularly effective as a treatment for depression. However, this may be because people with depression find it hard to communicate in the way required by psychoanalytic therapy.

Cognitive explanations

Beck's theory of depression

Depressed individuals feel as they do because their thinking is biased towards negative interpretations of the world.

Depressed people acquire a negative schema early on, which is activated when a situation is encountered that resembles the original one that led to the schema.

These schema are subject to irrational thinking, which lead to a *negative triad*, i.e. a pessimistic view of the self, world and future.

Cognitive therapies do work with depression…

Butler and Beck reviewed 14 meta-analyses and concluded that 80% of adults benefited from cognitive therapy (compared to control groups), lending support to the claim that depression has a cognitive basis.

There is research support for this explanation…

Hammen and Krantz found depressed women made more logical errors, and Bates *et al.* found that depressed participants who were given negative automatic thought statements became more depressed.

However…

Although research such as this demonstrates a link between negative thoughts and depression, it does not mean that the link between the two is a causal one.

Learned helplessness

Depression may be learned when a person tries but fails to control unpleasant experiences. As a result, they acquire a sense of being unable to exercise control over their life, and so become depressed.

Depressed people show a depressive attributional style, i.e. failures considered to be *internal, stable* and *global* (Abramson *et al.*).

There is research support for this explanation…

Hiroto and Seligman compared three groups. One received an unpleasant loud noise, controlled by pressing a button. A second received a noise that they could not control, and a third no noise. Later, all three groups received a controllable noise, which they could turn off by pressing a button. The 'no control' group took the noise without responding, while the other two groups escaped it by pressing the button.

This finding supports the claim that people may develop the view that they can't control unpleasant life events and so develop depression.

Hopelessness

Abramson *et al.* explains depression in terms of pessimistic expectations of the future. The 'hopeless' person expects bad rather than good things to happen in important areas of their life.

There is research support for this explanation…

Kwon and Laurenceau found that people with a negative attributional style also showed more of the symptoms of depression when stressed.

This may be more common in women in men, as during their social development they may be taught to think negatively about themselves, which may explain why more women suffer from depression than men.

Sociocultural explanations

Life events and depression

Life events may act as a trigger in individuals who have a genetic vulnerability for depression.

A depressive attributional style acts as a diathesis that predisposes the person to interpret events in ways that bring about depression.

There is evidence to support this explanation…

Brown and Harris found that episodes of depression were almost always preceded by a major life event. Vulnerability factors such as the lack of a close confiding relationship make depression more likely.

However, there is a problem with this explanation…

Depression may be a consequence of negative life events, but may also be their cause. When depressed, a person may become overwhelmed by life stressors, which are a direct result of their illness.

Social networks and social skills

Depressed individuals often report having sparse social networks (making them less able to handle negative life events).

They may also lack social skills (which means they may elicit rejection from others) (Joiner *et al.*).

There is evidence to support this explanation…

Research suggests that poor social skills may play a causal role in the development of depression.

Low social competence has been found to predict the onset of depression in primary age children (Cole).

Poor interpersonal problem-solving skills have been found to lead to an increased incidence of depression among adolescents (Davila *et al.*).

Chapter 10

Overview	
Explanations of depression	
	Biological therapies for depression
Depression	> Therapies for depression	> Psychological therapies for depression

Biological therapies for depression

Antidepressants

How do they work?

Depression is caused by insufficient amounts of neurotransmitters (serotonin and noradrenaline) available in the brain.

Antidepressants work either by reducing the rate of re-absorbtion or by blocking the enzyme which breaks down these neurotransmitters in the synapse.

This increases the amount of the neurotransmitters available to excite neighbouring nerve cells.

Tricyclics (TCAs)

These block the transporter mechanism that reabsorbs serotonin and noradrenaline into the presynaptic cell after it has fired.

As a result, more neurotransmitters are left in the synapse, prolonging their action.

SSRIs

Instead of blocking the reuptake of different neurotransmitters, they block mainly serotonin and so increase the availability of serotonin at the synapse.

Evidence comes from the success of SSRIs such as *Prozac*, which reduce the symptoms of depression.

Phases of treatment:

- Treatment of current symptoms takes place during the *acute phase*.
- Once symptoms have diminished, treatment enters a *continuation phase*.
- A *maintenance phase* is recommended for individuals with history of depression.

Effectiveness of TCAs versus SSRIs...

Both TCAs and SSRIs have been shown to produce a more significant reduction in depressive symptoms compared to a placebo (Arroll *et al.*).

SSRIs may only be effective in cases of severe depression...

Kirsch *et al.* concluded that only in cases of the most severe depression was there any significant advantage to using SSRIs over a placebo.

However...

This may be because, among moderately depressed individuals, even the placebo appeared to offer them *some* hope, which contributed to a lessening of symptoms. For the severely depressed, the expectation of anything working was absent, thus removing any placebo effect.

Appropriateness of TCAs and SSRIs...

SSRIs have an important advantage over TCAs with respect to tolerability. SSRIs are better tolerated than TCAs, therefore patients are more likely to continue with treatment and recover (Montgomery *et al.*).

Antidepressants are not suitable for children and adolescents...

Double blind studies (e.g. Geller *et al.*) have consistently failed to demonstrate the superiority of antidepressant medications over placebos when given to children and adolescents.

There may be an increased risk of suicide...

A review of studies (Barbui *et al.*) found that, although the use of SSRIs increased the risk of suicide among adolescents, the risk was decreased among adults, and particularly so for adults aged 65+ where it appeared to have a protective effect against the risk of suicide.

There is a publication bias... and an age bias...

Turner *et al.* claim that research that shows a positive outcome of antidepressant treatment is more likely to be published, thus exaggerating the benefits of antidepressant drugs.

Depression in the elderly is often misdiagnosed because natural changes mask its symptoms. As a result, antidepressant medication is less likely to be prescribed, even when needed.

Electroconvulsive therapy (ECT)

ECT is generally used in severely depressed patients for whom psychotherapy and medication have proved ineffective.

It is used when there is a risk of suicide, because ECT often has much quicker results than antidepressant drugs.

ECT in practice:

- In unilateral ECT, an electrode is placed on the non-dominant side of the brain and another on the forehead.
- The patient is injected with a barbiturate to make them unconscious during ECT, then given a nerve-blocking agent to prevent fractures during the seizure.
- A small amount of current is passed through the brain for half a second.
- This creates a seizure, which affects the whole brain.

The mechanism of ECT

It is the seizure rather than the shock that produces an improvement in symptoms.

The seizure appears to restore the brain's ability to regulate mood. It may do this by enhancing the transmission of neurochemicals, or by improving blood flow in the brain.

Effectiveness of ECT...

Research (e.g. Gregory *et al.*) has shown that when ECT is compared to 'sham' ECT, there tends to be a significant difference in outcome in favour of real ECT.

ECT is effective in cases of treatment-resistant depression (Folkerts *et al.*) although other studies have found no significant improvement following the administration of ECT for treatment-resistant depression (Hussain).

ECT versus antidepressants...

A review of 18 studies with 1,144 patients comparing ECT with antidepressant medication showed that ECT is more effective in the short-term treatment of depression (Scott).

However...

None of these trials compared ECT with the newer types of antidepressants such as the SSRIs.

Appropriateness of ECT... side effects...

Rose *et al.* concluded that at least one-third of patients complained of persistent memory loss after ECT. A Department of Health report in 2007 found that, among those receiving ECT in the previous 2 years, 30% reported that it had resulted in permanent fear and anxiety.

ECT may help the elderly...

Benek-Higgins *et al.* claim that depression in elderly people is often misdiagnosed because its symptoms are masked by natural changes in these individuals. However, ECT can be effective and is well-tolerated in the elderly. A meta-analysis (Mulsant *et al.*) found a significant improvement in 83% cases where ECT was used with elderly patients.

Chapter 10

Overview
Explanations of depression
Biological therapies for depression

Depression   >   Therapies for depression   >   Psychological therapies for depression

Psychological therapies for depression

Cognitive behavioural therapy (CBT)

Maladaptive cognitions

CBT emphasises the role of maladaptive thoughts and cognitions in the origins and maintenance of depression.

The aim of CBT is to identify and alter these maladaptive cognitions, as well as any dysfunctional behaviours that may be contributing to the depression.

CBT is focused on current problems and current dysfunctional thinking.

Thought catching

Individuals are taught to see the link between their thoughts and their feelings.

During CBT they are taught to challenge this association between emotion-arousing events and the 'automatic' negative thoughts that accompany them.

By challenging these dysfunctional thoughts, and replacing them with more constructive ones, clients may reduce the symptoms of their depression.

Behavioural activation

This is based on the common sense idea that being active leads to rewards that act as an antidote to depression.

A characteristic of depression is that depressed people no longer participate in activities that they previously enjoyed.

In CBT, therapist and client identify potentially pleasurable activities and deal with any cognitive obstacles.

Effectiveness of CBT...

A meta-analysis by Robinson *et al.* found that CBT was superior to no-treatment control groups. However, when these control groups were divided into waiting list (i.e. no treatment at all) and placebo groups, CBT was not significantly more effective than placebos at reducing depressive symptoms.

The problem of attrition...

Hunt and Andrews examined five meta-analyses and found the median drop-out rate to be 8%. If participants drop out because they feel therapy isn't helping, then the outcomes for the remaining participants will appear artificially positive, as they are more highly motivated.

Effectiveness depends on therapist competence...

Therapist competence appears to explain a significant amount of the variation in CBT outcomes. Kuyken and Tsivrikos lend support to this claim, concluding that as much as 15% of the variation in outcome can be attributed to therapist outcome.

Appropriateness of CBT...

CBT has been successfully applied to elderly populations, juveniles and depressed adolescents. When combined with antidepressants, CBT is particularly effective at reducing the symptoms of depression and reducing suicidal thoughts and behaviour (March *et al.*).

The appropriateness of computer- and phone-based therapies...

The cognitive aspect of CBT has been shown to be as effective as other forms of psychotherapy when administered by computer programs, such as 'Beat the Blues' (Selmi *et al.*).

Mohr *et al.* carried out a meta-analysis of 12 studies and found that psychotherapy conducted over the phone significantly reduced the symptoms of depression compared to a non-treatment control group, although it was only half as effective as face-to-face psychotherapy.

A particular advantage of computer- and phone-based psychotherapy is the low drop-out rate compared with face-to-face CBT.

Psychodynamic interpersonal therapy (PIT)

The nature of PIT

Hobson emphasised that the mutual task of therapist and client was to engage in a therapeutic 'conversation'.

In this 'conversation', problems are relived in the present and resolved within the therapeutic relationship.

Hobson believed that depression arises from disturbances in personal relationships, and can only be modified effectively within another relationship – the therapeutic relationship.

Components of PIT

There are seven interlinking components:

- *Exploratory rationale* – Interpersonal difficulties identified and links with current problems explored.
- *Shared understanding* – The therapist tries to understand what client is feeling.
- *Staying with feelings* – Feelings are recreated within the therapeutic environment.
- *Focusing on difficult feelings* – Client may not display appropriate emotion.
- *Gaining insight* – Therapist points out patterns in different types of relationship.
- *Sequencing of interventions*, e.g. context of feelings is established before sharing insights.
- *Change during therapy* is acknowledged and encouraged by therapist.

Effectiveness of PIT...

Paley *et al.* showed that, as a treatment for depression, outcomes for PIT were at least equivalent to those achieved with CBT. However, they acknowledged that changes in significant life events were not monitored during the study, therefore any observed reductions in depressive symptoms could not be attributed solely to the therapeutic effects of PIT. The *Collaborative Psychotherapy Project* (Barkham *et al.*) found that PIT was effective in reducing the severity of depressive symptoms, but after 12 months, patients showed a tendency for symptoms to recur, thus limiting its long-term effectiveness.

Appropriateness of PIT...

The importance of relational processes – Guthrie argues that PIT is particularly important in the treatment of cases of depression that result from dysfunctional relationships (e.g. between parent and child).

Research has consistently shown that the quality of the relationship between therapist and client is an important determinant of the outcomes of therapy. For example, Horvath and Bedi found that the better the quality of the relationship between therapist and client, the greater the client change.

A maintenance therapy – PIT is used effectively as a preventive measure by focusing on the period after the acute depression has passed. Once the individual is in remission and is relatively symptom-free, he or she begins to take on more responsibilities and has increased social contact.

PIT helps individuals to reduce the stresses associated with remission and thereby lower the risk of recurrence.

Phobic disorders

Division A   Overview
Classification and diagnosis of phobic disorders

Division B   Explanations of phobic disorders
Biological explanations of phobic disorders
Psychological explanations of phobic disorders

Division C   Therapies for phobic disorders
Biological therapies for phobic disorders
Psychological therapies for phobic disorders

Issues, debates and approaches
In the Psychopathology section (Section A) of the Unit 4 exam there is no explicit credit given to issues, debates and approaches. This doesn't mean that such material would not be creditworthy (it would) but it means it is not required. So, in this chapter we have not specifically identified IDA.

Specification

Phobic disorders	
Overview	• Clinical characteristics of phobic disorders.
	• Issues surrounding the classification and diagnosis of phobic disorders, including reliability and validity.
Explanations	• Biological explanations of phobic disorders, for example genetics, biochemistry.
	• Psychological explanations of phobic disorders, for example behavioural, cognitive, psychodynamic and socio-cultural.
Therapy	• Biological therapies for phobic disorders, including their evaluation in terms of appropriateness and effectiveness.
	• Psychological therapies for phobic disorders, for example behavioural, psychodynamic and cognitive-behavioural, including their evaluation in terms of appropriateness and effectiveness.

Classification and diagnosis of phobic disorders

Clinical characteristics of specific phobic disorders

Diagnosis

- *Fear* – Marked and persistent fear that is excessive or unreasonable.
- *Immediate response* – Exposure to phobic stimulus provokes an immediate anxiety response, e.g. a panic attack.
- *Self-awareness* of the excessive nature of the fear, which distinguishes phobia from delusional mental illness (e.g. schizophrenia) where the individual is not aware of the unreasonableness of their behaviour.
- *Interferes with normal functioning* – The avoidance of or distress in the feared situation interferes with the person's normal routine, occupation or relationships.
- *Duration* – In individuals under age 18 years the duration of symptoms is at least 6 months.

Reliability

Reliability refers to the consistency of a measuring instrument, such as a questionnaire or scale, to assess how fearful a person is about certain objects/experiences.

Inter-rater reliability

Skyre *et al.* assessed inter-rater reliability for diagnosing social phobia by asking three clinicians to assess 54 patient interviews obtained using the *Structured Clinical Interview* (SCID-I). There was high inter-rater agreement (+.72). SCID is a semi-structured interview requiring extensive training to administer, which may explain the high reliability.

Test–retest reliability

Hiller *et al.* reported satisfactory to excellent diagnostic agreement in a test–retest study using the *Munich Diagnostic Checklist* (MDC).

High reliability can be explained…

SCID is a semi-structured interview requiring extensive training to administer which may explain the high reliability.

There is some evidence of poor reliability…

Kendler *et al.* interviewed phobic individuals (face-to-face or over the telephone). Over a 1-month interval (test–retest) there was a mean agreement of +.46. Reliability over 8 years was even lower (+.30).

This may be explained…

Kendler *et al.* suggest that low test–retest reliability might be due to the poor recall by participants of their fears (sometimes over-exaggerating fears and sometimes under-exaggerating them).

Alternatively, low inter-rater reliability might occur because interviewers differ in their interpretation of the severity of symptoms, so that some interviewers might conclude that a symptom is clinically significant, whereas others might conclude that the severity does not exceed the clinical threshold and therefore a diagnosis is not made.

Reliability can be improved using computer diagnosis…

Computerised scales may be preferable because the presence of another person can create fears of negative evaluation.

Computerised scales also mean there is less of an effect of interviewer expectations on the patient's answers (Kobak *et al.*).

However…

Validity may be reduced when using computerised scales because clinicians play an important role in facilitating the disclosure of troubling information (Heimberg *et al.*).

Validity

Validity refers to the extent that a diagnosis represents something that is real and distinct.

Comorbidity suggests the diagnostic category is not very useful, e.g. when deciding what treatment to advise. Kendler *et al.* found high levels of comorbidity between social phobias, animal phobias, generalised anxiety disorder and depression.

Concurrent validity establishes the value of a new measure of phobic symptoms by correlating it with an existing one.

For example, Herbert *et al.* found that the *Social Phobia Anxiety Inventory* (SPAI) correlated well with the other measures.

Construct validity establishes validity by looking to see if individuals with key target behaviours are diagnosed as phobic.

For example, we might expect social phobics to underestimate their ability to cope in social situations.

The implications of low reliability and/or validity…

Research on phobic disorders (e.g. considering the effectiveness of a particular treatment) requires a reliable and valid means of assessing the disorders in the first place. If the means of assessing the disorder have low reliability/validity then the research using these assessment tools will also be low in reliability/validity.

Research on comorbidity is supported by…

Up to 66% of patients with one anxiety disorder are also diagnosed with another anxiety disorder (Eysenck). The implications are that the diagnosis should simply be 'anxiety disorder' rather than phobia or obsessive compulsive disorder (OCD).

Culture differences…

Taijin-kyofusho (TKS) is a culturally distinctive phobia recognised in Japan. This is a social phobia where an individual has a fear of embarrassing others in social situations. In the UK, a person exhibiting such symptoms would not be diagnosed with a social phobia, indicating the effect of cultural experiences on the diagnosis of a disorder.

Support for concurrent validity…

Mattick and Clarke showed that their Social Phobia Scale (SPS) correlated well with other standard measures of phobias (varying between +.54 and +.69).

Support for construct validity…

Beidel *et al.* found the SPAI correlates well with behavioural measures of social phobia (e.g. ease of public speaking) and lacks association with behaviours unrelated to social phobia.

However…

Perhaps this is not surprising because the inventory includes questions about cognitions and behaviours across a range of fear-producing situations. This means it is likely to correlate with behaviours associated with social phobias.

Chapter 11

Overview

| Explanations of phobic disorders | > | Biological explanations of phobic disorders |
| Phobic disorders | > | Therapies for phobic disorders | | Psychological explanations of phobic disorders |

Biological explanations of phobic disorders

Genetic factors

Family studies

Fyer et al. found that probands had three times as many relatives who also experienced phobias compared to normal controls.

Solyom et al. found that 45% of phobic patients had at least one relative with the disorder compared to 17% of normal controls.

Relatives usually have the same disorder as the proband, e.g. Ost found that 64% of blood phobics had a least one relative with the same disorder.

Twin studies

Torgersen compared MZ and same-sex DZ twin pairs (85 pairs) where one twin (the proband) had an anxiety disorder with panic attacks. Such disorders were five times more frequent in MZ twin pairs.

Inherited tendencies

Various suggestions include:

• High levels of arousal in the ANS, which creates increased amounts of adrenaline and this leads to an oversensitive fear response (adrenogenic theory).

• Dopamine pathways in the brain may predispose some people to be more readily conditioned, so that they are more likely to acquire phobias easily.

• Abnormal serotonin activity modulates those areas of the brain involved in the fear response, such as the amygdala.

Some phobias have a greater genetic component than others...

Kendler et al. estimated a 67% heritability rate for agoraphobia, 59% for blood/injury, 51% for social phobias and 47% for animal phobias.

Torgerson actually only found 31% concordance (which is very low) for MZ twins in terms of anxiety disorders and almost no concordance for DZ twins.

Cultural differences...

Brown et al. found that phobic disorders were more common among African-American than white American participants, even when socioeconomic factors were controlled. This shows that environmental/social factors are important.

The diathesis-stress model...

It is likely that genetic factors predispose an individual to develop phobias, but experience plays a role in triggering such responses.

One of the problems with family and twin studies...

They fail to control for shared experiences. MZ twins are likely to share more similar experiences (environments) than DZ twins because, for example, they are likely to have more similar interests even when reared apart (interests often are related to inherited tendencies).

There is research support...

Children with signs of behavioural inhibition at birth (dislike of unfamiliar situations) were found later to have higher ANS activity and develop significantly more anxiety disorders (Biederman et al.).

Successful drug therapies for phobics include drugs that block activity of the adrenergic system (beta-blockers), reducing anxiety.

Brain scanning techniques have been used to measure the density of dopamine reuptake sites. Tiihonen et al. found a significantly lower number of such sites in patients with social phobia than in normal controls, which would lead to abnormally low levels of dopamine.

However...

This does not show that such differences actually cause phobias in the first place, e.g. drugs may be treating symptoms that have arisen as an effect rather than the cause of phobias.

An evolutionary approach

Ancient fears and modern minds

Ancient fears (e.g. snakes, heights) were dangers to our distant ancestors. Modern phobias are often related to these ancient fears rather than modern dangers (e.g. guns, electricity) because these have not been around enough to have influenced adaptive selection (Marks and Nesse).

Prepotency

Experiencing anxiety after an event has happened would not be an adaptive response, therefore animals have evolved a response to potential threats.

Prepotency refers to the tendency to respond prior to direct experience, e.g. to respond anxiously to snake-like movement.

Preparedness

An innate readiness to learn about dangerous situations is more flexible than inheriting rigid behavioural responses to specific situations.

Seligman argued that animals, including humans, are biologically prepared to rapidly learn an association between particular (i.e. potentially life-threatening) stimuli and fear, and once learned this association is difficult to extinguish.

Biological 'preparedness' may be linked to ancient fears...

Rhesus monkeys rapidly develop a fear of snakes if they see another rhesus monkey showing fear towards a snake, but the same doesn't happen if fear is shown towards a flower (Mineka et al.).

The evolutionary approach doesn't explain clinical phobias...

Merckelbach et al. found that most of the clinical phobias in their survey of phobias were rated as non-prepared rather than prepared.

There is research support...

Öhman and Soares showed that people who were fearful of snakes or spiders showed a greater fear response (SNS activity measured by GSR) when shown masked (not immediately recognisable) pictures of snake/spiders. This shows that people respond to prepotent signals.

Bennett-Levy and Marteau asked participants to rate animals (e.g. for sliminess), and found that fear was due to discrepancy with the human form and aversive stimulus configuration (e.g. hissing), i.e. prepotent signals.

There is mixed research support...

McNally reviewed laboratory studies (participants were conditioned to fear prepared and unprepared stimuli). The participants showed resistance to extinction of fear responses conditioned by 'prepared' stimuli, but evidence for rapid acquisition was, at best, equivocal.

A simpler, non-evolutionary explanation...

Davey proposed that fears are based on an expectancy bias – the expectation that fear-relevant stimuli (e.g. past experience of unpleasantness) will produce negative consequences in the future. There is no need to invoke past evolutionary history. This explains the acquisition of 'modern' phobias (e.g. phobia of hypodermic needles).

Chapter 11

Overview
Explanations of phobic disorders   >   Biological explanations of phobic disorders
Phobic disorders   >   Therapies for phobic disorders
Psychological explanations of phobic disorders

Psychological explanations of phobic disorders

Psychodynamic approach

Freud proposed that a phobia was the conscious expression of repressed conflicts. The ego deals with conflict by repressing the undesirable emotions into the unconscious mind. Such repressed thoughts can be expressed by projecting them onto a neutral object or situation, e.g. a dog or social situation. Therefore the individual displays a fear of dogs or social situations, rather than expressing their real fear.

For example, the case study of Little Hans concerned a boy who had become terrified of horses. Freud suggested that Hans' phobia developed because Hans projected a real fear (that his mother would leave him) onto horses (because he heard a man say 'Don't put your finger to the white horse or it'll bite you' and Hans also once asked his mother if she would like to put her finger on his penis).

The Little Hans case study has been criticised...
A case study concerns one unique individual and therefore can't be generalised to the wider population.

The Little Hans study lacked objectivity because both Hans' father and Freud interpreted the evidence according to their expectations about the origins of phobias.

Hans' phobia could be explained in terms of classical conditioning (Hans associated horses with feeling scared).

However there is other research support...
Bowlby found that agoraphobics often had early experiences of family conflict. He suggested that such conflict leads a young child to feel very anxious when separated from their parents (separation anxiety). Such fears are suppressed but later emerge as agoraphobia.

Whiting et al. studied the occurrence of phobias in other cultures and concluded that they were more common in societies that had a structured form of child-rearing. The reason may be because stricter, structured parenting might lead to children having to repress desires.

The fact that therapies that simply target the symptoms of phobia (such as systematic desensitisation) are not 100% successful may be because they fail to deal with the underlying causes of the phobias.

Behavioural approach

Classical conditioning
Little Albert developed a fear of white furry objects because he experienced:

- A furry rat (neutral stimulus, NS) being associated with a loud noise (unconditioned stimulus, UCS).
- UCS produced an unconditioned response (UCR) of fear.
- The furry object (now a conditioned stimulus, CS) acquired the same properties (conditioned response, CR) so that when Albert saw it he cried, presumably because he was scared.

Operant conditioning
Two-process theory (Mowrer) suggests that phobias are (1) acquired through classical conditioning and (2) maintained through operant conditioning, where the avoidance of the phobic stimulus reduces fear and is thus reinforcing (negative reinforcement).

There is research support...
People with phobias often do recall a specific incident when their phobia first appeared, e.g. being bitten by a dog (Sue et al.).

However...
Not everyone who has a phobia can recall such an incident, though it may be that such traumatic incidents have been repressed (Öst).

Not everyone who is bitten by a dog develops a phobia of dogs (Di Nardo et al.), though perhaps only those with a genetic vulnerability for phobias would be affected by such events (diathesis-stress model).

Biological 'preparedness'...
Bergman failed to condition a fear response in infants by pairing a loud bell with wooden blocks. It may be that fear responses are only learned when the neutral stimulus is an 'ancient fear' (e.g. an animal).

Cultural differences...
The behaviourist approach can account for cultural differences because, for example, each society offers its own culture-specific role models that influence which phobias might be acquired.

Social learning
Phobias may also be acquired through imitating the behaviour of others, e.g. seeing a parent responding to a spider with extreme fear may lead a child to acquire a similar behaviour because the behaviour appears rewarding.

There is research support...
In one study (Bandura and Rosenthal) an observer watched a model apparently experiencing pain every time a buzzer sounded. The observer later demonstrated an emotional reaction to the sound.

We can conclude that...
Different phobias may be the result of different processes, e.g. Sue et al. found that agoraphobics were most likely to explain their disorder in terms of a specific incident, whereas arachnophobics were most likely to cite modelling as the cause.

Cognitive approach

Phobias may develop as the consequence of irrational thinking, e.g. a person in a lift may think 'I could become trapped in here and suffocate' (an irrational thought).

Beck et al. proposed that such irrational thoughts create anxiety and it is the fear of being in a situation of high anxiety that creates a phobia. Phobics tend to overestimate their fears, increasing the likelihood of phobias.

There is research support for dysfunctional assumptions...
Gournay found that phobics were more likely than normal people to overestimate risks, suggesting that they are predisposed to develop phobias because of their cognitive style.

The success of CBT as a treatment for phobia...
It can be argued that, if a therapy changes the dysfunctional assumptions a person has and this leads to a reduction to their phobia, then the dysfunctional assumptions may originally have caused the disorder.

Chapter 11

Overview
Explanations of phobic disorders
Phobic disorders > Therapies for phobic disorders >

Biological therapies for phobic disorders
Psychological therapies for phobic disorders

Biological therapies for phobic disorders

Chemotherapy

Antianxiety drugs – Benzodiazepines

Benzodiazepines (BZs) (e.g. *Valium, Diazepam*) slow down the activity of the central nervous system by enhancing the activity of GABA, a neurotransmitter that has a general quietening effect on many of the neurons in the brain.

They do this by locking into GABA receptors on the outside of receiving neurons, which opens a channel to increase the flow of chloride ions into the neuron. Chloride ions make it harder for the neuron to be stimulated by other neurotransmitters.

Antianxiety drugs – Beta-blockers

Beta-blockers (BBs) reduce the activity of adrenaline (part of SNS response to stress).

BBs bind to receptors on the cells of the heart and other parts of the body that are usually stimulated during arousal. By blocking these receptors, it is harder to stimulate these cells, so the heart beats slower and blood vessels do not contract so easily, resulting in a fall in blood pressure, and less feeling of anxiety.

Antidepressants

SSRIs (e.g. *Zoloft, Prozac*) are currently the preferred drug for treating anxiety disorders (Choy and Schneier). They increase levels of the neurotransmitter serotonin that regulates mood/anxiety.

MAOI (monoamine oxidase inhibitor), an older class of antidepressants, is more effective with some patients (Lader and Petursson). *Monoamine oxidase* (MAO) is the enzyme responsible for breaking down monoamine neurotransmitters (e.g. serotonin and dopamine) so an inhibitor prevents this happening, leading to higher levels of monoamines in the synaptic gap.

The effectiveness of antianxiety drugs…

Kahn *et al.* found that BZs were more effective than placebos in reducing anxiety.

Hildalgo *et al.* found that BZs were more effective than antidepressants in reducing the anxiety associated with phobic reactions.

Research studies (e.g. Liebowitz *et al.*) have shown that BBs can also provide an effective means of anxiety control.

However…

Some studies have shown that the benefits may be largely explained in terms of placebo effects, e.g. Turner *et al.* found no difference between BBs and placebo groups in terms of reduced heart rate, feelings of nervousness and so on.

The effectiveness of antidepressant drugs…

MAOIs have been found to be more effective than placebos and more effective in the reduction of anxiety than BBs (Liebowitz *et al.*).

SSRIs led to improved levels of self-rated anxiety when compared to a placebo treatment (Katzelnick *et al.*).

Aouizerate *et al.* concluded that SSRIs provide relief for social phobics in 50%–80% of cases, a level fairly similar to BZs, but SSRIs are preferable because there are fewer side effects.

Appropriateness of chemotherapy… Not a cure…

Drugs can't provide a complete treatment as they focus on symptoms.

Side effects…

BZs may cause increased aggressiveness and long-term impairment of memory – although recent research (Kindt *et al.*) has proposed that such negative effects might be used to remove anxiety-causing memories.

- BBs have few side effects.
- SSRIs are linked to increased suicides in adolescents (Barbui *et al.*).
- MAOIs have a number of side effects, e.g. dizziness, insomnia.

Addiction…

BZs may become addictive, even when only low doses are given. A maximum use of 4 weeks is recommended (Ashton).

Ethical issues…

The issue of informed consent concerns the extent to which patients are not informed about the fact that drugs may not actually be much better than placebos.

Psychosurgery

Capsulotomy and cingulotomy

These surgical interventions sever connections to malfunctioning parts of the brain to reduce anxiety levels.

The *capsule* and the *cingulum* are both parts of the limbic system, the region of the brain that is associated with emotion.

The surgeon inserts a probe through the top of the skull and pushes it to the capsule or cingulum, which is located deep in the brain. The leading tip of the probe burns away small portions of tissue.

Such operations are irreversible and only performed as a last resort.

Deep brain stimulation (DBS)

Wires are placed in target areas (capsule and cingulum) and connected to a battery in the patient's chest. When the current is on the target circuits are interrupted.

Deep brain stimulation involves no tissue destruction, though the wires are permanent.

Effectiveness of psychosurgery…

Ruck *et al.* studied 26 patients with long-term non-obsessive anxiety disorders (e.g. panic disorder, social phobia). Following a capsulotomy, the patients showed significant reductions in anxiety.

However…

The negative symptoms were greater than expected, e.g. seven patients attempted to commit suicide after surgery.

Appropriateness of psychosurgery…

Psychosurgery is rarely suitable for phobias and then only for extreme cases that have proved otherwise untreatable and that interfere with normal day-to-day functioning.

Deep brain stimulation may offer a better, non-permanent solution.

Szasz criticised psychosurgery generally because the psyche is not something that is physical and therefore it is illogical to suggest that it can be operated on.

Ethical issues…

The irreversible nature of psychosurgery raises ethical concerns because of physical harm and difficulties with gaining informed consent. Patients with severe mental illness are not in a position to give such consent because of their distorted thinking, and relatives may not be fully informed about the risks and therefore unable to truly provide informed consent.

Chapter 11

Overview
Explanations of phobic disorders   Biological therapies for phobic disorders
Phobic disorders   > Therapies for phobic disorders   > Psychological therapies for phobic disorders

Psychological therapies for phobic disorders

Behavioural therapy: Systematic desensitisation (SD)

Key principle

Phobias are perpetuated because the anxiety created blocks any attempt to re-experience the stimulus. Wolpe developed a technique where the feared stimulus is reintroduced gradually.

Counterconditioning

The patient is taught relaxation techniques and then given the opportunity to experience the feared stimulus while relaxed, forming a new association that runs counter to the original association. Wolpe also called this 'reciprocal inhibition' because the relaxation inhibits the anxiety.

Desensitisation hierarchy

Therapist and patient construct a series of imagined scenes, each one progressively more fearful. They then work through this hierarchy, relaxing and mastering each stage before moving on to the next.

Different forms of SD

In vivo desensitisation – confronting feared situations directly.

Covert (also known as in vitro) desensitisation – imagining the feared stimuli.

Effectiveness of SD...

Research has found that SD is successful for a range of phobic disorders, e.g. McGrath et al. found about 75% success rates.

Capafóns et al. found overall success for 41 aerophobics receiving two 1-hour sessions per week over a 12–15-week period, using in vivo and covert techniques, but SD was not 100% effective.

In vivo techniques are more successful than covert ones (Menzies and Clarke), although often a number of different exposure techniques are involved – in vivo, covert and also modelling where the patient watches someone else who is coping well with the feared stimulus (Comer).

However...

Öhman et al. suggest that SD may not be as effective in treating phobias that have an underlying evolutionary survival component (e.g. fear of the dark or dangerous animals) than in treating phobias that have been acquired as a result of personal experience.

Appropriateness of SD...
Strengths...

SD requires less effort from the patient than other psychotherapies (such as REBT, below).

SD can be self-administered, a method that has proved successful with, for example, social phobia (Humphrey).

Symptom substitution...

SD may appear to resolve a problem but suppressing symptoms may result in other symptoms. However, there is no evidence of this (Langevin).

Are the ingredients of SD necessary?...

Positive expectancies may be the most important ingredient, e.g. Klein et al. found SD and supportive psychotherapy equally effective for patients with either social or specific phobias.

It may not be appropriate to generalise from animal research...

SD was based on research conditioning cats. In humans, fear may not be produced as simply because expectations play a greater role.

Rational-emotive behaviour therapy (REBT)

Key principle

Ellis proposed that phobias occur because of irrational thinking.

Therefore treatment should make thinking rational (R) and also address emotional (E) and behavioural (B) problems (= REB).

ABC model (Ellis)

A = Activating event (situation that results in feelings of frustration and anxiety) e.g. friend ignores you in the street.

B = Irrational beliefs arising from A, e.g. your friend must have decided he doesn't like you; no one likes you, you are worthless.

C = Self-defeating consequences, e.g. avoid social situations in the future.

Disputing

Beliefs (not activating events) lead to self-defeating consequences. Therefore REBT focuses on disputing the beliefs, e.g.:

• Logical disputing – e.g. 'Does thinking this way make sense?'
• Empirical disputing – (evidence based) e.g. 'Where is the proof that this belief is accurate?'
• Pragmatic disputing – (usefulness) e.g. 'How is this belief likely to help me?'

The phobic moves from catastrophising ('All spiders will kill me') to more rational interpretations ('It is rare to encounter a poisonous spider'). This helps the phobic become more self-accepting.

Effectiveness of REBT...

REBT has generally done well in outcome studies (i.e. studies designed to measure responses to treatment), e.g. a meta-analysis by Engels et al.

Ellis claimed a 90% success rate, taking an average of 27 sessions to complete.

NICE identified CBT (of which REBT is an example) as the first-line approach in treating anxiety disorders.

However...

Emmelkamp et al. concluded that REBT was less effective than in vivo exposure treatments, at least for agoraphobia.

Appropriateness of REBT...
Not suitable for all...

Ellis believed that sometimes people who claimed to be following REBT principles were not putting their revised beliefs into action and therefore the therapy was not effective.

Ellis also suggested that some people simply do not want the direct sort of advice and cognitive effort associated with REBT.

There is research support...

Research has found that people who hold irrational beliefs form inferences that are significantly less functional than those that are formed by people who hold rational beliefs (Bond and Dryden).

On the other hand, it may be that irrational beliefs are counterproductive but realistic, e.g. Alloy and Abrahmson found that depressed people gave more accurate estimates of the likelihood of a disaster than 'normal' controls (calling it the 'sadder but wiser' effect).

Obsessive compulsive disorder

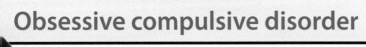

Division A   Overview
Classification and diagnosis of OCD

Division B   Explanations of OCD
Biological explanations of OCD
Psychological explanations of OCD

Division C   Therapies for OCD
Biological therapies for OCD
Psychological therapies for OCD

Issues, debates and approaches

In the Psychopathology section (Section A) of the Unit 4 exam there is no explicit credit given to issues, debates and approaches. This doesn't mean that such material would not be creditworthy (it would) but it means it is not required. So, in this chapter we have not specifically identified IDA.

Specification

Obsessive compulsive disorder (OCD)	
Overview	• Clinical characteristics of OCD. • Issues surrounding the classification and diagnosis of OCD, including reliability and validity.
Explanations	• Biological explanations of OCD, for example genetics, biochemistry. • Psychological explanations of OCD, for example behavioural, cognitive, psychodynamic and socio-cultural.
Therapy	• Biological therapies for OCD, including their evaluation in terms of appropriateness and effectiveness. • Psychological therapies for OCD, for example behavioural, psychodynamic and cognitive-behavioural, including their evaluation in terms of appropriateness and effectiveness.

Classification and diagnosis of OCD

Clinical characteristics

Obsessions create anxiety.

- Recurrent, intrusive thoughts or having impulses that are perceived as inappropriate or forbidden (DSM-IV-TR), e.g. the idea that germs are everywhere or having the impulse to shout out.
- More than excessive worries about real-life problems.
- Perceived as uncontrollable, which creates more anxiety.
- Recognised as the product of the patient's own mind, rather than thought insertions.
- Ignored, suppressed or neutralised with other thoughts/actions.

Compulsions aim to deal with obsessions, but also create anxiety.

- Repetitive behaviours or mental acts that aim to reduce the anxiety that accompanies an obsession (DSM-IV-TR), e.g. hand washing (overt behaviour) or counting (mental act).
- Not connected in any realistic way to what they are trying to neutralise.

Further criteria

- *Obsessions and compulsions recognised by patients as excessive* or unreasonable (doesn't apply to children).
- *Product of patient's own mind* – The obsessions or compulsions are recognised as a product of the patient's own mind (i.e. not placed in their mind, as in schizophrenia).
- *OCD is only diagnosed* if no other physiological cause or if symptoms not better explained by another disorder.

Reliability

Reliability refers to the consistency of a measuring instrument, such as a questionnaire or scale to assess how fearful a person is about certain objects/experiences.

Shorter test–retest reliability is better…

Kim *et al.* reported that good test–retest reliability over the short-term (2 weeks). Short-term reliability may be more important because we would expect symptoms to change over longer periods (i.e. not find consistency).

Inter-rater reliability

The *Yale-Brown Obsessive Compulsive Scale* (Y-BOCS) is a semi-structured interview that can be used to assess symptom severity.

Woody *et al.* used Y-BOCS to assess 54 OCD patients and found good internal consistency.

Computerised scales are also reliable…

Online versions of Y-BOCS yield reliability scores similar to interviewer-administered versions (Baer *et al.*).

Problems with self-report…

Some OCD patients may lack awareness of the severity and frequency of their symptoms, therefore the validity of any diagnosis is likely to be improved by interviewing close friends/partners.

Test–retest reliability

Woody *et al.* found reliability of +.64 (obsessions subscale) and +.56 (compulsions subscale), over an average of 48.5 days.

However…

The symptoms of OCD (unlike other mental disorders) are observable and concrete, so easier for patients to identify.

Validity

Validity refers to the extent that a diagnosis represents something that is real and distinct. Also a scale should measure what it aims to measure.

There may be cultural bias in the diagnosis of OCD…

The symptoms of OCD are often shaped by a patient's culture of origin, e.g. contamination fears in India may relate to fears about touching a person from a lower social caste.

However…

Matsunaga *et al.* studied Japanese OCD patients and found symptoms similar to those in the West, suggesting OCD transcends culture.

Comorbidity suggests the diagnostic category is not very useful, e.g. when deciding what treatment to advise.

Rosenfeld *et al.* found that patients diagnosed with OCD had higher Y-BOCS scores than patients with other anxiety disorders and normal controls, i.e. it does distinguish OCD patients from others.

Some studies have found evidence of comorbidity…

Woody *et al.* found poor discrimination with depression, i.e. patients diagnosed with OCD were also often diagnosed with depression.

This suggests that the diagnostic category is not very useful, e.g. when deciding what treatment to advise.

Interviews may be better than questionnaires…

OCD patients may be fearful of handling questionnaires because they are contaminated (Anthony and Barlow).

An experienced clinician can distinguish between simple worries and pathological obsessions (Brown *et al.*), whereas patients may not be able to.

Internal validity of questionnaires

OCD patients may be embarrassed or feel afraid that an interviewer will take symptoms as a sign of a deeper psychosis, and therefore might not produce honest answers to questionnaires and this reduces the validity of any such questionnaire.

Internal validity may be increased using computer diagnosis…

Computerised scales for assessing OCD may be preferable because the presence of another person creates fears of negative evaluation.

Computerised scales also mean there is less effect of interviewer expectations on the patient's answers (Kobak *et al.*).

ICD may have lower validity than DSM…

Steinberger and Schuch used DSM and ICD to diagnose patients – using DSM 95% were diagnosed as OCD whereas only 46% diagnosed using ICD.

Chapter 12

Overview	
Explanations of OCD >	Biological explanations of OCD
Obsessive compulsive disorder > Therapies for OCD	Psychological explanations of OCD

Biological explanations of OCD

Genetic factors

Family studies

Nestadt et al. found that people with a first-degree relative with OCD had a five times greater risk of having OCD at some time in their lives, compared to the general population.

OCD patients and their relatives found it difficult to control repetitive responses on a reaction test, suggesting such behaviours might be inherited (Menzies et al.).

Twin studies

A meta-analysis of 14 twin studies found that MZ twins were twice as likely as DZ twins to develop OCD if their co-twin had the disorder (Billett et al.).

The COMT gene

COMT (catechol-O-methyltransferase) terminates dopamine activity. Karayiorgou et al. found that a variation in the COMT gene occurred in 50% of the male OCD sufferers tested, 10% of the females and only 16% of the normal population.

Inherited tendencies

Various suggestions include:

- *The worry circuit* (frontal cortex) – The caudate nucleus suppresses 'worry' signals from the orbitofrontal cortex (OFC) to the thalamus. If the caudate nucleus is damaged the thalamus is 'worried'.
- *Low levels of serotonin* – Antidepressant drugs that increase serotonin reduce OCD symptoms (Pigott et al.), whereas those drugs that don't affect serotonin don't reduce OCD symptoms (Jenicke).
- *High levels of dopamine* – Drugs that increase dopamine induce stereotyped movements in animals resembling the compulsive behaviours found in OCD patients (Szechtman et al.).

There is evidence for a strong genetic component...

Concordance rates are higher for OCD than many other disorders, e.g. 87% concordance for MZ twins for OCD (Carey and Gottesmann) compared with 46% for schizophrenia (McGuffin et al.).

However...

Concordance rates are not 100%, which means that environmental factors must play a role too – particularly when it comes to determining specific symptoms (it is obsessive behaviours that run in families rather than the manifestation, e.g. hand washing).

Comorbidity...

OCD symptoms are also found in other disorders, e.g. autism (stereotyped behaviours), anorexia nervosa (obsessive behaviour).

In particular OCD appears to be one form of expression of the same gene that determines Tourette's syndrome, as both conditions appear to run in the same families (Pauls and Leckman).

There is research support...

Schindler et al. confirmed the link between OCD and the COMT gene, but not the gender differences found by Karayiorgou et al.

Other candidate genes are being discovered all the time, e.g. a gene involved in serotonin production (SLC6A4) (Wendland et al.) and a gene (SAPAP3) absent in mice that compulsively groom themselves (Welch et al.).

There is research support...

- PET scans show greater activity in the *OFC-caudate nuclei loop* in OCD patients (compared with controls) and this increase is correlated with the severity of OCD (Schwartz et al.).
- SSRIs reduce dopamine levels in the basal ganglia and this is positively correlated with a reduction of OCD symptoms (Kim et al.).
- OCD patients (and their close relatives) have reduced grey matter in key regions of the brain including the OFC (Menzies et al.).

However...

A recent study (Moritz et al.) found that OCD patients did not perform abnormally on cognitive tasks related to the OFC.

Links between the worry circuit and serotonin and dopamine...

Serotonin plays a key role in the OFC and caudate nuclei, therefore low serotonin would cause these areas to function poorly (Comer).

Dopamine is the main neurotransmitter of the basal ganglia. High levels of dopamine lead to overactivity in this region (Sukel).

An evolutionary approach

Adaptive basis

Obsessions and compulsions might be an exaggeration of behaviours that are adaptive. Marks and Nesse suggest:

- *Grooming behaviour* reduces parasitism and smoothes social interaction. OCD patients often wash and groom endlessly.
- *Concern for others* decreases ostracism from the group. OCD patients are often concerned with fear of harming others.
- *Hoarding* guards against future shortages. OCD patients excessively store things.

Harm-avoidance strategies

Abed and de Pauw suggest that a particular mental module evolved (the *Involuntary Risk Scenario Generating System*, IRSGS), which allows individuals to imagine certain potential risks before they happen and thus be able to deal more effectively with them when they do happen. An extremely sensitive IRGS could lead to OCD.

There is supporting evidence...

The fact that OCD is so widespread across cultures (see facing page) suggests that it may have some evolutionary significance, i.e. it may be adaptive.

Limitations of evolutionary explanations...

Evolutionary explanations are often criticised for being determinist, but this is a misunderstanding of such explanations – in the case of OCD the suggestion is that our evolutionary past simply predisposes us to worry which, when excessive, leads to abnormal behaviour (an ultimate explanation) but the disorder only develops if there are proximate triggers.

Predictions from the theory have research support...

Obsessional patients should be less prone to risk taking because overactivity of IRSGS would warn them of the dangers associated with such activities and thus lead to risk avoidance. Evidence from Osborn suggests that this is the case.

There should be an increased risk of OCD at biologically critical life stages because that would be the time when the IRSGS would be generating lots of new risks. There is evidence to support this, such as increased risk for OCD during pregnancy (Buttolph et al.).

Chapter 12

Overview	
Explanations of OCD >	Biological explanations of OCD
Obsessive compulsive disorder >	Therapies for OCD	Psychological explanations of OCD

Psychological explanations of OCD

Psychodynamic

Freud's explanation

OCD arises when unacceptable wishes and impulses from the id are only partially repressed and so provoke anxiety.

People with OCD use defence mechanisms to reduce their anxiety:

- *Isolation* from undesirable wishes and impulses, but sometimes the id dominates and the impulses intrude as obsessional thoughts.
- *Undoing* unacceptable id impulses (symbolically) using compulsive acts, e.g. compulsive hand washing, to undo.
- *Reaction formation* – Adopting behaviours that are exactly the opposite of the unacceptable impulses.

There is research support…

Freud analysed the case study of the Rat Man who had obsessive fears about harm coming to his fiancée and her father. In order to fend off his obsessional fantasies, the Rat Man felt compelled to commit certain acts such as moving a rock from the path of a carriage. Freud explained this in terms of the patient's conflicting thoughts about his fiancée and her father, e.g. he loved the father but also wished him dead so he could inherit his money.

Negative effects on OCD recovery…

Salzman suggests that the therapy derived from Freud's explanation, psychoanalysis, may actually have a negative effect on OCD recovery, which challenges the Freudian explanation.

An alternative is to use a short-term psychodynamic therapy. These tend to be more direct and action-oriented and therefore reduce the tendency in OCD patients to 'think too much'.

Behavioural

Obsessions

Mowrer explained the acquisition of fears in two-process theory:

Classical conditioning – The neutral stimulus (NS) becomes associated with anxiety, e.g. a child is told that eating food from the floor (NS) is disgusting and thereafter all dirty items create anxiety.

Operant conditioning – Avoiding a feared stimulus (negative reinforcement) leads to positive outcomes and is thus reinforced.

There is research support…

Mowrer's theory predicts that OCD patients are predisposed to rapid conditioning. This was demonstrated in a study (Tracy et al.) where participants were tested for OCD symptoms and divided into an 'OCD-like' group and a control group. The OCD-like participants were conditioned more rapidly (using an eye blink task).

Problems with using a non-clinical population…

OCD-like participants (a 'non-clinical') group are sometimes used in research on OCD for ethical and practical reasons (because of difficulties using people with OCD). It may not be appropriate to generalise the data from such studies to understanding clinical cases of OCD.

Compulsions

If a behaviour becomes associated with reduction of anxiety, this behaviour is reinforced and repeated in future.

Compulsive rituals are learned from accidental associations.

There is research support…

OCD patients were asked to carry out a 'prohibited' activity (e.g. touching something dirty) and allowed to either carry out their compulsive act or delay this. If they delayed, their anxiety levels were found to persist for a while, but then gradually decline.

Rachman concluded that compulsive behaviours serve an important function, because they provide quicker relief from anxiety than waiting.

Cognitive

Obsessions – Intrusive thoughts

People with OCD find it difficult to dismiss 'normal' intrusive thoughts (e.g. harming others, danger from germs). This leads to self-blame and an expectation that terrible things will happen as a result (Salkovskis).

Such individuals also often have depression, which weakens their ability to distract themselves from these intrusive thoughts (Frost and Steketee).

There is research support…

People with OCD do have maladaptive thought patterns, for example:

- They believe that they can and should have total control over their world (Bouchard et al.).
- Students with OCD symptoms more likely to self-blame and have intrusive thoughts (Pleva and Wade).
- They have more intrusive thoughts than 'normal' people (Clark).
- They report trying to do things that will neutralise unwanted thoughts (Freeston et al.).

Compulsions – Neutralising anxiety

In order to avoid the anticipated consequences of intrusive thoughts, the individual must 'neutralise' them, e.g. washing their hands after feeling contaminated by dirty objects.

However, such behaviours provide only temporary relief and then anxiety builds up again. Every time a neutralising thought or act is repeated it becomes harder to resist because of the relief it provides, and it becomes a compulsion.

This is like an addiction – the more you do it, the more you have to do it again.

Gender issues…

In males, it appears that early brain injury may be associated with OCD and Tourette's.

In females, OCD and *trichotillomania* (pulling hair out) often appear after childbirth and pregnancy.

This suggests that *Obsessive compulsive spectrum disorders* may have different triggers in men and women (Lochner and Stein).

Reductionism…

There is a tendency in all these psychological (and biological) explanations to suggest that anxiety disorders can be reduced to a simple set of principles, such as repressed anxieties or classical conditioning. It is important to recognise that the 'real' explanations are likely to consist of a combination of a number of different explanations.

Chapter 12

Overview		Biological therapies for OCD
Explanations of OCD		
Obsessive compulsive disorder	>	Therapies for OCD	>	Psychological therapies for OCD

Biological therapies for OCD

Chemotherapy

Antidepressants

Antidepressant drugs (e.g. SSRIs and tricyclics) increase levels of serotonin, which may normalise the 'worry circuit' (a possible cause of OCD (see page 98).

SSRIs block the transporter mechanism that re-absorbs serotonin into the pre-synaptic cell after it has fired, resulting in more serotonin at the synapse. Tricyclics block noradrenaline as well.

Antianxiety drugs

Benzodiazepines (BZs) reduce anxiety by enhancing the activity of GABA (gamma-amino-butyric-acid). GABA locks onto receptors on the outside of receiving neurons and this opens a channel that increases the flow of chloride ions into the neuron. Chloride ions make it harder for the neuron to be stimulated by other neurotransmitters, thus slowing down its activity and making a person feel relaxed.

Other drugs

D-Cycloserine is an antibiotic used in the treatment of tuberculosis, which appears to enhance the transmission of GABA and thus reduce anxiety (Kushner et al.). It is particularly effective when used in conjunction with psychotherapy.

Effectiveness of chemotherapy...

Tricyclics are regarded as more effective than SSRIs in the treatment of OCD (Koran et al.) but tricyclics tend to have more side effects (e.g. hallucinations and irregular heartbeat) so they are more likely to be used as a second-line treatment.

However, some studies have found SSRIs are comparable in effectiveness to clomipramine (a tricyclic) (Zohar and Judge).

Soomro et al. reviewed 17 studies of the use of SSRIs with OCD and found them to be more effective than placebos in reducing the symptoms of OCD as measured with Y-BOCS.

However... Most treatment studies are only of three to four months duration and therefore little long-term data exists (Koran et al.).

Appropriateness of chemotherapy...
Strengths and limitations of chemotherapy...

Chemotherapy requires little effort and is effective in the short term, but it does not provide a lasting cure, e.g. Maina et al. found that patients relapsed within a few weeks if medication was stopped.

There are considerable side effects even with SSRIs, e.g. nausea, headache and insomnia are common (Soomro et al.).

Psychotherapy may be preferable...

Koran et al. conducted a comprehensive review of treatments for OCD concluding that, although drug therapy is more commonly used, psychotherapies such as CBT should be tried first.

Psychotherapy is particularly useful in reducing compulsions. In fact, behavioural therapy can have the same effect on the brain as drugs – reducing activity in the caudate nucleus (Schwartz et al.).

Psychosurgery

Capsulotomy and cingulotomy

These surgical interventions sever connections to malfunctioning parts of the brain to reduce anxiety levels.

The capsule and the cingulum are both parts of the limbic system, the region of the brain that is associated with emotion. The cingulum links the orbitofrontal cortex (OFC) to the caudate nucleus. The capsule is part of the limbic system involved with emotion and anxiety.

The surgeon inserts a probe through the top of the skull and pushes it to the capsule or cingulum, which is located deep in the brain. The leading tip of the probe burns away small portions of tissue.

Such operations are irreversible and only performed as a last resort.

Deep brain stimulation (DBS)

Wires are placed on target areas of the brain. The wires are connected to a battery in the patient's chest. When the current is on this interrupts the target circuits in the brain, such as the 'worry circuit'.

Transcranial magnetic stimulation (TMS)

TMS, like DBS, avoids destruction of brain tissue. A large electromagnetic coil is placed above the scalp near the forehead. This creates painless electric currents that stimulate the frontal cortex, a region of the brain associated with the worry circuit and mood regulation.

Effectiveness of cingulotomy...

Dougherty et al. found that up to 45% of patients studied (total 44) who were previously unresponsive to medication and behavioural treatments for OCD, were at least partly improved after a cingulotomy.

However... Such findings may be biased because they are 'unblinded', i.e. the researchers know the treatment received by patients and their expectations may influence their judgment (Koran et al.).

A further criticism is that... Psychosurgery may affect behaviour more globally, e.g. reducing motivation levels (Sachdev and Hay) and this (rather than surgery) may explain reduced OCD symptoms.

Effectiveness of TMS...

Greenberg et al. used 20 minutes of TMS to treat 12 OCD patients, resulting in a reduction of compulsive urges lasting at least 8 hours.

However... When OCD patients were given either TMS or sham TMS there was no measurable difference afterwards, as assessed using Y-BOCS (Rodriguez-Martin et al.). This suggests that the earlier success might be due to a placebo effect.

Appropriateness of psychosurgery...

Szasz criticised psychosurgery; a psychological state of mind is not physical and thus it is illogical to suggest that it can be operated on.

Permanent psychosurgery is associated with severe side effects ranging from personality changes and seizures to transient mania.

However... Nyman et al. followed up OCD patients who received a capsulotomy at a hospital in Sweden between 1978 and 1990. Their IQ test performance, in general, remained intact.

Ethical issues...

The irreversible nature of psychosurgery and the difficulties with providing informed consent raise ethical concerns, as in the case of Mary Lou Zimmerman, who had both a capsulotomy and cingulotomy resulting in loss of function (e.g. she couldn't walk). Her family sued the clinic (and won) because they had not been sufficiently informed of the dangerous and experimental nature of the surgery.

Chapter 12

Overview
Explanations of OCD
Biological therapies for OCD
Obsessive compulsive disorder > Therapies for OCD > Psychological therapies for OCD

Psychological therapies for OCD

Behavioural therapy

Exposure and response prevention therapy (ERP)

The behaviourist approach suggests that obsessions and compulsions are acquired through conditioning and therefore, in order to recover, patients must unlearn these behaviours. ERP aims to provide opportunities for re-conditioning.

1. Exposure

Anxieties persist because of negative reinforcement. This can be unlearned by forcing a patient to experience the stimulus and learn, using relaxation, that it no longer produces anxiety.

The patient is presented with the feared stimulus repeatedly until anxiety subsides ('habituation'). Exposures may move gradually from least to most threatening, in vivo or in vitro (covert) as in systematic desensitisation (see page 92).

2. Response prevention

At the same time, the patient is prohibited from engaging in the usual compulsive response. This is important for the patient to recognise that anxiety can be reduced without the compulsive ritual.

Mode of action

Typically, ERP consists of 13–20 weekly sessions (March et al.). Patients are then encouraged to continue using the ERP techniques and to apply them to new situations as they arise.

Effectiveness of ERP…

Albucher et al. report that between 60% and 90% of adults with OCD have improved considerably using ERP.

For people with mild OCD, self-directed ERP may be an effective alternative to therapist-led ERP. One computer-based program, BT STEPs, was found to be more effective than relaxation training alone, but less effective than therapist-guided ERP (Greist et al.).

ERP is most effective when combined with other therapies…

Drug therapy – Foa et al. found that a combination of *clomipramine* (a tricyclic) and ERP was more effective than either alone. Wilhem et al. also found that simultaneous administration of *d-cycloserine* (see facing page) substantially improves the effectiveness of ERP.

Cognitive therapy (e.g. discussing dysfunctional beliefs) improves the effectiveness of ERP, especially in preventing relapse (Huppert and Franklin). In fact, Koran et al. point out that in many instances ERP inevitably involves some informal cognitive techniques.

However…

One review of research (Foa and Kozak) concluded that ERP alone was found to be equally effective to ERP with drugs. In both conditions (without or with drugs) patients were doing equally well at a 2-year follow-up.

Appropriateness of ERP…
Not suitable for all…

Not all patients are helped by ERP, e.g. it has not been found to be successful with patients who are too depressed (Gershuny et al.), nor with patients who have certain types of OCD, such as patients with severe hoarding behaviour (Steketee and Frost).

Success depends on effort…

The success of ERP depends on the effort made by the patient and their willingness to do the 'homework' – not all patients are willing to commit to this kind of effort. This leads to a substantial refusal rate that may artificially elevate the apparent success of ERP because only those patients who are willing to 'be helped' may agree to participate.

Cognitive therapy (CT)

Obsessions

A CT therapist questions patients about their obsessions, e.g. asking a patient why they think shaking hands will pass on germs. Such beliefs can then be challenged and re-interpreted so that shaking hands is no longer experienced as an anxiety-producing activity.

Compulsions

A CT therapist also questions patients about the value of their compulsive behaviour(s), e.g. challenging the belief that hand washing guards against infection. When this belief is challenged and confronted as false, it can help control the behaviour.

Thought records

Patients are required to keep a daily record of their intrusive thoughts (e.g. where they were when they had the thought, what they felt) and about what they did to challenge the intrusive thoughts and compulsive responses.

This helps patients consider their dysfunctional beliefs. The therapist challenges unrealistic beliefs so that the patient will come to recognise the irrational nature of their beliefs and responses.

Effectiveness of CT…

CT is rarely used on its own, although Wilhelm et al. found a significant improvement in 15 patients who used CT alone over 14 weeks.

Ellis believed that sometimes people who claimed to be following the principles of CT were not putting their revised beliefs into action and therefore the therapy was not effective.

Appropriateness of CT…
Not suitable for all…

CT, like ERP, involves patient effort and is therefore not suitable for everyone. Ellis suggested that some people simply do not want the direct sort of advice that CT practitioners tend to dispense. They prefer to share their worries with a therapist, without getting involved with the cognitive effort that is associated with recovery.

There is research support…

Research has found that people who hold irrational beliefs form inferences that are significantly less functional than those that are formed by people who hold rational beliefs (Bond and Dryden).

On the other hand, it may be that irrational beliefs are counterproductive but realistic. For example, Alloy and Abrahmson found that people with depression (and some people with OCD are depressed) gave more accurate estimates of the likelihood of a disaster than 'normal' controls.

Ethical issues in research…

Ideally, research should involve a comparison between treatment and no treatment, e.g. O'Kearney et al. reported on four studies where ERP combined with CT was compared either to a placebo therapy or waiting list (two of the studies found no benefit). The issue is that it is unethical to withhold effective treatment, which makes research difficult.

Media psychology

Division A   Media influences on social behaviour
Media influences on prosocial behaviour
Media influences on antisocial behaviour
The effects of computers and video games

Division B   Media and persuasion
Explaining the persuasive effects of media
Explanations for the persuasiveness of television advertising

Division C   The psychology of 'celebrity'
The attraction of celebrity
Research into intense fandom

Issues, debates and approaches

In the Psychology in Action section (Section B) of the Unit 4 exam there is no explicit credit given to issues, debates and approaches. This doesn't mean that such material would not be creditworthy (it would) but it means it is not required. So, in this chapter we have not specifically identified IDA.

Specification

Media psychology	
Media influences on social behaviour	• Explanations of media influences on prosocial and antisocial behaviour. • The positive and negative effects of computers and video games on behaviour.
Media and persuasion	• The application of Hovland-Yale and Elaboration Likelihood models in explaining the persuasive effects of media. • Explanations for the persuasiveness of television advertising.
The psychology of 'celebrity'	• The attraction of 'celebrity', including social psychological and evolutionary explanations. • Research into intense fandom, including celebrity worship and celebrity stalking.

Chapter 13

Media influences on social behaviour	>	Media influences on prosocial behaviour
Media and persuasion		Media influences on antisocial behaviour
Media psychology	>	The psychology of 'celebrity'		The effects of computers and video games

Media influences on prosocial behaviour

Explanations

Exposure to prosocial behaviour

There is clear evidence of prosocial content in children's TV programmes.

Greenberg et al. analysed popular children's programmes in the US and found the same number of prosocial and antisocial acts in any hour.

There is research support for this...

Woodard found that US TV programmes for preschool children did have high levels of prosocial content; 77% of the programmes surveyed contained at least one prosocial lesson.

However...

The survey also found that only four of the top 20 most watched TV programmes for under 17s contained any prosocial lessons.

Acquisition of prosocial behaviours and norms

We learn by observation how to do things and when it is acceptable to do them.

Prosocial acts are likely to *reinforce* established social norms rather than contrast with them.

We are more likely to be rewarded for imitating prosocial than antisocial acts.

There is research support for this...

Research (e.g. Mares and Woodard) has found that children are most affected when they are shown the exact steps for a prosocial behaviour. This most probably is because young children are better able to remember concrete acts than abstract lessons of 'niceness'.

However...

Learning prosocial *norms* (rather than specific behaviours) from the media appears to be less common, except when viewing is accompanied by follow-up discussion.

Developmental factors

Research suggests that many of the skills involved in prosocial behaviour (e.g. perspective-taking, empathy) develop in later childhood.

This means that younger children may be less affected by prosocial portrayals in the media than older children.

Research challenges this view...

Despite the expectation that younger children would be least affected by prosocial programming, the meta-analysis by Mares (see below, left) found that the weakest effect was for adolescents and the strongest effect for primary school children.

However...

The expectation that the media has an effect on young children may be unrealistic because they are likely to be more strongly affected by home experiences than by media exposure.

Parental mediation

For many children, the effect of television viewing is mediated by the presence of a parent (as co-viewer).

Austin argued that effective mediation involves the parent discussing the programme with the child, explaining ambiguous or disturbing material and following up concepts from the TV.

Real-world application...

Sesame Street aimed to use prosocial programming to nurture prosocial behaviour in inner city children. However, it was children from higher socioeconomic backgrounds who benefitted the most from this series, presumably because of parental mediation with this group.

However, not all forms of parental mediation work...

Valkenburg et al. suggest that only 'instructive mediation' is effective in enhancing prosocial messages in television programmes. They argue that when engaging in 'social co-viewing', parents and children might watch together but would not discuss the content.

Behavioural effects

A meta-analysis (Mares)

Mares examined research published between 1966 and 1995. She discovered four main behavioural effects of prosocial television:

- *Altruism* (e.g. sharing, offering help). Children who viewed prosocial content behaved more altruistically than those who viewed neutral or antisocial content.
- *Self-control* (e.g. resistance to temptation, task persistence). When exposed to a model demonstrating self-control, children subsequently showed higher levels of their own self-control.
- *Positive interaction* (e.g. friendly, peaceable conflict resolution). Children who watched prosocial programmes behaved more positively towards other children.
- *Anti-stereotyping*. Programmes which featured counter-stereotypical themes resulted in children becoming less stereotyped or prejudiced in their attitudes.

Television is not the only source of prosocial messages...

Although most research has focused on television, Mares and Woodard argue that other forms of media have prosocial effects, e.g. children's stories have traditionally carried prosocial messages. Young children are fond of reading these stories over and over again, which reinforce the message.

There are limitations in the effectiveness of prosocial messages...

Mares also found that children tend to imitate prosocial acts directly with little evidence of generalisation to other forms of prosocial behaviour, whereas aggressive acts are generalised (to other forms of antisocial behaviour). This lack of generalisation therefore limits the overall effectiveness of prosocial messages in the media.

Antisocial messages can overshadow prosocial messages...

Mixing prosocial and antisocial messages appears to reduce the effectiveness of the prosocial message. Mares and Woodard found that children who watched mixed messages behaved more aggressively than those who watched aggressive content only.

Real-world application...

The Walt Disney Corporation has produced a set of DVDs specially aimed at babies, yet Zimmerman et al. claim that watching such DVDs can actually lead to poorer developmental outcomes. The *American Academy of Pediatrics* recommend no television at all for children under 2 years, as it is associated with attention and behaviour problems later in life.

Chapter 13

Media influences on social behaviour	>	Media influences on prosocial behaviour
Media and persuasion		Media influences on antisocial behaviour
Media psychology >	The psychology of 'celebrity'	The effects of computers and video games

Media influences on antisocial behaviour

Observational learning and imitation

Children observe actions of media models and may later imitate these behaviours, especially if they admire and identify with the model.

Television may also inform viewers of the positive and negative consequences of violent behaviour.

The more real that children perceive violent televised scenes to be and the more they believe the characters are like them, the more likely they will be to try out the modelled behaviours.

There is research support...

A meta-analysis of media violence research (Paik and Comstock) found a highly significant relationship between television violence and imitation of aggressive behaviour. The greatest effect was evident in preschool children, and the effect for males was slightly higher than it was for females.

Methodological problems with research...

Bandura's research on observational learning also supports the claim that children learn specific acts of aggression from exposure to violent media, but laboratory studies like Bandura's suffer from the problem of demand characteristics.

Cognitive priming

Immediately after watching a violent programme, a viewer is primed to respond aggressively because a network of memories involving aggression is retrieved.

Frequent exposure to scenes of violence may lead children to store scripts for aggressive behaviour, and these may be later recalled if any aspect of the original situation is present.

There is research support...

The importance of cognitive priming was demonstrated in a study by Josephson, where hockey players were deliberately frustrated and then shown a violent or non-violent film where an actor held a walkie-talkie. In a subsequent hockey game, the boys behaved most aggressively if they had seen the violent film and the referee in their game was holding a walkie-talkie. Presumably the walkie-talkie acted as a cue for a network of aggressive memories to be retrieved.

Desensitisation

Under normal conditions, anxiety about violence inhibits its use. Media violence, however, may stimulate aggressive behaviour by desensitising children to the effects of violence.

The more televised violence a child watches, the more acceptable aggressive behaviour becomes for that child.

Frequent viewing of television violence may cause children to be less anxious about violence and perceive it as normal.

There is research support...

Cumberbatch argues that people might get 'used' to screen violence but there is no evidence that a person will also get used to violence in the real world. He claims that screen violence is more likely to make children 'frightened' (anxious and afraid of violence) than 'frightening'.

Gender bias in media effects research...

Effects research tends not to use representative samples (e.g. male students) but then makes generalisations about all viewers.

The inherent gender bias in these studies is often hidden behind gender-neutral terms such as 'college students' or 'viewers' when describing the population from which the sample is drawn.

Lowered physiological arousal

The arousal stimulated by viewing violence is unpleasant at first, but children who constantly watch violent television become used to it, and their emotional and physiological responses decline.

As a result, they do not react in the same way to violent behaviour, and so are less inhibited in using it.

Huesmann and Moise report that boys who are heavy television watchers show lower than average physiological arousal in response to new scenes of violence.

There is an alternative explanation for the role of arousal...

Zillman's excitation-transfer model explains the role of physiological arousal in a different way. According to this model, arousal creates a readiness to aggress in real-life situations because the excitation from one situation (watching violence on TV) is transferred to another (e.g. a response to provocation in real life).

Some theorists (e.g. Feshbach and Singer) believe that watching violence has positive rather than negative effects. They suggest that arousal allows one to release pent-up aggression (i.e. it is cathartic).

There is research support for justification...

Many TV programmes have mixed pro- and antisocial messages, for example the 1980s television series The A-Team portrayed good guys behaving violently, thus, justifying the use of violence.

Justification

Violent behaviours on television may provide a justification for a child's own violent behaviour or it may provide moral guidelines concerning what is acceptable and what is unacceptable.

Children who behave aggressively may watch violent television to relieve their guilt and justify their own aggression.

When violence is justified or left unpunished, the viewer's guilt or concern about consequences is also reduced.

Viewing television violence may also produce attitude change and suggest that problems can be solved through aggressive behaviour.

Liss and Reinhardt suggest that the negative effects of such programmes support the concept of justification. The use of aggression by prosocial characters lends an aura of moral justification to their violence, with which children readily identify.

The anti-effects lobby...

There is growing concern that the media are unreasonably the focus of blame for violent behaviour. The evidence does not always support the hypothesis that media violence leads to violent behaviour.

Belson, for example, interviewed more than 1,500 adolescent boys, and found that those who watched least television when they were younger were also least aggressive in adolescence. However, boys who watched most television were less aggressive (by about 50%) than boys who watched moderate amounts. This suggests that the link between watching television and aggression is unpredictable.

Chapter 13

Media influences on social behaviour	>	Media influences on prosocial behaviour
Media and persuasion		Media influences on prosocial behaviour
Media psychology	>	The psychology of 'celebrity'	The effects of computers and video games

The negative effects

Video games and aggression

Experimental studies

Lab experiments have found short-term increases in levels of physiological arousal, hostile feelings and aggressive behaviour following violent game play compared to non-violent game play (Gentile and Stone).

Longitudinal studies

Anderson et al. surveyed children aged between 7 and 9 years at two points during the school year. Children who had high exposure to violent video games became more verbally and physically aggressive and less prosocial.

Meta-analyses – Several meta-analyses have found a consistent link between violent game play and aggressive behaviour. Gentile and Anderson found larger effects in more recent studies possibly because violent video games have become more violent over time.

There are methodological problems with the research…

A major weakness of research in this area is that researchers cannot measure 'real-life' aggression directly so must use measures of aggressive behaviour that may have no relationship to real-life aggression, and can only measure short-term effects. Longitudinal studies are able to observe real-life patterns of behaviour and document both short-term and long-term effects, but participants may be exposed to other forms of media violence (e.g. TV) during the course of the study, so the influence of violent video game play alone is uncertain.

Why might there be an effect?…

Research has yet to establish a reliable causal link between violent game play and aggressive behaviour. The 'bi-directional model' (Gentile et al.) states that, although playing violent video games may cause an increase in aggressive behaviour, it is just as likely that people who already possess personality traits that orientate them towards aggressive behaviour, preferentially select violent video games for recreational purposes.

Computers: Facebook use

Facebook use and college grades

Karpinski found that the majority of students who use Facebook every day underachieved by as much as an entire grade compared with those who do not use the site. The link between lower grades and Facebook use was found even in graduate students.

Facebook friends and stress

Charles found 12% of students experienced anxiety linked to their use of Facebook. They reported stress from deleting unwanted contacts, the pressure to be humorous and worrying about the proper type of etiquette toward different friends.

The link between Facebook use and grades may be complicated…

Karpinski acknowledges that her study does not suggest that excessive Facebook use directly causes lower grades, merely that there is some relationship between the two. She suggests that perhaps Facebook users may simply be prone to distraction.

Greenfield argues that social networks such as Facebook 'infantilise' the brain by shortening the attention span and providing constant instant gratification, although evidence for this claim is yet to be provided.

Facebook use may be a triggering factor for some people…

The stress associated with Facebook use has been supported in a case study of an 18-year-old asthmatic man whose condition was stable until he split up with his girlfriend and she erased him from her Facebook page (D'Amato et al.). This indicates that social network sites can be a triggering factor for stress reactions in vulnerable individuals.

The positive effects

Video games and prosocial behaviour

Helping behaviour

Playing a prosocial game can increase helping behaviour. Greitemeyer and Osswald found that participants who played a prosocial video game subsequently displayed significantly more prosocial behaviour than those who played an aggressive game or a neutral game.

Multiplayer games and social commitment

Kahne et al. – majority of those who listed The Sims as a favourite game said they learned about problems in society and explored social issues while playing computer games.

Lenhart et al. – 64% of those who played multiplayer games such as Halo committed to civic participation (compared to 59% of 'solo' players).

Why don't prosocial video games have more of an effect?…

Greitemeyer and Osswald suggest that, although prosocial games can lead to increased prosocial behaviour, people who play video games are much less likely to experience this type of game, partly because they are seen as less attractive.

There are methodological limitations with this research…

A problem in game research concerns the lack of controls for young people's prior civic commitments and prosocial activities. The lack of random exposure to civic gaming opportunities (i.e. people choose these games rather than being randomly allocated to them) limits our ability to make claims about how playing prosocial games influences the development of social and civic responsibilities.

Real-world application: Therapeutic applications of video games…

The Virtual Iraq computer 'game' allows soldiers suffering from post-traumatic stress disorder to relive and confront psychological trauma. Playing Tetris can help to reduce memory flashbacks after traumatic events (Holmes et al.). Games like Tetris reduce flashbacks because they compete with the same sensory channels needed to form the traumatic memory.

Computers: Facebook use

Facebook and self-esteem

In a study of students, Gonzales and Hancock found that Facebook walls could have a positive influence on self-esteem, because feedback posted on them by others tends to be overwhelmingly positive.

How does Facebook increase self-esteem?…

The Hyperpersonal Model (Walther) explains why these positive effects occur. It states that self-selection of the information we choose to represent ourselves (e.g. through photos and personal details) can have a positive influence on self-esteem. Social networks offer people an opportunity for positive self-esteem as feedback left on their 'wall' is invariably positive.

Explaining the persuasive effects of media

The Hovland-Yale model

Hovland *et al.* found effective persuasion could be achieved by focusing on who (the source) says what (the message) to whom (the audience).

Attractive sources are not necessarily the most influential…

Research on product endorsement has shown that celebrities are not as effective as we might imagine, given the predictions of the Hovland-Yale model. O'Mahony and Meenaghan found that celebrity endorsements were not regarded as particularly convincing or believable, and did not significantly increase the persuasive communication of the advert.

Applying the Hovland-Yale model

The source – Research has shown that expert and attractive sources are more persuasive than non-expert and less attractive communicators (Petty and Cacioppo).

Message – Messages are more effective if we think they are not intended to persuade and if they create a moderate level of fear. Putwain and Symes found that when fear appeals emphasised a 'mastery' approach they were positively related to examination performance. If perceived as threatening they were negatively related to examination performance.

The audience – Low- and high-intelligence audiences are less easily persuaded than those with moderate intelligence. With intelligent audiences, presenting both sides of an argument is more effective. Younger people are more susceptible to persuasive messages than adults or the elderly, e.g. Martin found that younger children did not understand the persuasive intent of advertisements.

Fear appeals do work…

Fear appeals can be persuasive if they do not petrify the audience with fear and if the audience is informed how to avoid the danger. This was supported in a real-life anti-drug campaign. In 2008, the Australian government 'ICE' campaign used moderate fear but also emphasised choice and opportunities for positive attitude formation and change. Seventy-eight per cent of 13–24 year olds felt that the campaign had changed how they felt about drugs.

There are methodological problems with this approach…

Much of the early research carried out by Hovland *et al.* used students and army personnel. It is inappropriate to generalise from these samples to the general population as they had an age and education profile which was untypical of the general public. The experimenters were also able to cut off other stimuli and demand the complete attention of participants, something that real-life sources rarely have.

Gender bias in persuasion research…

Research suggests that women are more susceptible to persuasive communications than men. Sistrunk and McDavid claim that women are easily persuaded because in most studies the topic used was one with which men were more familiar. Women would not be so susceptible to persuasive communications if the topic was one with which they were familiar (and men were not). Karabenick provided evidence to support this claim, i.e. males were more influenced with feminine content.

Elaboration-likelihood model (ELM)

Central route – Effective when audience is motivated to think about the message and focus on the quality of the arguments. This route is more likely to produce lasting attitude change.

Peripheral route – Effective when audience not motivated to think about the message, focus on peripheral factors. This route produces only temporary attitude change.

Some people have high need for cognition and so focus on quality of arguments rather than their context (Cacioppo and Petty).

There are lessons to be learned from the online shopping study…

Lin *et al.*'s research finding contributes to a better understanding of the effect of online reviews. For marketing executives, the peripheral route perspective demonstrates the importance of generating as many reviews as possible for a low need for cognition audience. Knowledge of the demographic profile of a target audience, e.g. their level of need for cognition, can also guide Internet marketers to design appropriate promotional materials and review formats in order to influence online shoppers effectively.

Applying the ELM

Online shopping – Students took part in an online shopping study. Each student had to select a mobile phone based on consumer reviews previously selected from the Amazon.com website. Consistent with ELM predictions, high need for cognition students placed greater importance on review quality rather than quantity of reviews when making a decision to purchase (Lin *et al.*).

Health campaigns – Vidrine *et al.* showed that need for cognition (NC) is also a relevant factor in real-life health campaigns. Students with higher NC were more influenced by a fact-based message about smoking risk (i.e. the central route), whereas participants with low NC were more influenced by the emotion-based message.

Peripheral route influence may only be temporary…

Penner and Fritzsche found that that no university students volunteered to help an AIDS victim with a school project. However, a week after Magic Johnson announced that he was HIV positive, the help rate soared to 83%. Four and a half months after the announcement, helping was back to pre-announcement levels, indicating that any change produced by this route is likely to be temporary.

Why do people sometimes take the peripheral route?…

Fiske and Taylor claim that human beings are cognitive misers in that they frequently rely on simple strategies when evaluating information and making decisions. If the content of a message is not personally important, then individuals are more likely to be influenced by contextual cues (such as celebrity endorsement). However, when the content is more important, they are better motivated to process the message more carefully (i.e. take a central route).

The implications of research applying ELM to health campaigns…

What is also clear from research on the ELM is that when people lack expertise about an issue (e.g. HIV risks or healthy eating), they are more likely to employ the peripheral route as they consider a health message. This helps to explain why health claims unsupported by research findings often appeal to many people.

Chapter 13

Media influences on social behaviour
Media and persuasion > Explaining the persuasive effects of media
Media psychology > The psychology of celebrity
Explanations for the persuasiveness of television advertising

Explanations for the persuasiveness of television advertising

Hard-sell and soft-sell advertising

Hard sell = presenting factual information about a product.

Soft sell = using subtle and creative persuasive techniques.

Snyder and de Bono found that hard-sell and soft-sell approaches had different effects on different types of people. People high in self-monitoring had more favourable attitudes to soft-sell adverts. People low in self-monitoring preferred more factual hard-sell approaches.

Product endorsement

Giles suggests that celebrities provide a familiar face, a reliable source of information that we feel we can trust because of the parasocial relationship that we have built up with that celebrity.

Celebrities are also seen as a neutral source of information and so perform the function of 'rubber stamping' the advertiser's claims.

Meenaghan found celebrity endorsements were not overly convincing or believable, with perceived credibility and expertise of the endorser being the 'source' characteristics with the greatest influence on consumer purchase intentions.

Children and advertising

Martin, in a meta-analysis of studies, found a strong positive correlation between age and understanding of persuasive intent. Older children better understood the persuasive intent of the commercials (compared to factual programmes) and trusted them less.

The importance of congruence

Bushman suggests that TV advertisements may be more persuasive if there is a congruence between the programme content and the content of the ad. This relationship can be explained in terms of the viewer's motives for watching a particular TV programme. Commercials that are consistent with this motive would be easier to recall, and therefore their message would be more persuasive.

Sex, violence and persuasion

Advertisers are interested in making their commercials persuasive for viewers in the 18–34 years age bracket. Because they watch less television than older viewers, advertisers tend to embed their commercial messages in programmes that younger viewers like to watch, e.g. those that contain violence or sex. The content of these programmes appears to impair memory for advertising shown during commercial breaks (Bushman), reducing their persuasiveness.

Hard-sell versus soft-sell techniques…

Okazaki *et al.* carried out a meta-analysis to test whether 'hard-sell' or 'soft-sell' advertisements were more persuasive in terms of attitude towards a product. Hard-sell techniques were more believable because they focused on specific, factual information. However, they also had a greater potential to irritate viewers by being more direct and confrontational, decreasing their ability to persuade.

Soft-sell techniques are focused more on generating positive emotions, and were associated with more positive attitudes toward the product than hard-sell techniques.

Does product endorsement work?…

Research suggests that celebrity product endorsement is not that effective. Martin *et al.* found that their student participants were more convinced by a television endorsement from a fictional fellow student when buying a digital camera than by one from a celebrity.

In a study of the 'persuasiveness' of more than 5,000 TV commercials, Hume concluded that celebrity endorsement did not significantly increase the persuasive communication of the advert.

There are limitations in celebrity endorsement research…

Erfgen claims that a celebrity might be portrayed as endorsing a product in a number of different ways – explicitly, implicitly or in a co-present way where the celebrity and product are depicted together without further explanation. Research has not considered these different endorsement modes in order to determine whether one type is more persuasive that the others.

The impact of advertising…

Giles points out that television and cinema advertising is successful because adverts generally have a captive audience. However, unlike cinema audiences, television audiences have more options open to them, which may limit the effectiveness of television advertising.

Comstock and Scharrer found that 80% of viewers left the room during adverts, and when programmes were recorded, viewers tended to fast-forward through the adverts, thereby minimising their impact, which may limit the effectiveness of TV advertising.

There are cultural differences in the persuasiveness of children's advertising…

Pine and Nash found significantly fewer gift requests (in letters to Santa) among Swedish children than among children from the US. The researchers suggest that the lack of direct advertising to Swedish children (where direct advertising to under-12 is banned by law) is the reason for this difference.

Gender bias in advertising and its consequences…

Gender stereotypes in television advertising reinforce the traditional role of women as caretakers, wives or subordinates (Scharrer *et al.*).

As a result, gender stereotyped television advertisements promote acceptance of current social arrangements, no matter how biased or inappropriate these representations might be.

Disentangling media and other effects…

The influence of peers inevitably shapes the subsequent buying (or pestering) behaviour of children. Consequently, it becomes difficult, if not impossible, to confidently predict a direct causal relationship between exposure to advertisements and subsequent consumer behaviour among children.

Measuring the persuasiveness of advertisements…

For an advert to be effective, it should lead to an actual purchase of the product being advertised. What is measured in research, however, is not the actual behaviour (product purchase) but the related attitude (liking, intention) that may or may not lead to an actual purchase.

The attraction of celebrity

Social psychological explanations

Parasocial relationships

An individual is attracted to another individual, but the target individual is usually unaware of the existence of the person who has created the relationship.

A parasocial relationship is particularly appealing to some individuals because it makes few demands. They do not run the risk of criticism or rejection, as might be the case in a real relationship.

What determines the likelihood of a parasocial relationship?

Schiappa et al. concluded that parasocial relationships were most likely to form with television celebrities who were seen as attractive and similar in some way to the viewer.

If the celebrity acted in a believable way, viewers were able to compare how they would behave in similar situations.

The 'absorption–addiction model'

Maltby et al. identified three levels in people's attraction to celebrities:

• Entertainment-social – Fans are attracted to a celebrity because of their perceived ability to entertain and to become a source of social interaction and gossip.

• Intense-personal – This aspect of celebrity worship reflects intensive and compulsive feelings about the celebrity.

• Borderline-pathological – Typified by uncontrollable behaviours and fantasies about the celebrity, with the person believing there is a real relationship between themselves and the celebrity.

Parasocial relationships may not be dysfunctional…

It is commonly believed that parasocial relationships with celebrities are dysfunctional (i.e. based on loneliness). However, Schiappa et al. found that loneliness was not a predictor of parasocial relationships.

Benefits of parasocial relationships with celebrities…

Such relationships provide media models of social behaviours (e.g. generosity) and an opportunity to learn cultural values (e.g. importance of marriage) from them.

Perse and Rubin studied parasocial relationships with soap opera characters and found that, because people are exposed to the same characters over and over again, one benefit of parasocial interaction is a perceived reduction in uncertainty about social relationships.

The absorption–addiction model: links to mental health…

Maltby et al. used the Eysenck Personality Questionnaire to assess the relationship between level of celebrity worship and personality. The entertainment-social level was associated with extraversion and the intense-personal level was associated with neuroticism.

As neuroticism is related to anxiety and depression, this explains why higher levels of celebrity worship are related to poor mental health.

Attachment style and parasocial relationships…

Cole and Leets reported that individuals with anxious-ambivalent attachment were most likely, and avoidant individuals least likely to enter into parasocial relationships. Coles and Leets claim individuals with anxious-ambivalent attachment style turn to TV characters as a means of satisfying 'unrealistic and unmet relational needs'.

Parasocial relationships and eating disorders…

Maltby et al. found that parasocial relationships with celebrities influenced body image among female adolescents. Teenage girls who had parasocial relationships with celebrities who were slim and were seen as having a 'good body shape' tended to have a poor body image, which consequently predisposed them to eating disorders.

Evolutionary explanations

Attraction to creative individuals

Humans have a love of novelty (neophilia).

Therefore mate choice in the EEA could well have favoured creative courtship displays from males, which would have evolved through the process of sexual selection, favouring minds prone to creativity and fantasy.

This would explain characteristics that are uniquely developed in humans, e.g. art, music and humour. Because musicians, artists and actors display these talents in abundance, we are drawn to them.

Celebrity gossip

The exchange of social information about group members might have been adaptive for early humans living in social groups.

DeBacker suggests 'gossip' served to create bonds within groups, manipulate the reputation of rivals, and exchange information about potential mates.

Barkow suggests that our minds are fooled into regarding media characters as being members of our social network, thus celebrities trigger the same gossip mechanisms that have evolved to keep up with the affairs of ingroup members.

Evidence for an evolved love of creativity…

Shiraishi et al. discovered an enzyme correlated with novelty-seeking tendencies. Genetic differences mean that people produce different variations of the enzyme MAOA. The researchers found that one form of this enzyme was significantly associated with higher scores of novelty seeking, suggesting that there may be a genetic origin for neophilia and our attraction to creative people.

The arbitrary nature of sexual selection explanations…

Suggesting that a love of novelty, and therefore an attraction to creative people, arose because early females preferred creative behaviour in potential mates tells us nothing about why they would prefer it. Sexual selection explanations are arbitrary because they argue that traits are preferred simply because they would have been 'attractive'. Such explanations do not provide an adequate adaptive reason why traits such as creativity in music, art and humour would have been attractive to ancestral members of the opposite sex.

Research support for the adaptive role of celebrity gossip…

De Backer et al. surveyed more than 800 participants to test evolutionary explanations for celebrity gossip. Participants reported that gossip was seen as a useful way of acquiring information about social group members. Media exposure was also found to be a strong predictor of interest in celebrities.

De Backer et al. concluded that media exposure would lead to the misperception that celebrities were actually a part of the social network, thus explaining the interest in celebrity gossip.

Chapter 13

Media influences on social behaviour
Media and persuasion
The attraction of celebrity

Media psychology > The psychology of 'celebrity' > Research into intense fandom

Research into intense fandom

Celebrity worship

Measuring celebrity worship

Most research on celebrity worship has used the *Celebrity Attitude Scale* (CAS).

Maltby *et al.* used this scale to produce the three levels of parasocial relationships described on page 105: *entertainment-social*, *intense-personal* and *borderline-pathological*.

How common is celebrity worship?

Maltby *et al.* found that, in a sample of 372 people aged 18–47:

• 15% were at the 'entertainment-social' level of celebrity worship.
• 5% at the 'intense-personal' level.
• Less than 2% would be considered 'borderline pathological'.

Developmental problems

Celebrity worship is associated with less-desirable developmental outcomes.

Maltby *et al.* found celebrity worshippers have lower levels of psychological wellbeing than non-worshippers.

Scores on the 'entertainment-social' subscale of the CAS predicted patterns of social dysfunction and scores on the 'intense-personal' subscale predicted both depression and anxiety scores.

The limited benefits of celebrity worship…

Cheung and Yue found that teenagers who 'worshipped' key family members, teachers and other individuals with whom they came into regular contact, tended to demonstrate higher levels of self-esteem and educational achievement than teenagers who worshipped television stars.

This is understandable given that the admiration of those who are able to provide tangible benefits and inputs to the adolescents' lives would be more likely to provide a greater positive impact than those celebrities with whom they enjoy only a parasocial relationship.

Negative consequences of celebrity worship…

Research (e.g. Phillips) has shown that high-profile celebrity suicides are often followed by increased numbers of suicides among the general population.

Sheridan *et al.* claim that pathological worshippers are often drawn to more entertaining, even antisocial celebrities. We might, therefore, expect fans of more rebellious celebrities to seek to emulate them with negative consequences for the worshipper.

An evolutionary explanation for celebrity worship…

Evolutionary psychologists suggest that it is natural for humans to look up to those individuals who receive attention because they have succeeded in our society. Gill-White claims that it makes a good deal of evolutionary sense to value individuals according to how successful they are, because whoever is getting more of what everybody wants is probably using above-average methods to get them, therefore would serve as a valuable role model.

Celebrity stalking

Stalking

Stalking involves repeated and persistent attempts to impose unwanted contact or communication on another person.

Types of celebrity stalker

Stalkers may develop a love obsession or fixation with a celebrity. Stalkers of this type suffer from delusional thought patterns and many suffer from a mental disorder, such as schizophrenia. Since most are unable to develop normal personal relationships through more conventional means, they retreat into a life of fantasy relationships with the celebrity.

Parasocial bereavement

Parasocial bereavement is the grief felt at the death of a celebrity. Giles and Naylor analysed tributes left on the BBC website following the death of Diana, Princess of Wales, and BBC presenter Jill Dando.

These tributes revealed the nature of the parasocial relationships formed with these two celebrities, and the depth of feeling that some people felt toward them.

Attachment style

Individuals with a 'pre-occupied' attachment style have a poor self-image and a positive image of others. Meloy claims that individuals with this type of attachment style may engage in celebrity stalking because they overvalue others and perceive that contact with celebrities will show that they are acceptable and valued. This, in turn, would challenge their negative views of self.

Anti-stalking legislation has its limitations…

Despite the introduction of legislation, a continuing problem is that many of the strategies employed by celebrity stalkers (e.g. being in the same place as the celebrity) are basic rights and freedoms guaranteed by law. Similarly, as fans are encouraged to be adoring it becomes difficult to assess when fan behaviour actually becomes stalking.

Explaining stalking in terms of insecure attachment…

Tomin measured stalkers' retrospective childhood attachment styles and their current adult attachment. To find out whether stalkers detained under the Mental Health Act were less securely attached than non-stalkers, she compared them to two other groups: 24 people detained in the same way but with no history of stalking, and a non-clinical community sample of 33. It was found that the stalkers had significantly more evidence of insecure adult attachment styles than the control group.

Stalking may reflect an underlying psychopathology…

Stalkers sometimes behave irrationally towards their victims, in ways that suggest an underlying psychopathology (Cupach and Spitzberg). Those who score high on the borderline-pathological subscale of the CAS are more likely to endorse irrational items such as: 'If I were lucky enough to meet my favourite celebrity, and he/she asked me to do something illegal as a favour, I would probably do it.'

Real-world application: psychological profiles and clinical interventions…

Roberts found that individuals with a 'preoccupied' attachment style had an increased likelihood of approach behaviour towards celebrities.

This has important implications, including being able to draw a psychological profile of an unknown offender after persistent attempts to contact a particular celebrity. Clinical interventions may be designed for persistent offenders to help them overcome their attachment difficulties.

The psychology of addictive behaviour

Division A Models of addictive behaviour
The biological approach applied to smoking and gambling
The cognitive approach applied to smoking and gambling
The learning approach applied to smoking and gambling

Division B Vulnerability to addiction
Risk factors in the development of addiction
Media influences on addictive behaviour

Division C Reducing addictive behaviour
The theory of planned behaviour
Types of intervention

Issues, debates and approaches
In the Psychology in Action section (Section B) of the Unit 4 exam there is no explicit credit given to issues, debates and approaches. This doesn't mean that such material would not be creditworthy (it would) but it means it is not required. So, in this chapter we have not specifically identified IDA.

Specification

The psychology of addictive behaviour	
Models of addictive behaviour	• Biological, cognitive and learning approaches to explaining initiation, maintenance and relapse, and their applications to smoking and gambling.
Vulnerability to addiction	• Risk factors in the development of addiction, including stress, peers, age and personality. • Media influences on addictive behaviour.
Reducing addictive behaviour	• The theory of planned behaviour as a model for addiction prevention. • Types of intervention and their effectiveness, including biological, psychological and public health interventions.

Models of addictive behaviour > The biological approach
Factors affecting addictive behaviour   The cognitive approach
The psychology of addictive behaviour > Reducing addictive behaviour   The learning approach

The biological approach

Gambling

Initiation

The role of genetics – Studies have shown that pathological gambling runs in families. A twin study by Shah *et al.* found evidence of genetic transmission of gambling in men. Black *et al.* found that the first-degree relatives of pathological gamblers were more likely to suffer from pathological gambling than more distant relatives, demonstrating a genetic link.

Maintenance

The pituitary-adrenal response – Pathological gambling is associated with an underactive pituitary-adrenal response to gambling. Paris *et al.* found, pathological gamblers demonstrated no cortisol increase in response to gambling stimuli.

Sensation-seeking – Individual differences in optimal amounts of stimulation (Zuckerman). High sensation-seekers have a lower appreciation of risk and anticipate arousal as more positive than do low sensation-seekers, and so are more likely to gamble.

Relapse

Boredom avoidance – Blaszczynski *et al.* found that poor tolerance for boredom may contribute to repetitive gambling.

Pathological gamblers had significantly higher boredom proneness scores than a control group of non-gamblers. There were no significant differences between the different types of gambling (e.g. horses betting, slot machines, etc.).

Genetics can explain individual differences in gambling…

This explains why some people develop pathological gambling yet others who have the same experiences and life pressures do not. Some people are more vulnerable to develop an addiction or are more resistant to treatment because of their genetic predisposition (the diathesis-stress model).

Genetic explanations ignore environmental factors…

Explaining pathological gambling in terms of biological factors alone ignores the importance of external factors (e.g. peer pressure) in the development of gambling behaviour. It is more likely that addictive gambling is a product of biological factors, which may predispose some people to excessive gambling, plus external factors, together with the interaction between them.

There are explanatory limitations of the biological approach…

Biological explanations cannot explain why some types of gambling are more addictive than others. Breen and Zimmerman found that it took about 1 year before people were at risk of becoming addicted to online or video gambling, but about 3 years before people were at risk of developing compulsive gambling addiction to horse racing.

There is research evidence for the role of sensation-seeking…

Bonnaire *et al.* found that pathological gamblers who bet at racetracks had significantly higher scores on sensation-seeking than those who played games available in cafés. The researchers concluded that there are two clinically distinct subgroups of gamblers. One (racetrack gamblers) gamble for the arousal produced by the game. The other (café gamblers) gamble to avoid boredom.

Biological explanations of addiction are reductionist… as they reduce

a complex phenomenon, such as gambling, down to a relatively simple level of explanation, i.e. an imbalance of brain chemicals or the influence of specific genes. There are potential advantages to this approach (e.g. it allows researchers to study the family history of addiction or offers possibilities for effective treatment). However, this approach also has its limitations as it ignores all other potential influences (e.g. irrational thought processes, social context, etc.).

Smoking

Initiation

The role of genetics – Family and twin studies estimate the heritability of tobacco smoking to be between 39% and 80%. Vink *et al.* – individual differences in smoking initiation due to 44% genetic and 56% environmental influences.

Study of identical twins and same-sex fraternal twin pairs estimate heritability for regular smoking at 42% (Boardman *et al.*)

Maintenance

The effects of nicotine – Regular tobacco use is linked to individual differences in nicotine metabolism (Vink *et al.*). Nicotine causes the release of dopamine, which creates short-lived feelings of pleasure. This must be repeated to avoid withdrawal symptoms.

Pre-natal exposure to nicotine – mothers who smoked heavily during pregnancy doubled the risk of their child becoming addicted to tobacco if they did begin smoking. (Buka *et al.*)

Relapse

Xian *et al.* found 54% of the risk for quit failure is attributed to heritability. Research has attempted to identify specific gene clusters associated with quit success and with nicotine dependence, with the aim of matching specific anti-smoking treatments with the smokers most likely to benefit from them.

There is supporting evidence for genetic influence on smoking…

This comes from an Icelandic study (Thorgeirsson *et al.*). They identified a specific gene variant on chromosome 15 that influenced the number of cigarettes smoked per day, nicotine dependence and the risk of developing smoking-related diseases. This suggests that genetic factors may not determine smoking initiation, but make it more likely that some smokers will become dependent on nicotine once they do start smoking.

There are limitations of biological explanations…

A problem for biological explanations of addiction is that they neglect other possible determining factors, including the social context of smoking behaviour. However, by regarding smoking addiction as a biological problem, this creates the possibility that it may be treated by various pharmacological methods.

A genetic approach has implications for treatment…

Individuals found to have a higher genetic risk of smoking addiction could then be advised to change their behaviour (e.g. stop smoking) or seek medical treatment to reduce their chances of developing smoking-related diseases. However, Gartner *et al.* suggest that, at present, screening for genetic susceptibility to smoking is unlikely to be successful, given the relatively small reported associations between specific genes and smoking addiction.

The effectiveness of medication for smoking cessation may be moderated by a person's genetic makeup…

Smokers with Asp40 variant of the mu-opioid gene are twice as likely to quit smoking with higher-dose nicotine replacement therapy (NRT) than they are with lower-dose NRT. Smokers with the more common Asn40 variant are equally likely to stop smoking regardless of NRT level. Genetic testing might allow therapists to choose the most appropriate cessation therapy to maximise the likelihood of quitting successfully (Lerman *et al.*).

Chapter 14

Models of addictive behaviour	>	The biological approach
Factors affecting addictive behaviour		The cognitive approach
The psychology of addictive behaviour	>	Reducing addictive behaviour	The learning approach

The cognitive approach

Gambling

Initiation

Self-medication – Gelkopf *et al.* propose that individuals use different forms of pathological behaviour (e.g. alcohol, gambling) to 'treat' the psychological symptoms from which they suffer.

The activity an addict chooses tends to be one that is perceived as helping with a particular problem.

Maintenance

The role of irrational beliefs – Problem gamblers may have irrational perceptions about their ability to influence the outcomes of their gambling.

Cognitive distortions associated with gambling include the 'gambler's fallacy' and illusions of control.

Pathological gamblers may also show an exaggerated self-confidence in their ability to 'beat the system' with success being attributed to personal ability or skill, and failure to chance.

Relapse

Recall bias and the *'just world'* hypothesis – Pathological gamblers tend to remember and overestimate wins while underestimating or rationalising losses (Blanco *et al.*).

A string of losses does not act as a disincentive for future gambling because such individuals believe they will eventually be rewarded for their efforts.

They could relapse because of a belief that they 'deserve' to win, having lost so often on previous occasions (the 'just world hypothesis').

There is research support for the self-medication explanation...

Li *et al.* found that, compared to pathological gamblers who gambled for pure pleasure, pathological gamblers who gambled to escape the painful reality of life were significantly more likely to have other substance dependencies. Pathological gamblers motivated by self-medication usually have substitute means to satisfy their goal, whereas those who gamble for pure pleasure do not.

There are problems determining cause and effect...

The self-medication model argues that some form of psychological distress must precede the problem activity, as one necessitates the use of the other. There is some evidence for this, e.g. a depressive disorder is evident in the majority of pathological gamblers (Becona *et al.*).

This correlation between depression and gambling does not mean that depression is the cause of gambling. It is possible that depression is a consequence of personal and financial costs of pathological gambling.

Research challenges the role of irrational beliefs...

Possessing relevant knowledge does not make people less susceptible to cognitive distortions. Benhsain and Ladouceur found no difference in students trained in statistics or a non-statistical field, in their susceptibility to irrational gambling-related cognitions.

Delfabbro *et al.* found that pathological gamblers were more irrational in some forms of gambling related cognition, but were just as accurate as non-gamblers in estimating the odds of winning.

The are implications for treatment from this approach...

The evidence that there is more than one motivation for becoming a pathological gambler implies that there should be differing approaches to helping in their treatment, depending on their motivation for gambling.

For example, for self-medicating gamblers, it might be more beneficial to treat any underlying mood problem or mental disorder before attempting to get them to quit gambling.

As irrational beliefs play a key role in gambling, cognitive therapy corrects these cognitive errors, which reduces the motivation to gamble.

Smoking

Initiation

Expectancy theories propose that a behaviour escalates into addiction because of the expectations that an individual has about the costs and benefits of that activity.

Adolescent smokers report smoking when they are experiencing negative moods (Kassel *et al.*) and expect that smoking will decrease the intensity of their negative mood (Brandon and Baker).

Maintenance

Automatic processing – as an addiction develops, an activity is influenced less by conscious and more by unconscious expectancies (automatic processing). This would explain the loss of control that many smokers experience and the difficulties they experience in abstaining.

Expectancies can also be manipulated to prevent relapse (e.g. Tate *et al.*)

Relapse

Expectations of the costs and benefits of smoking affect an individual's readiness to quit and also the likelihood of them relapsing after they have quit.

Individuals who perceive smoking to have many benefits and quitting to have relatively few are the ones most likely to relapse after quitting.

There is a distinction between 'addiction' and 'excess'...

Much of the research relating to expectancy theory is concerned more with excesses of a particular behaviour rather than addiction to it. Research might focus on 'problematic behaviour', such as heavy smoking or excessive gambling, but does not consider 'loss of control'.

Addiction normally involves the individual being unable to control their behaviour, in which case it is not clear what role that expectancies might play in the development of this loss of control.

Changing expectancies helps prevent relapse...

Studies on the effectiveness of nicotine patch treatment on smoking cessation have revealed inconsistent findings. Moolchan *et al.* found that use of nicotine patches could increase cessation rates and reduce relapse rates, but only when accompanied by cognitive-behavioural therapy to change the positive expectancies associated with smoking.

Expectancies are important in maintaining smoking behaviour...

Juliano and Brandon found that smokers reported greater expectancies that cigarettes would alleviate their negative mood states and craving. They were also perceived as having a positive effect on weight control compared with the different forms of nicotine replacement therapy (NRT) available. Smokers' positive expectancies for the effects of smoking do not generalise to NRT, which might explain its modest success rate for smoking cessation.

There is a publication bias linked to expectancy theory...

The focus of research into expectancy theory and addiction has largely been on positive research findings, with negative results receiving far less attention. This constitutes a publication bias, in that the selective publication of positive results gives an unrepresentative view of a particular research area, particularly when contradictory findings are frequent.

Chapter 14

Biological models of addiction

| Models of addictive behaviour | > | The biological approach |

Factors affecting addictive behaviour

The cognitive approach

| The psychology of addictive behaviour | > | Reducing addictive behaviour | | The learning approach |

The learning approach

Gambling

Initiation

Operant conditioning – Griffiths argues that gamblers playing slot machines become addicted because of the rewards they experience, e.g. psychological (a near miss) and social rewards (peer praise).

Gamblers generally lose but do not always behave rationally, and greater weight may be given to the experience of winning.

Maintenance

Intermittent reinforcement – People continue gambling because of intermittent reinforcement characteristic of most types of gambling. They become used to long periods without reward and their gambling is reinforced by the occasional payout.

Social approval – Gambling may also be maintained because reinforcement is provided in the form of social approval from peers and family members of problem gamblers (Lambos *et al.*).

Relapse

Conditioned cues – Addicts learn to associate other stimuli with their gambling behaviour. If an individual comes into contact with one of these conditioned cues, they are at a higher risk of relapse.

Approach-avoidance conflict – Gambling has positive and negative consequences for the individual. Whether they gamble when faced with the urge is related to their ability to control the arousal and delay need for reinforcement.

Operant conditioning can't explain all forms of gambling…

A problem for explanations of gambling based on operant conditioning is that it is difficult to apply the same principles to all forms of gambling. For example, some forms of gambling have a short time period between behaviour and consequence (e.g. scratch cards) whereas others (e.g. sports betting) have a much longer period between bet and outcome, which is also less to do with chance and more to do with the skill of the individual.

There are different types of pathological gambler…

Behaviourally conditioned gamblers pathway start gambling because of exposure to gambling in role models or peer groups. They show the least severe gambling associated difficulties of any pathological gamblers and are motivated to seek treatment (Blaszczynski and Nower).

Emotionally vulnerable gamblers have accompanying anxiety and/or depression and a history of poor coping skills. Their accompanying psychological dysfunction makes them resistant to change and requires treatment for their underlying vulnerabilities as well as the gambling.

The learning approach can only explain why some people become addicted…

This approach explains addiction in terms of consequences of gambling behaviour. Although this may explain why some people initially engage in a potentially addictive behaviour, there are aspects of gambling addiction that are not dealt with by this explanation. Many people gamble at some time and experience the reinforcements associated with gambling, but few become addicts. This suggests that there are other factors involved in the transition from gambling behaviour to gambling addiction.

The occasional reinforcement of gambling may be enough…

Positive consequences are likely to be occasional rather than consistent, as gambling will not always produce a desired positive mood state or relieve a negative one. Individuals tend to learn adaptive behaviours that work to their advantage on average. Provided that engaging in a particular behaviour such as gambling produces the desired consequences occasionally then a pattern of addictive behaviour will become established.

Smoking

Initiation

Availability of role models – Social learning theory explanations propose that young people begin smoking because of the social role models around them who smoke. They then learn to expect positive physical and social consequences from smoking.

Popularity as a positive reinforcer – Popularity among peers can be a positive reinforcer in the initiation of smoking. Mayeux *et al.* found a relationship between smoking at age 16 and boys' popularity 2 years later.

Maintenance

Repetition leads to a conditioned association between the sensory aspects of smoking and the reinforcing effects of nicotine. These sensory cues become conditioned stimuli and activate the same brain areas as nicotine, making cessation difficult.

Relapse

Conditioned cues – Cues associated with receiving nicotine, e.g. the smell of cigarette smoke, increase the likelihood that the smoker will respond by smoking.

Refusal self-efficacy – Those who smoke frequently have less confidence in their ability to abstain (Lawrance and Rubinson) and are more likely to relapse.

There is research support for the importance of role models…

Peer group influences appear to be the primary influence for adolescents who smoke. DiBlasio and Benda found that adolescents who smoked were more likely to 'hang out' with other adolescents who also smoked.

Karcher and Finn found that youth whose parents smoked were almost twice as likely to take up smoking, and up to 8 times more likely to smoke if their close friends smoked than if they didn't.

There is support for the importance of conditioned cues…

Thewissen *et al.* tested the importance of environmental contexts in the urge to smoke. In one room, they repeatedly presented 33 smokers with a cue predicting smoking, whilst in a second room they presented a cue predicting smoking unavailability. Consistent with expectations, results supported the view that a cue predicting smoking later led to a greater urge to smoke.

The role of conditioned cues has implications for treatment…

Drummond *et al.* propose a treatment based on the fact that cues associated with smoking are an important factor in the maintenance of that habit. Cue exposure, involves presenting the cues without the opportunity to engage in the smoking behaviour. This leads to stimulus discrimination, as without the reinforcement provided by the actual nicotine, the association between the cue and smoking is extinguished.

There is a gender bias in smoking research…

Nerín de la Puerta and Jané argue there is a gender bias in research relating to smoking addiction. The onset of smoking and development of smoking addiction follows a different pattern in men and women according to López *et al.* They found that women start smoking later than men, and that there are gender related differences in relation to both the stages and context of smoking. Explanations of smoking addiction generally fail to address these gender differences.

Chapter 14

Models of addictive behaviour | Risk factors in addiction
Factors affecting addictive behaviour | > | Media influences on addictive
The psychology of addictive behaviour | > | Reducing addictive behaviour | behaviour

Risk factors in the development of addiction

Stress

Everyday stress

People report that they drink, smoke, use drugs, gamble, etc. as a means of coping with daily hassles, such as relationship problems.

Stressors may contribute to initiation and continuation of addictions, and to relapse after long periods of abstinence (NIDA).

Traumatic stress

People exposed to severe stress (e.g. parental loss or child abuse) are more vulnerable to addictions. Post traumatic stress disorder (PTSD) is also linked to addiction. Driessen et al. found 30% of drug addicts and 15% of alcoholics also suffered from PTSD.

Smoking may actually increase rather than decrease stress...

Many smokers smoke to reduce stress, yet smoking may actually increase stress levels. Stress may be a risk factor for smoking addiction but smoking doesn't have the desired effect in reducing the stress.

Part of the reason may be because the periods in between cigarettes can be stressful. Smokers get a sudden urge for another cigarette and the desire to have one can be a considerable cause of mental strain.

Stress may create vulnerability in some but not all people...

Cloniger suggested that there are two different kinds of alcoholics: type 1 individuals primarily drink to reduce tension (and are more prone to anxiety/depression), type 2 alcoholics drink primarily to relieve boredom (and have a tendency towards risk taking). Therefore, stress may explain vulnerability for some (type 1s) but not all people.

Peers

Peer pressure is cited as a reason for why adolescents start taking drugs or smoking. Transitions to increased levels of smoking are linked to peer approval and encouragement together with the message that smoking is an activity that promotes popularity.

Two theories explain this:

Social learning theory (SIT) – Smoking is learned through the observation of others and subsequent imitation of their behaviour. Once smoking behaviour starts, an individual's experiences with it then determine whether it persists.

Social identity theory – Group members adopt behaviours important to the social identity of the group. If status as 'smoker' or 'non-smoker' is central to the social identity of the group, individuals are likely to be similar to one another in smoking habits.

There is research support for the role of peer pressure...

The importance of social context in smoking is supported by research. Research supports the claim that exposure to peer models increases the likelihood that teenagers will begin smoking (Duncan et al.).

There is also support for the claim that perceived rewards such as social status and popularity are instrumental in why adolescents begin smoking. These rewards remain important while they develop their smoking addiction (Eiser et al.).

There is a lack of support for SIT as an explanation of smoking...

Although there is evidence to support the claim that adolescents are motivated to begin smoking because of stereotypes they hold of adolescents in general (Michell), little is known about the extent to which these groups influence their members to smoke. Nor do we know whether adolescents conform to the behaviours of their social group when these conflict with their own concerns to lead a healthy lifestyle.

Age

The influence of peers on smoking and drug use decreases in later adolescence, and close friends and romantic partners become increasingly important as an influence on attitudes and behaviours (Brown et al.).

Peers have a greater impact on young adolescents, while romantic partners play a greater role later on.

There are ethical issues in addiction research...

Research on sensitive topics creates ethical issues for the researcher. One of these is the 'threat of sanction', which involves the possibility that research may reveal information that is incriminating in some way. Researchers must weigh up the potential benefits (e.g. possibilities for helping addicts) against potential risks (e.g. further discrimination).

Personality

The concept of an 'addictive personality' can explain why some people become addicted when others don't, despite the fact that both try the same experience.

Neuroticism and psychoticism

Francis found a link between addiction and high scores on neuroticism (prone to negative affect) and psychoticism (prone to hostility and impulsivity).

Tri-dimensional theory of addictive behaviour (Cloniger)

Personality traits that predispose individuals towards substance dependence:

• novelty seeking
• harm avoidance
• reward dependence.

Research on the addictive personality is correlational only...

Some personality traits may be common amongst addicts, however this does not mean they cause addictive behaviour. Teeson et al. suggest it is difficult to disentangle the effects of personality on addiction from the effects of addiction on personality.

There is evidence for personality as a cause of addiction...

Research has found evidence that personality causes addiction. Belin et al. placed rats in a device where they could self-administer doses of cocaine. One group were sensation-seekers and immediately started taking large doses. A second group, who were high in impulsiveness, started with lower doses but they were the ones to become addicted.

Impulsivity rather than sensation-seeking causes addiction...

Weintraub et al. assessed individuals suffering from Parkinson's disease (PD). Individuals with PD are treated with drugs that increase dopamine levels to combat their symptoms. A side effect appears to be a 3.5 fold increase in impulse-control disorders, including gambling and sex addiction. This study suggests that high levels of dopamine lead to impulsivity and also may cause addiction.

Addictions may be more rewarding for people with a hypersensitive dopamine system...

Buckholtz et al. found that addictions may be more rewarding for people with certain personality types because they have a more hypersensitive dopamine response system. A heightened response to an anticipated reward (e.g. from drugs or gambling) could make such individuals less fearful about the consequences of their behaviour.

Chapter 14

	Models of addictive behaviour	Risk factors in addiction
	Factors affecting addictive behaviour >	Media influences on addictive behaviour
The psychology of addictive behaviour >	Reducing addictive behaviour	

Media influences on addictive behaviour

Research into film representations of addiction

Sulkunen

Method: 61 scenes from 47 films were analysed regarding addictions to alcohol, drugs, tobacco, gambling and sex.

Results: The enjoyment of drugs was frequently contrasted with the dullness of ordinary life. The competent use of drugs was represented as a way of alleviating a particular problem, e.g. in *Human Traffic*, the use of ecstasy was portrayed as a way of resolving relationship problems for two of the main characters.

Waylen *et al.*

This study suggests that media representation of smoking can influence teenagers to take up the habit.

Method: Researchers examined 360 of the top US box office films released between 2001 and 2005, including those that depicted smoking.

Results: They found that teenagers who watched films showing actors smoking were more likely to start smoking themselves. Even after controlling for social factors such as whether their parents or peers smoked, the researchers found a significant relationship between adolescent smoking and the number of films they had seen depicting smoking.

Do film portrayals affect behaviour?...

Sargent and Hanewinkel surveyed a total of 4,384 adolescents who were re-surveyed a year later. They found that of those individuals who had not smoked when first surveyed, exposure to movies with smoking over the intervening year was a significant and strong predictor of whether they had begun to smoke when re-surveyed one year later.

The importance of film representations of addiction...

Byrne argues that films such as *Trainspotting* are important because they educate both addicts and the general public about addiction by creating stereotypes.

He draws a parallel with the fact that the dominant image of ECT comes not from the public information literature of the Royal College of Psychiatrists, but from the 1975 film *One Flew Over the Cuckoo's Nest*.

An alternative perspective...

Boyd argues that films actually often represent negative, rather than positive, consequences of addiction. For example, illegal drug use and addiction, claims Boyd, are depicted by physical deterioration (e.g. unkempt bodies), sexual degradation (e.g. prostitution), violence and crime (e.g. murder) and moral decline (e.g. stealing from loved ones).

Ethical guidelines...

In the US, the Office for Substance Abuse Protection (OSAP) has developed guidelines about drugs for film and television writers. These recommend that writers should communicate all illegal drug use as unhealthy and harmful, that addiction should be presented as a disease and abstinence as a viable choice. There should be no references to 'recreational use of drugs', since no drug use is 'recreational'.

The role of media in changing addictive behaviour

A suitable role for the media

Television and the Internet have been identified as media that could be used to provide support for addicts and education about addiction. They are increasingly being used to promote healthy lifestyles and behaviour change such as smoking cessation and physical exercise.

Problem drinking TV programmes

Bennett *et al.* assessed the effect of the BBC programme *Psst... the Really Useful Guide to Alcohol*. Viewers showed improved alcohol-related knowledge, but did not show any change in attitude or in actual alcohol consumption.

Kramer *et al.* assessed the effectiveness of *Drinking Less? Do it Yourself!*, a 5-week television self-help intervention designed to reduce problem drinking. They found that the intervention group were more successful than a control group in achieving low-risk (rather than high-risk) problem drinking, a difference maintained at a 3-month follow-up.

Antidrug campaigns

In 2008, a television and Internet advertising campaign was launched in the UK to warn teenagers of the dangers of cocaine use. The adverts feature a fictional dog called Pablo, who is used by drug dealers to carry cocaine. The dog seeks out cocaine users to find out what happens to them after taking the drug.

Competitive media drives people to use drugs...

Brian Wilson, the creative genius behind the Beach Boys, used drugs such as cannabis and LSD as a creative influence. However, his use of cocaine, to which he became addicted, no longer contributed to the creative process, but was a form of self-medication as he struggled with the pressures of writing and touring. This shows how the competitive media drives some people to experiment with drugs as a creative influence, but they become victims of the drugs' addictive power (Belli).

There are methodological problems...

The Kramer *et al.* study involved an intervention group, who watched the *Drinking Less?* series, and a control group who watched the series later.
- The intervention group received weekly visits from the researchers; the extra attention may explain the positive outcome for this group.
- The waiting list group were aware they would receive treatment soon, so may have postponed their behavioural change, thereby artificially inflating the magnitude of the difference between the two groups.

Correlation isn't the same as causality...

Most of the evidence about media effects on addictive behaviour is correlational, i.e. exposure to depictions of drug and alcohol use in films and on television is related to addictive behaviour. However, this does not indicate a causal relationship between exposure and addiction.

Do antidrug campaigns work?...

Hornik *et al.* concluded that the $1 billlion US *National Youth Anti-Drug Media Campaign* not only failed but also had negative effects. Why?
- The messages in the campaign were not particularly novel.
- Antidrug advertising has an implicit message that drug use is commonplace. Johnston *et al.* found that youths who saw the ads took from them the message that their peers were using marijuana, and were then more likely to imitate marijuana use themselves.

The theory of planned behaviour (TPB)

Main assumptions

An individual's decision to engage in a particular behaviour can be directly predicted by their intention to engage in that behaviour. Intention is a function of three factors:

1. Behavioural attitude

The individual's attitude toward the behaviour in question. This is formed on the basis of beliefs about the consequences of performing this behaviour and an appraisal of the value of these consequences.

2. Subjective norms

The individual's subjective awareness of social norms relating to that particular behaviour, including the 'injunctive norm' (perceived right thing to do) and the 'descriptive norm' (what others actually do).

3. Perceived behavioural control

The more control people believe they have over a behaviour, the stronger their intention to actually perform it will be.

An individual with higher perceived behavioural control is likely to try harder and persevere.

The TPB has been criticised as being too rational…

It fails to take into account emotions, compulsions or other irrational determinants of human behaviour (Armitage et al.). The presence of strong emotions may help to explain why people sometimes act irrationally by failing to carry out an intended behaviour (e.g. stop drinking) even when it is in their best interest to do so (Albarracin et al.).

The TPB ignores other factors…

There are many other influential factors that are ignored by the TPB. Topa and Moriano suggest that group variables, such as identification with peers, could play a mediating role in any addictive behaviour.

Another element that is missing from the TPB is motivation. Klag studied 350 substance abusers in Australia and found that recovery was consistently more successful in individuals who had decided themselves to give up rather than people who were coerced (e.g. a court sentence).

There are methodological issues with the TPB…

When attitudes and intentions are assessed by questionnaires responses may be affected by self-presentational biases, thus they may turn out to be poor predictors of actual behaviour (Albarracín et al.).

The research on the TPB is almost entirely correlational. This means it is not clear whether any one component of the model (e.g. behavioural attitude, perceived behavioural control) has caused behaviour change.

TPB as a model for addiction prevention

Changing behavioural attitude

The US Office of National Drug Control Policy launched a campaign to lower teenage marijuana use. A review of this campaign attributes its success to its influence in creating a different attitude toward the effect of marijuana use.

Changing subjective norms

Anti-drug campaigns often give adolescents data about the percentage of people engaging in drug taking behaviour. Accurate statistical information should correct subjective norms as part of an effective campaign (Wilson and Kolander).

Perceived behavioural control

Godin et al. found the three elements of the TPB explained intentions, whereas perceived behavioural control was the most important predictor of actual behaviour.

Self-efficacy

The TPB proposes that intentions to change behaviour will be stronger in people who have an increased sense of control. Self-efficacy has been shown to be important in many aspects of addiction prevention.

Promoting health behaviour change

Webb et al. analysed 85 studies of internet-based interventions and concluded that those based on a theoretical model, especially the TPB, tended to have greater success.

Addiction to sun

White et al. examined sun protection intentions and behaviours of young people in Australia. Results showed the TPB components were significant predictors of intentions to engage in sun protection, and these intentions were significant predictors of actual sun protection behaviour.

The TPB does not distinguish between intention and expectation…

A distinction should be made between behavioural intention (a person's plans about their future behaviour), and behavioural expectation (the perceived likelihood of performing a particular behaviour). Although intention may have a causal effect on behaviour, a behavioural expectation is less likely to do so (Armitage and Conner).

The TPB predicts intention rather than behaviour change…

Armitage and Conner's meta-analysis of studies using the TPB found that this model was successful in predicting intention to change rather than actual behavioural change. This suggests that the TPB is primarily an account of intention formation rather than specifying the processes involved in translating the intention into action.

This has implications when trying to change addictive behaviours…

In the context of changing risky behaviours such as drug taking or gambling, therefore, we can make a distinction between a motivational phase that results in the formation of a behavioural intention, and a post-decisional phase which involves behavioural initiation and maintenance (Abraham et al.).

Alcohol and drugs can produce a discrepancy between measured intention and actual behaviour…

Attitudes and intentions related to health behaviours (e.g. gambling or unprotected sex) tend to be measured when sober, whereas actual risky behaviour is often performed when under the influence of alcohol or drugs. MacDonald et al. found that when participants had taken alcohol they did then show increased intentions to engage in unprotected sex and other risky behaviours. One reason for this may be that alcohol tends to decrease cognitive capacity so that only the most obvious characteristics of a situation are attended to.

Control is not important for all behaviours…

Perceived behavioural control is more important when issues of control are associated with actually performing a task. Specifically, this depends on whether the performance of a particular behaviour requires specific resources, abilities, skills etc. For example, voting behaviour or eating convenience food are both behaviours where perceived behavioural control is less important in determining behaviour as they don't require any specific abilities. However, for other behaviours, such as losing weight or giving up smoking, perceived behavioural control is an important predictor of behaviour (Netemeyer et al.).

Types of intervention

Biological interventions

Heroin addiction and methadone

Methadone mimics the effects of heroin but is less addictive. A drug abuser is given slowly increasing amounts of methadone to improve tolerance. Then the dose is decreased until the addict no longer needs methadone or heroin.

Problems with methadone treatment…

Some drug addicts can become as reliant on methadone as they were on heroin, thereby substituting one addiction for another.

The use of methadone remains controversial. Statistics show more than 300 methadone-related deaths in the UK in 2007. Because methadone consumption is often unsupervised, this has created a black market in methadone, with addicts selling their doses for only £2.

Drug treatments for gambling addiction

In the UK drug treatments have not been approved for gambling but there is evidence that they may be effective.

SSRIs increase serotonin levels. Hollander *et al.* found that gamblers treated with SSRIs showed improvements compared to a control group.

Naltrexone (a dopamine receptor antagonist) reduces the rewarding and reinforcing properties of gambling, thus reducing the urge to gamble.

Drug treatments for gambling addiction…

The Hollander study involved only ten people. A larger and longer study (Blanco *et al.*), involving 32 gamblers over 6 months, failed to demonstrate any superiority for the drug treatment over a placebo.

Use of naltrexone led to decreases in gambling thoughts and behaviours after 6 weeks of treatment (Kim and Grant).

Intervention bias…

Cohen and Cohen describe a phenomenon called the 'clinician's illusion' – clinicians believe that addictions are difficult to treat because they only tend to come across addicts when their condition is well advanced, too severe to effectively respond to treatment.

Psychological interventions

Reinforcement

One way to reduce addiction is to reward people for not engaging in the behaviour.

Sindelar *et al.* tested people on methadone treatment programmes (also received counselling). One group was rewarded each time they tested negative for drugs. At the end of the programme the reward group had 60% more negative urine samples than the control group.

Reinforcement does not address underlying problems…

Although research such as the Sindelar *et al.* study have shown the effectiveness of reinforcement therapies for reducing addictive behaviour, such interventions do nothing to address the problem that led to the addiction in the first place.

This means that although a specific addictive behaviour might have been reduced, it is possible that the person may engage in a different addictive behaviour instead. A drug addict may, for example, turn to alcohol, but in most cases new addictions tend to be subtle including compulsive spending or even developing dependent relationships.

Cognitive-behavioural therapy (CBT)

The main goal of CBT is to help people change the way they think about their addiction, and learn new ways of coping more effectively.

For example, in gambling addiction cognitive errors (e.g. believing one can control and predict outcomes) play a part in maintaining gambling. Such errors are corrected by CBT.

Research support for CBT…

Ladouceur *et al.* randomly allocated 66 pathological gamblers to a cognitive therapy or to a waiting list control group. Afterwards 86% of the treatment group were no longer classed as pathological gamblers and had increased self-efficacy.

Sylvain *et al.* evaluated treatments that target cognition as well as behaviour. Pathological gamblers were given cognitive therapy, social skills training and relapse prevention resulting in improvements after treatment, with these gains maintained at 1-year follow-up.

Public health interventions

The NIDA study

Government-sponsored intervention projects such as the US National Institute on Drug Abuse (NIDA) *Collaborative Cocaine Treatment Study* are designed to intervene in the cycle of personal and social problems associated with drugs.

Public health interventions…

The NIDA intervention led to reduced cocaine use, with an associated reduction in other behaviours (e.g. unprotected sex in addicts leading to a reduction in HIV) (Crits-Christoph *et al.*).

Conclusions…

Research has not tended to show that any one type of psychological treatment is superior to any other. Psychological therapies appear more effective when combined with a pharmacological treatment.

Telephone smoking 'Quitlines'

Stead *et al.* found that smokers (sample =18,000) who received repeated Quitline calls increased their odds of stopping smoking by 50% compared to smokers who only received self-help materials and/or brief counselling.

Real-world application of Quitlines…

Military personnel deployed abroad (e.g. Iraq) often increase smoking or take it up for the first time (Boos and Croft). Beckham *et al.* found that a combination of Quitline counselling and nicotine replacement therapy was highly effective in treating US military veterans.

Prevention of youth gambling

Messerlian *et al.* proposed a prevention model based on research into pathological gambling in adolescents and young adults using denormalisation, protection, prevention and harm-reduction principles. For example, programmes based on prevention include early identification strategies as an attempt to avert at-risk youth from escalating towards pathological gambling.

A public health approach to youth gambling is important because…

It is a proactive approach to addressing a potentially devastating social issue. Research has demonstrated that problem gambling during adolescence can lead to adverse outcomes, such as strained relationships, delinquency and criminal behaviour, depression and even suicide (Derevensky and Gupta).

Anomalistic psychology

Division A   The study of anomalous experience
Pseudoscience and parapsychology
Methodological issues

Division B   Explanations for anomalous experience
Coincidence and probability judgements
Superstitious behaviour and magical thinking
Personality factors in anomalous experience

Division C   Research into exceptional experience
Psychic healing and psychic mediumship
Out-of-body and near-death experiences

Issues, debates and approaches
In the Psychology in Action section (Section B) of the Unit 4 exam there is no explicit credit given to issues, debates and approaches. This doesn't mean that such material would not be creditworthy (it would) but it means it is not required. So, in this chapter we have not specifically identified IDA.

Specification

Anomalistic psychology	
• The study of anomalous experience	• Pseudoscience and the scientific status of parapsychology. • Methodological issues related to the study of paranormal cognition (ESP, including Ganzfeld) and paranormal action (psychokinesis).
• Explanations for anomalous experience	• The role of coincidence and probability judgements in anomalous experience. • Explanations for superstitious behaviour and magical thinking. • Personality factors underlying anomalous experience.
• Research into exceptional experience	• Psychological research into and explanations for psychic healing, near-death and out-of-body experiences, and psychic mediumship.

Chapter 15

The study of anomalous psychology	>
Explanations for anomalous experience	Pseudoscience and parapsychology
Anomalistic psychology	>	Research into exceptional experience	Methodological issues

Pseudoscience and parapsychology

A pseudoscience is a field of study that claims to be a science but lacks certain important characteristics:

Lacks falsifiability

The aim of the scientific method is to test hypotheses. Proof is only possible through falsification and therefore hypotheses must be falsifiable.

Some paranormal claims cannot be falsified, e.g. because they are 'jealous phenomena' which disappear when studied by non-believers.

Paranormal research is not the only pseudoscience...

Freud's theory has been criticised because many of his hypotheses are unfalsifiable, e.g. his view that all men have repressed homosexual tendencies cannot be disproved. If you do find men who have no repressed homosexual tendencies then it could be argued that they have them, it's just the tendencies are so repressed they are not apparent.

It could also be argued that psychology itself is not scientific. Koch reviewed the state of psychological research and concluded that such research has resulted in verifiable descriptions of behaviour but the explanations derived from such research are more opinion than fact.

Lacks carefully controlled, replicable research

A high level of control is essential to determine causal relationships, but is often lacking in paranormal research – see studies of ESP and psychokinesis, discussed on the facing page.

Replication is the means by which findings can be confirmed as valid. However, paranormal findings are not often replicated, especially when studies are conducted by non-believers, e.g. Ritchie *et al.* (sceptics) failed to replicate Bem's experiment on backwards causation.

Using scientific methods may be 'just dressing up'...

Miller suggests that psychologists have deluded themselves about being scientists. Just because they use the appropriate terms and methods, they are doing no more than just 'dressing up'. The same criticisms could be made of parapsychology.

Lacks a theory to explain the effects

The aim of scientific research is to construct explanations for observations made about the world. Many paranormal phenomena have not, as yet, been given explanations that are likely.

The *Society for Psychical Research* acknowledges that scientific respectability will not be attained until there is some agreed theoretical basis for paranormal phenomena.

Parapsychological research is respectable...

Mousseau compared articles in peer-reviewed parapsychology journals with journals covering respectable mainstream science.

She concluded that parapsychology journals came out better because, for example, they did report negative findings (a necessary part of the scientific process). She found no mainstream articles that reported negative findings, a case of selective reporting.

She also found that 43% of the parapsychology articles produced empirical data compared to mainstream rates of 64%. The rate is lower but it still shows that a significant proportion of parapsychological research is embracing the goals of science.

Burden of proof misplaced

With paranormal phenomena the requirement to provide proof is with the sceptic rather than the believer (in true science the burden of proof is with the believer).

Such proof (or disproof) is often difficult, e.g. because it is difficult to prove that a photo is fake or that the hypotheses lacks falsifiability.

Parapsychology is recognised as a science...

The *American Association for the Advancement of Science* (AAAS), the largest general scientific society in the world, accepted the *Parapsychological Association* (PA) as an affiliated member in 1969. This appears to confirm its scientific status.

Lack ability to change

In science, explanations are adapted as a result of hypothesis-testing, whereas anomalous experiences have continued to be explained in the same way for centuries despite a lack of evidence.

Ethical issues... where's the harm?...

There are three reasons to be concerned about paranormal research:
- Some people make a lot of money out of unfounded claims.
- As a society we should be encouraged to ask for evidence rather than respond to trends and superstitions which, in the past, have resulted in dangerous practices, e.g. the persecution of witches or the punishment of mental patients.
- On the positive side, thorough research may lead to valuable discoveries, e.g. acupuncture is now accepted as a valuable therapy due to research that has demonstrated repeatable results.

Methodological issues

Extrasensory perception (ESP)

The Ganzfeld technique – A method developed by Honorton to study ESP. It aims to suppress sensory input so ESP can be better accessed. The sensory deprivation is typically achieved by placing a subject in a red-lit room, with half ping pong balls over their eyes and earphones playing white noise. The sender, in another room, telepathically transmits an image. The receiver selects the image from a choice of four, or describes the image and an independent judge has to match the received image to images that were sent.

Researcher bias
Woofitt found that sceptical researchers didn't encourage the 'receivers' to elaborate their images whereas interviewers who believed in psi often did, which led to more positive results. The sheep–goat effect leads to investigator bias.

The sheep-goat effect could be explained…
It could be argued that positive results from non-sceptical researchers are due to 'jealous phenomena' only appearing in the presence of a non-sceptic, rather than being due to expectations.

However…
Hyman argued that, even if significant effects are found, these are meaningless unless some explanation can be offered.

Lack of control
Ganzfeld studies criticised for being poorly controlled, e.g. poor soundproofing (receiver could hear video played to sender) and non-random order of target selections (first one displayed more likely to be selected).

Autoganzfeld was developed to improve control…
An automated computer system selects and displays the targets. Therefore the experimenter is blind as to which target has been selected and cannot unconsciously influence the target selected by a judge as a match. The receiver is also placed in a soundproof steel-walled and electromagnetically shielded room.

Biased analysis
Honorton analysed 28 Ganzfeld studies, finding results better than chance.

Hyman (a sceptic) used a different method of analysis, concluding there was no effect.

Honorton et al. reported the results of 11 autoganzfeld studies involving eight different researchers. The studies produced a hit rate of 34%, a statistically significant effect.

However conflicting findings have continued…
Milton and Wiseman reviewed 30 other well-controlled Ganzfeld studies and found no significant effects.

The file–drawer effect
Paranormal researchers have been accused of leaving studies with negative results out of meta-analyses (i.e. filing them away). This biases any conclusions reached.

This review was subsequently criticised because, Bem et al. claimed, the review included studies that had not followed the Ganzfeld protocol. When these inconsistent studies were removed, and some more recent studies added, a significant result was again obtained by Bem et al.

Fraud
Sargent was accused of fraud in ESP research but his work was still included in Honorton's review.

Fraud is not unique to paranormal research…
Playfair suggests that many noted scientists have resorted to data-fudging, but Hines counter-argues that fraud has been more common in parapsychology than other areas of scientific investigation.

Psychokinesis (PK)

Random event generator (REG), an electronic coin flipper. Volunteers asked to produce more heads than tails, or vice versa.
Split-beam laser – Participants invited to influence the activity of a split-beam laser on the web (Stevens).

Lack of control
Ideal controls would be, for example, having two researchers, true randomisation of targets and using independent recording of targets.

Hansel examined 30 PK studies, only 13 produced positive results and none of these were adequately controlled.

In contrast, many of the studies returning negative results did apply controls.

There is contradictory evidence…
A meta-analysis of over 500 studies of micro PK found no significant relationship between methodological quality of a study (e.g. size of sample) and the outcome (Radin and Nelson).

Bosch et al. (neither sceptics or believers) looked at the highest quality studies and still found no significant effects.

Positive results may due to a small band of investigators…
Radin and Nelson found that 91 investigators were involved in their 500 studies. About 50% of these were conducted by the same 10 researchers, suggesting this is not a small group of investigators.

The effect of expectations
Participants were shown a video of a fake psychic placing a bent key on a table. Those who heard the psychic say the key was continuing to bend later were more likely to report further bending than participants in a no-expectation condition (Wiseman and Greening).

The file drawer effect is unlikely…
Positive PK results have been attributed to selective reporting (research papers are 'filed away in a drawer'), but Radin and Nelson calculated that there would need to be 10 unpublished studies with negative effects for each of the 500 published studies in order to nullify the effect.

Radin et al. found that the average number of unreported studies per investigator was only about one. Therefore the file–drawer effect is unlikely to explain the positive findings.

Ecological validity
Using REG to test PK may be inappropriate because the original claims for PK are about observable physical changes and REG concerns unobservable changes.

The effect size should be increasing not decreasing…
Usually, if there is a real effect, the size of the effect becomes greater over time because scientists are progressively better able to identify and control extraneous variables. Increasing control has had the opposite effect in paranormal research (Bierman).

Chapter 15

	The study of anomalous psychology	Coincidence and probability judgements
	Explanations for amomalous experience >	Superstitious behaviour and magical thinking
Anomalistic psychology >	Belief in exceptional experience	Personality factors in anomalous experience

Coincidence and probability judgements

The role of coincidence in anomalous experience

Illusion of causality

People assume (rightly or wrongly) that things that happen at the same time have a causal relationship.

Illusion of causality may have adaptive significance...

Understanding causality is adaptive because, e.g. you might avoid eating a poisonous mushroom. But may sometimes lead to Type 1 errors: rejecting the null hypothesis ('mushrooms have no effect') when it is true. Such Type 1 errors are tolerated in order to avoid Type 2 errors (eating a mushroom that is actually poisonous). Foster and Kokko argue that an advantage persists as long as the occasionally correct response has a large adaptive benefit.

Illusion of connection

Links are made between events that are unrelated, or patterns detected where none exist.

There is biological support for the tendency to make links...

Brugger *et al.* found that people with high dopamine levels were more likely to interpret coincidental events as having meaning. Giving *L-dopa* (a drug that increases dopamine levels) to sceptics had the same effect (but had no effect on believers).

The illusion of connection is also adaptive

Always better to think you see a tiger that is hidden in the grassland than miss it – an ability that may underlie creativity. Thalbourne found that believers are more creative than sceptics who may even lose out because they fail to detect meaningful connections.

Illusion of control

Explanations for coincidence give a sense of order and increase feelings of control.

Believers show a greater illusion of control (e.g. Ayeroff and Abelson).

There is research support...

Whitson and Galinsky found that reduced control led participants to detect patterns where there were none and form illusory correlations between unrelated events.

General cognitive ability or intelligence

Lower intelligence might mean being less accurate at judging whether a psychic event in fact has a normal explanation.

Research (e.g. Gray) has found that believers have lower levels of academic performance than sceptics.

Some research has found the opposite...

A survey of *New Scientist* readers (more than half hold a science degree) found that 67% regarded ESP either as an 'established fact' or 'a likely possibility' (Evans).

In general research has not found a difference in terms of cognitive ability (except for syllogistic reasoning) (Wiseman and Watt).

The role of probability judgements in anomalous experience

Probability misjudgement (cognitive illusions – Blackmore and Troscianko).

Believers (sheep) more than sceptics (goats) tend to underestimate statistical likelihood on probability judgement tasks (see below). Therefore they are likely to reject coincidence as an explanation and prefer anomalous explanations.

Probability judgement tasks

• *Repetition avoidance* – Sheep tend to underestimate statistical likelihood when asked to generate a string of random numbers (e.g. they avoid consecutive repeats) (Brugger *et al.*).

• *Questions about probability*, e.g. the birthday party paradox – how many people would you need at a party to have a 50:50 chance that two of them have the same birthday (not counting year)? More goats than sheep got this right on a multiple choice test (the answer is 23) (Blackmore and Troscianko).

• *Conjunction fallacy* – Participants given 'conjunction vignettes' (descriptions of occasions where two events co-occur, such as getting food poisoning after eating eggs). Then asked to indicate the probability of such events co-occurring. Sheep made more conjunction errors than goats (Rogers *et al.*).

Sheep may be no worse than goats at probability judgement...

Blackmore asked over 6000 participants to identify which of 10 statements were true for them and for a randomly selected other person (e.g. 'I have a scar on my left knee'). Sheep gave higher answers for both self and others but all participants overestimated the number of statements true for others, suggesting that probability misjudgement is not unique to believers.

One reason for contradictory findings is...

Different researchers assess belief and non-belief differently, e.g. using the *Paranormal Belief Scale* involves a wide range of paranormal beliefs whereas Blackmore just asked about ESP.

The findings are correlational...

Just because there is a link between probability misjudgment and belief doesn't mean that it causes anomalistic belief.

It might be low cognitive ability rather than probability misjudgement...

Musch and Ehrenberg controlled for differences in general cognitive ability and found this reduced the difference between believers and non-believers on probability judgment tasks to zero. So it may be that poor probability judgments are due to low cognitive ability and not a component in paranormal belief.

An alternative explanation...

Kahneman and Tversky suggest that people use various heuristics (strategies to solve problems) such as representativeness.

For example, some people understand that short runs of tossing a coin will not be representative of theoretical probability of 50:50 whereas other people expect short runs to match the theoretical probability (the gambler's fallacy).

Chapter 15

The study of anomalous psychology	Coincidence and probability judgements
Explanations for amomalous experience >	Superstitious behaviour and magical thinking
Anomalistic psychology >	Belief in exceptional experience	Personality factors in anomalous experience

Superstitious behaviour and magical thinking

Explanations for superstitious behaviour

Type 1 and 2 errors

Causal thinking is adaptive, e.g. learning to link poisonous mushrooms with illness.

Such thinking leads to Type 1 errors (rejecting a true null hypothesis) which are 'tolerated' in order to avoid disastrous Type 2 errors (being ignorant of causal relationships).

These explanations don't account for cultural superstitions…

The explanations on the left only account for how individuals acquire personal superstitions. There are also culturally transmitted superstitions, e.g. the number 7 is lucky in the UK whereas in Thailand it's the lucky number 9.

It may be that people adopt cultural superstitions because they provide a sense of control. Whitson and Galinsky showed that a reduced sense of control leads to the development of superstitions.

Behaviourist explanation

Skinner proposed that superstitious beliefs develop through operant conditioning where an accidental stimulus-response link is learned.

Such beliefs are maintained because of negative reinforcement – avoidance of potential disaster results in a sense of relief which is reinforcing.

This explanation has been supported…

Skinner observed that pigeons appeared to learn ritual (superstitious) behaviours when certain random behaviours were coincidentally associated with getting food.

However…

Staddon and Simmelhag showed that ritual behaviours in pigeons were unrelated to food rewards. The 'rituals' were produced as frequently before any reinforcement takes place as afterwards.

Illusion of control

Whitson and Galinsky created a sense of high or low control by asking one group of participants to think of past events where they felt in control, the other group thought of events where they didn't feel in control.

Then they were asked to judge probabilistic events. Found that reduced control led participants to detect patterns where there were none.

On the other hand…

Matute found that human participants did learn superstitious behaviour in the way suggested by Skinner. An uncontrollable noise was appeared to be stopped by pressing one of a variety of buttons. Participants later tried to press the same button.

There are advantages of having an illusion of control…

It means we actively confront unpredictable circumstances rather than withdraw from them.

Damisch *et al.* found that the activation of good-luck-related superstitions led to enhanced performance on a variety of tasks (such as motor dexterity and memory) and suggest that such superstitions increase one's self-efficacy (belief in your own competence).

Explanations for magical thinking

Psychodynamic explanation

Magical thinking is a form of childlike thought where inner feelings are projected onto the outer world. In adults, such behaviour is a defence mechanism where regression is a means of coping with anxiety (Freud).

Research supports magical thinking…

Pronin *et al.* asked students to put pins in a voodoo doll to make someone else get a headache. Afterwards they said they felt more responsible for apparent headaches in a confederate who had been behaving stupidly and made them feel angry, i.e. they felt their angry feelings were the cause.

Dual processing theory

Children's thinking is intuitive, adults are rational but continue to sometimes use intuitive thinking.

There are benefits of magical thinking…

Magical thinking may act like a placebo – it creates a positive expectation and this alone can account for improvements. This is called a self-fulfilling prophecy – things turn out as we expected just because of our expectations (Rosenthal and Jacobsen).

Animism

Children ascribe feelings to inanimate objects (Piaget).

There are costs of magical thinking…

Magical thinking is sometimes listed as one of the characteristics of schizophrenia (Weinberger and Harrison), which suggests it might be an element in the separation from reality experienced by schizophrenics.

Nominal realism

Children have difficulty separating the names of things from the things themselves (Piaget). Continues in adults, e.g. people find it difficult to drink from a glass labelled 'cyanide' even when they know it's sugar (Rozin *et al.*).

There are also costs of not having magical thinking…

People who are depressed generally show less magical thinking, called *depression realism*. Both a lack of magical thinking and *anhedonia* (the inability to experience pleasure) have been linked to low levels of dopamine, a neurotransmitter that is high in both schizophrenics and believers in the paranormal (Mohr *et al.*).

Law of contagion

Things having been in contact continue to act on each other even after physical contact ceases.

Rozin and Nemeroff relate this to an evolved fear of contagion. It would be adaptive to avoid touching something that had been in contact with a diseased person, leading to the belief that psychological and physical properties can pass between people via the things they touch.

Real-world application…

Vamos suggests that people don't agree to organ donation because they associate it with death (*law of contagion*). If organ donation was associated with extending people's lives, donation rates might increase.

Chapter 15

The study of anomalous psychology | Coincidence and probability judgements
Explanations for amomalous experience > | Superstitious behaviour and magical thinking
Anomalistic psychology > Belief in exceptional experience | Personality factors in anomalous experience

Personality factors in anomalous experience

Eysenck's personality factors

Neuroticism

Research has found a link between paranormal beliefs and neuroticism (tendency to experience negative emotional states) (e.g. Williams *et al.*).

Paranormal beliefs may act as a defence mechanism to create a distance from reality and reduce negative states.

Extraversion

Honorton *et al.* conducted a meta-analysis of 60 published studies relating extraversion to ESP and found an overall positive correlation.

Extraverts seek stimulation to increase brain arousal levels. They may respond better to new stimuli than introverts and therefore are more open to paranormal experiences, which increases their belief.

Results vary with different methods of assessment...

If different subscales of the *Paranormal Belief Scale* are used, different personality traits emerge as being significant.

For example...

Wiseman and Watt found neuroticism was only related to those paranormal beliefs associated with bad luck, i.e. neuroticism doesn't explain all paranormal beliefs.

Francis *et al.* found that high psychoticism did correlate with unconventional paranormal beliefs such as astrology and psychokinesis.

A more imaginative personality

Fantasy proneness is the tendency to become so deeply absorbed in a fantasy that it feels as if it actually happened.

Evidence suggests that believers are more fantasy prone, e.g. Dixon *et al.* demonstrated a link between belief and mental imagination.

Wiseman *et al.* found believers were more deeply absorbed in a séance despite knowing it to be fake. This may explain why they reported a table had moved.

Validity of research studies...

Belief in the paranormal is measured using a set of statements about paranormal phenomena, e.g. the *Paranormal Belief Scale*, which covers various phenomena such as belief in UFOs and the Loch Ness monster. This may not be a valid measurement because it covers such a wide range of different beliefs.

Paranormal beliefs may satisfy a psychological need...

French and Kerman found a relationship between childhood trauma, fantasy proneness and paranormal beliefs. Paranormal beliefs may provide a necessary 'illusion' of control.

Schizotypy

Irwin and Green found a link between paranormal belief and *schizotypy* (e.g. the tendency to have hallucinations and disordered thinking).

Is belief a sign of mental disorder?...

The link with schizotypy implies that belief in the paranormal is in some sense pathological. However, this isn't very surprising because the characteristics of schizotypy overlap with the characteristics of paranormal beliefs. So people who gain high scores on scales for paranormal beliefs are likely to get high scores on tests for schizotypy.

Some research has found a positive correlation between paranormal belief and mental health, e.g. self-actualisation (Clarke).

Suggestibility

Suggestibility is the inclination to accept the suggestions of others, e.g. to be easily hypnotised.

Since some paranormal phenomena are the result of deceptions (e.g. from psychic mediums), suggestible people might be more likely to believe.

Hergovich found a positive correlation between suggestibility and score on a paranormal belief scale.

There is supporting research evidence...

Clancy *et al.* found that people who claimed to have experienced an alien abduction were also found to be more suggestible, in particular they were more susceptible to false memories when compared to people who hadn't had such experiences.

It may be that some reports of paranormal experiences are actually false memories...

Paranormal experiences and beliefs may occur because people who have strong imaginations (e.g. those who are more creative) create a memory of events, such as sightings of UFOs, and then they believe them to be true, i.e. they hold a false memory.

Creative personality

Thalbourne found a correlation between creative personality and paranormal beliefs in a meta-analysis of 15 studies. People who are more creative may be more able to make links between unrelated items, a characteristic that may underlie paranormal experiences.

There is evidence to support this...

French and Wilson gave 100 participants a questionnaire. Four of the five items were about real events but one was fictitious (it was a faked CCTV recoding of the first Bali bombing – there was no recording), 36% of the participants claimed that they had seen the recording that was in fact fictitious. These participants had scored higher on a test of paranormal belief and experience.

Other personality factors

Believers are also found to have:
- *External locus of control* (e.g. Allen and Lester).
- *Field dependence*, such people may rely less on detail (Hergovich).
- *Higher sensation seeking*, also linked to extraversion (Kumar *et al.*).
- *Dissociation* (separation of feelings and thoughts into different streams of consciousness) (Gow *et al.*).

It may be that only some forms of psi correlate positively...

Wolfradt found that superstition correlates positively with an external locus of control, whereas psychokinesis correlates negatively. This might explain why some studies (e.g. Davies and Kirkby) have found a positive correlation between an internal locus of control and paranormal belief.

On the other hand...

Groth-Marnat and Pegden found that superstition was associated with an internal locus of control, and an external locus of control was associated with spirituality and precognition subscales.

Psychic healing and psychic mediumship

Research into psychic healing

Explanations

- *Energy fields* – Therapeutic touch (TT) works by detecting and re-aligning a patient's aura (energy field) without touching their body.
- *Anxiety reduction* – Beneficial effects of contact with a sympathetic person. Social support is known to reduce stress and anxiety, and enhance the effectiveness of the immune system (e.g. Kiecolt-Glaser).
- *Placebo effect* – Real, measurable improvement occurs as a result of believing that an effective treatment has been received.

Research studies

- *Therapeutic touch and prayer* – Wirth compared wound healing in patients treated with TT or with no treatment. The patients were not aware of the treatment they received (eliminating placebo effects). Patients treated with TT healed faster.
- *Therapeutic touch tested through a screen* – TT practitioners should be able to detect the energy field of a person's hand but when 21 TT practioners were tested by placing their hands through two holes in a screen, they correctly identified another hand only 44% of the time (Rosa et al.).
- *The effects of prayer* – Wirth found that infertile women were twice as likely to become pregnant if they were prayed for by a Christian stranger than those who weren't prayed for (Cha et al.).

Belief in psychic healing may explain some of its success…

Lyvers et al. recruited 20 volunteers suffering from chronic back pain and randomly assigned them to a control group or a group who received treatment from a psychic healer. They found no evidence for psychic healing but did find evidence that believers were more likely to think they had received healing benefits.

There is a lack of support for the placebo effect…

Benson et al. studied patients recovering from cardiac surgery. One group of patients acted as a control and the other two groups were told prayers were being said for them. In fact only one group was prayed for; the other group were the placebo group (they expected benefits). There was no benefit from the placebo effect. In fact the only group to suffer more complications were those who were prayed for (i.e. there was actually a negative effect).

There are criticisms of the study by Rosa et al. …

TT supporters point out that the study was designed by a 9-year-old girl, although it was published in a reputable journal.

TT supporters have also claimed the study was invalid because the experimenter was not ill, which might affect their aura (Hines).

However…

Long et al. repeated the study with ordinary people (not TT practitioners) and a distance of only 3 inches. The results were better than chance, possibly because of body heat. Glickman and Gracely controlled body heat and the results were just at the chance level, suggesting body heat, not an aura, is the explanation.

There are criticisms of Wirth and his research…

Various issues question the scientific honesty of the research:

- The study of wound healing has not been replicated (Wirth et al.).
- Researchers who wished to discuss his research have failed to be able to contact Wirth (Solfvin et al.).
- One of the authors of the prayer study withdrew his name saying he had nothing to do with the study and Wirth's co-author (Cha) has been accused of plagiarism in another journal.

Nevertheless, worryingly, the study continues to be cited and taken as evidence for the power of prayer (Flamm).

Research into psychic mediumship

Explanations

- *Sensitivity to cues* – Mediums are good at picking up information (cold reading).
- *The Barnum effect* – A medium (cold reader) relies on general statements, e.g. 'I see a recent loss of life' or 'I see the letter J'. Sitters then often offer elaborations.
- *Fraud* – Mediums use complex and convincing strategies to fool their clients.

Research studies

- *Schwartz et al.* – Five mediums gave readings to two women who had recently had several bereavements. The readings were judged as 83% and 77% accurate by the two women and 36% by students.
- *Rock and Beischel* – Six mediums spoke on the phone to a sitter. They could only asked questions about a loved one. There were differences in the information collected, related to whether they had been told the loved one was alive or dead, showing their clairvoyant abilities.

The apparent success of mediums can be explained…

Roe reports that many sitters are aware of the deceptions used by mediums but nevertheless remain convinced they are genuine.

In a mock séance conducted by Wiseman et al. (see page 120) believers tended to be taken in by events even though participants knew it was fake. This suggests that belief in psychic mediumship does not require a 'real' explanation.

The research is poor in quality…

Most people are content to believe in psychic mediumship without scientific proof, so there is less motivation to conduct well-controlled research.

There is contradictory evidence…

O'Keeffe and Wiseman arranged for five mediums to give readings for five sitters. Each sitter read all of the 25 readings that were produced and rated the personal relevance of each statement. The ratings were actually lowest for the statements written about them.

There are criticisms of the study by Schwartz et al. …

The accuracy of the medium's statements was demonstrated by comparing the ratings given by the sitters and students – however since the statements would have been geared towards older women who had experienced deaths in recent years it is not surprising that the students judged the statements as less accurate.

Out-of-body and near-death experience

Research into out-of-body experience (OOBE)

Out-of-body experience is the sensation of being awake and seeing your own body from a location outside your physical body. About 15–20% of people have experienced an OOBE (Blackmore).

Explanations

- *Paranormal explanations* – OOBEs due to a separation between mind and body, seen as evidence of a soul.
- *Biological explanations* – We usually view the world as if we were behind our eyes. If sensory input breaks down the brain tries to reconstruct the visual field using memory and imagination (Blackmore).

Research studies

- *Naturally occurring OOBEs* – Green studied 400 cases: 20% involved another body ('parasomatic' rather than 'asomatic'), 25% linked to psychological stress, 12% occurred during sleep.
- *Artificially induced OOBEs* – Alvarado reviewed lab studies where OOBEs were induced by, e.g. relaxation, hypnosis. The participants were asked to identify objects that were out of sight of their physical body. One person (Miss Z) was able to read out a randomly selected five-digit number placed in another room (Tart).
- *Biological studies* – Blanke et al. induced OOBEs accidentally by stimulating the *temporal-parietal junction* (TPJ) in a woman who suffered epilepsy in that region. Transcranial magnetic stimulation of the TPJ also results in OOBEs.

The evidence doesn't support paranormal explanations…

Alvardo's review did not find evidence that the parasomatic body had physically moved out of the physical body. Exceptional cases can be explained in terms of suspect methodology, e.g. the subject might have seen the target object prior to the test.

There is evidence that supports biological explanations…

Ehrssen demonstrated an OOBE by scrambling a person's visual and touch sensations using video displays so a person saw their own back as if they were sitting behind themselves.

Difficulties with studying OOBEs…

It is difficult to study natural OOBEs because they occur without predictability.

Even if a researcher was present, the OOBE would cease as soon as the subject reported it.

Therefore most research is conducted on artificially-induced OOBEs in lab settings which are not equivalent to natural OOBEs (Holden et al.).

Individual differences…

OOBEs are reported more often by individuals who are paranormal believers (Irwin), more fantasy prone, score higher on hypnotisability and on dissociation (ability to separate different aspects of conscious activity) (Gow et al., Irwin). Such characteristics go some way to explaining why such individuals have OOBEs.

There is no evidence to link OOBEs with mental illness, although OOBEs may make people feel they are losing their mind (Gabbard and Twemlow).

Research into near-death experience (NDE)

Near-death experience occurs when a person is close to death, or after fainting or in stressful situations.

Explanations

- *Psychological explanations*, e.g. viewing NDEs as a spiritual experience.
- *Endorphins* (released at times of pain or stress) lead to feelings of euphoria and detachment (Carr, 1982).
- *Hypoxia* (lack of oxygen) occurs, e.g. during cardiac arrest or fainting. This hypoxia might cause REM sleep intrusions that create a mixed sleep/awake state that could, like OOBEs, disrupt the integration of sensory information.
- *Flood of glutamate* – Brain reacts to hypoxia by creating a blockade to prevent neuronal death. This blockade is the NDE.

Research studies

- *Naturally-occurring NDEs* – Ring interviewed 100 people with NDEs, 60% of survivors reported a sense of peace, 33% reported OOBEs, a few said they had experienced a kind of 'life review'.
- *Nelson et al.* found that people with NDEs were more likely to experience REM intrusions.
- *Artificially induced NDEs* – Jansen found that the drug ketamine can produce the classic symptoms of NDEs, and triggers the same blockade as glutamate.

There is support for a psychological component…

The fact that NDEs are not experienced by all near-death patients means that the experience is separate from the near-death event and implicates a psychological component.

There is support for a spiritual component…

van Lommel et al. studied 344 cardiac survivors. Those who had an NDE regarded it as a spiritual experience.

However…

Just because it is a spiritual *experience* doesn't mean that it is caused by spiritual factors.

There are cultural differences…

Augustine found differences (e.g. in India NDEs sometimes involve encounters with Hindu figures) and there are similarities (e.g. going through a tunnel). Suggests that both psychological and biological factors involved.

Early studies may have lacked appropriate controls…

Interviewer bias may have affected the data collected, e.g. Moody reported NDEs as wonderful experiences, whereas more recent research has found that they are frightening.

Reductionism…

The reductionist view is that the experience of mind is the product of chemical processes. However, if mental experiences occur when the brain is inactive (e.g. in a NDE), this shows the mind is separate from the physical body (Parnia).

On the other hand…

Jansen says the real reductionism comes from those who attempt to 'draw a mystical shroud' over NDE, ignoring scientific explanations.

Research and scientific methods

Division A The application of scientific method in psychology

Major features of science
Validating new knowledge

Division B Designing psychological investigations

Selection and application of appropriate research methods
Reliability, validity and sampling
Ethical considerations in research

Division C Data analysis and reporting on investigations

Inferential analysis, probability and significance
Descriptive and inferential statistics
Analysis and interpretation of qualitative data
Designing and reporting investigations

Specification

This section builds on the knowledge and skills developed at AS level.

Psychological research and scientific method	
The application of scientific method in psychology	• The major features of science, including replicability, objectivity, theory construction, hypothesis testing, the use of empirical methods. • Validating new knowledge and the role of peer review.
Designing psychological investigations	• Selection and application of appropriate research methods. • Implications of sampling strategies, for example, bias and generalising. • Issues of reliability, including types of reliability, assessment of reliability, improving reliability. • Assessing and improving validity (internal and external). • Ethical considerations in design and conduct of psychological research.
Data analysis and reporting on investigations	• Appropriate selection of graphical representations. • Probability and significance, including the interpretation of significance and Type 1/Type 2 errors. • Factors affecting choice of statistical test, including levels of measurement. • The use of inferential analysis, including Spearman's Rho, Mann–Whitney, Wilcoxon, chi-square. • Analysis and interpretation of qualitative data. • Conventions of reporting on psychological investigations.

The application of scientific method in psychology

The major features of science

Empirical methods

Information is gained through direct observation or experiment rather than by reasoned argument or unfounded beliefs. This is important because the only way we know that things are true is through direct testing, i.e. empirical evidence.

Objectivity

Scientists' expectations should not affect results.

In order to achieve this research is conducted under controlled conditions.

In an experiment the independent variable is controlled to demonstrate causal relationships.

Replication

The validity of any study is demonstrated by exact replication. If the outcome is the same, this affirms the original results.

Theory construction

Science aims to use facts to construct theories, which will help us understand and predict the natural phenomena around us.

Hypothesis testing

A good theory must be able to generate testable expectations. These are stated in the form of a hypothesis.

If a scientist fails to find support for a hypothesis, then the theory requires modification:

- *Induction* (reasoning from particular to general).
  Observation → hypothesis → test → theory
- *Deduction* (reasoning from general to particular).
  Theory → hypothesis → test

Hypotheses can only be proved through falsification. Popper argued that no number of sightings of white swans can prove the theory that all swans are white, whereas the sighting of just one black swan will disprove it.

Scientific research is desirable…

Early psychologists sought to create a science of psychology to enable them to produce verifiable knowledge.

Psychology may share the goals of other sciences but…

Simply using the scientific method may be just 'dressing up', i.e. psychologists may be using the technical language of science but they are not engaged in real scientific research (Miller).

Perhaps at best psychology is a pseudoscience – but a dangerous one because psychologists can then claim their discoveries are fact (see pseudoscience on page 116).

Psychological research lacks objectivity and control…

In psychology the object of study reacts to the researcher, leading to problems that reduce validity, e.g. investigator bias and demand characteristics.

However, the *uncertainty principle* describes the fact that, even in physics, it is not possible to measure something without changing its 'behaviour' (Heisenberg).

Are the goals of science appropriate for psychology?…

The psychiatrist R.D. Laing, in discussing the causes of schizophrenia, claimed that science was inappropriate for psychology. Science takes a nomothetic approach, aiming to make generalisations, whereas Laing thought an idiographic approach was more appropriate to studying human behaviour.

This is supported by unsuccessful psychological explanations…

Psychological approaches to treating mental illness that are based on scientific principles have had only modest success, suggesting that the goals of science may not be appropriate.

Qualitative research…

Some psychologists advocate more subjective, qualitative methods of conducting research, but these methods can still be validated.

For example, data from interviews, qualitative content analysis, observations, etc. can be triangulated – the findings from these different methods are compared with each other as a means of verifying them and making them more objective.

Validating new knowledge

Peer review refers to the assessment of scientific work by others who are experts in the same field. The intention of peer review is to ensure that research is of high quality.

The *Parliamentary Office of Science and Technology* suggests that peer review may be used for:

- *Allocation of research funding* – Government and charitable bodies who fund research need to decide which research is likely to be worthwhile.
- *Publication of research in scientific journals and books* – Peer review aims to prevent incorrect or faulty data entering the public domain. Prior to peer review research was simply published and the burden of proof lay with opponents.
- *Assessing the research rating of university departments* – All University science departments are expected to conduct research, which is assessed in terms of quality (*research excellence framework*, REF). Future funding for the department depends on receiving good ratings from a peer review.

Unachievable ideal…

It isn't always possible to find an appropriate expert with the same specialist interest to review research.

Anonymity…

Anonymity allows a reviewer to feel they can be honest, but may result in dishonesty, e.g. if a person wishes to settle an old score. Some journals now use open reviewing.

Publication bias…

Peer review tends to favour the publication of positive results, possibly because editors want research with important implications to increase their journal's standing.

Preserves the status quo…

Peer review results in a preference for research that does not challenge existing theory.

Cannot deal with already published research…

Once research has been published it continues to be used even if later found to be fraudulent (e.g. Marc Hauser's research on cognitive abilities of monkeys).

An alternative…

Online blogs and journals invite comments from any reader as a means of peer reviewing.

Chapter 16

The application of scientific method in psychology	Selection of appropriate research methods
Designing psychological investigations	>	Reliability, validity and sampling
Research methods	>	Data analysis and reporting on investigations	Ethical considerations in research

Selection and application of appropriate research methods

Method/technique		Nature and use	Advantages and weaknesses
Experiments In all cases there is an IV and DV. Design: repeated measures, independent groups or matched pairs.	Laboratory experiment	IV is manipulated by an experimenter to observe its effect on the DV. Laboratory experiments are highly controlled.	+ Can draw causal conclusion. + Extraneous variables minimised. + Can be easily replicated. – Contrived, tends to lack mundane realism. – Investigator bias and participant effects.
	Field experiment	More natural surroundings, IV is directly manipulated by the experimenter. Field experiments are less controlled.	+ Can draw causal conclusion. + Usually higher ecological validity. + Avoids some participant effects. – Less control. – May have demand characteristics.
	Natural experiment	IV is not directly manipulated, participants not randomly allocated.	+ Allows research where the IV can't be manipulated for ethical/practical reasons. + Enables psychologists to study 'real' problems. – Cannot demonstrate causal relationships. – Inevitably there are many extraneous variables. – Investigator and participant effects.
Studies using a correlational analysis		Co-variables examined for positive, negative or zero correlation.	+ Can be used when it is not possible to manipulate variables. + Can rule out a causal relationship. – People often misinterpret correlations. – There may be other, unknown variables.
Observational techniques Design: the use of behavioural categories, and time or event sampling.	Naturalistic observation	Everything left as normal, all variables free to vary.	+ Can study behaviour where it isn't possible to manipulate variables. + High ecological validity. – Poor control of extraneous variables. – Observer bias, low inter-observer reliability.
	Controlled observation	Some variables (e.g. the environment) controlled by the researcher.	+ Can manipulate variables to observe effects. – Less natural, reduced ecological validity. – Investigator and participant effects. – Observer bias, low inter-observer reliability.
	Content analysis (quantitative or qualitative)	Indirect observation of behaviour based on written or verbal material such as interviews or TV.	+ High ecological validity because it is based on what people do. + Can be replicated easily because sources are publicly available. – Observer bias.
Self-report techniques Design: may involve open or closed questions.	Questionnaires	Set of written questions.	+ Can be easily repeated, so lots of people can be questioned. + Respondents may be more willing to reveal personal information. + Does not require specialist administrators. – Leading questions, social desirability bias. – Biased samples.
	Interviews (structured or unstructured)	In unstructured interviews, the questions are in reply to the respondent's answers, conducted in real time.	+ More detailed information collected. + Can access unexpected information. – Social desirability bias, interviewer bias, inter-interviewer reliability, leading questions. – Requires well-trained personnel.
Case studies		Detailed study of a single individual, institution or event. Involves many different techniques e.g. interviews, psychological tests.	+ Rich, in-depth data collected. + Used to investigate unusual instances of behaviour. + Complex interactions studied. – Lacks generalisability. – May involve unreliable, retrospective recall. – Researcher may lack objectivity.
Other methods		Cross-cultural studies, meta-analysis	

Chapter 16

The application of scientific method in psychology | Selection of appropriate research methods
Designing psychological investigations > | Reliability, validity and sampling
Research methods > | Data analysis and reporting on investigations | Ethical considerations in research

Reliability, validity and sampling

Reliability

Internal reliability is a measure of the extent to which something is consistent within itself (e.g. all questions on an IQ test should be measuring the same thing).

External reliability is a measure of consistency over several different occasions.

Experimental research

Reliability refers to the ability to repeat a study and obtain the same result, i.e. replication.

Replications are conducted to test the reliability/validity of the original result – if the same result is obtained a second time this shows that the result is more likely to be legitimate (i.e. valid).

It is essential that all conditions are the same when conducting a replication, otherwise, if the results are now different, this may be due to the changed conditions rather than a lack of validity.

Observational techniques

Observations should be consistent which means that ideally two observers should produce the same record.

Assessing reliability: inter-rater (or inter-observer) reliability is a measure of the extent to which two (or more) observers agree, calculated by dividing total agreements by total number of observations. Should be at least +.80.

Reliability can be improved through training observers in the use of, e.g. coding systems.

Self-report techniques

Internal reliability can be assessed using the split-half method – compare a person's performance on two halves of a questionnaire or test, there should be a close correlation in the scores from both halves of the test.

External reliability can be assessed using the test–retest method – a person is given a questionnaire/interview/test on one occasion and then this is repeated again after a reasonable interval (e.g. a week). If the measure is reliable the outcome should be the same.

Validity

Internal validity concerns what goes on inside a study – whether the researcher did test what they intended to test.

External (ecological) *validity* concerns things outside a study – the extent to which the results of the study can be generalised to other situations and people.

Experimental research

Internal validity is affected by extraneous variables (EVs) that act as an alternative IV. If changes in the DV are due to EVs rather than the IV, then conclusions about the effect of the IV on the DV are erroneous.

External validity can be affected by the contrived and artificial nature of laboratory experiments but this is not always true, e.g. in a memory task. It is often more important to consider issues such as whether the participants were aware they were being studied (reduces the realism of their behaviour) and whether the task itself was artificial and thus was low in mundane realism (reduces the generalisability of the results).

Observational techniques

Observations will not be valid (nor reliable) if the coding system/behaviour checklist is flawed, e.g. some observations may belong in more than one category, or some behaviours may not be codeable (reduces the internal validity of the data collected).

The internal validity of observations is affected by observer bias – what someone observes is influenced by their expectations. This reduces the objectivity of observations.

Observational studies are likely to have high ecological validity because they involve more natural behaviours.

Self-report techniques

Face validity: Does the test look like it is measuring what the researcher intended to measure? For example, are the questions obviously related to the topic?

Concurrent validity: This can be established by comparing performance on a new questionnaire or test with a previously established test on the same topic.

External validity of self-report techniques is likely to be affected by biased sampling strategies.

Sampling

Sampling techniques aim to select a representative sample from a target population in order to be able to generalise from the sample to the target population. A sample that is not representative is described as biased, i.e. leaning in one direction. A biased sample means that any generalisations lack external validity.

- *Opportunity sample* – Using those people who are most easily available. It is the easiest method to use but inevitably biased because the sample is drawn from a small part of the target population.
- *Volunteer sample* – Participants are selected by asking for volunteers, this can enable access to a variety of participants (e.g. advertisement in a newspaper), making the sample more representative. However, such samples are biased because participants are, e.g. likely to be highly motivated (= volunteer bias).
- *Random sample* – Participants are selected from a target population using a random number technique (e.g. the lottery method, names from a hat or using a random number generator). This method is potentially unbiased because all members of the target population have an equal chance of selection, but may be biased if some people refuse to take part.

- *Stratified and quota samples* – Subgroups (strata) within a population are identified (e.g. different age groups). Then a predetermined number of participants are taken from each subgroup in proportion to their numbers in the target population. In stratified sampling, this is done using random techniques, in quota sampling it is done using opportunity sampling. This method is more representative than other methods because there is proportional representation of subgroups. However, opportunity sampling may lead to bias.
- *Snowball sampling* – Start with a one or two people with, e.g. eating disorders and ask them to direct you to some other people with eating disorders and so on. This is useful when conducting research with participants who are not easy to identify but is prone to bias because only a limited section of the population is contacted.

Chapter 16

The application of scientific method in psychology	Selection of appropriate research methods
Designing psychological investigations >	Reliability, validity and sampling
Research methods >	Data analysis and reporting on investigations	Ethical considerations in research

Ethical considerations in research

Ethical issues with human participants

Ethical issues

- *Informed consent* – Participants must be given comprehensive information concerning the nature and purpose of a study and their role in it, in order that they can make an informed decision about whether to participate. However, such information might reveal the study's aims and affect participants' behaviour.
- *Deception* occurs when a participant is not told the true aims of a study (e.g. what participation will involve). Thus the participants cannot give truly informed consent. However, it might be argued that some deception is relatively harmless and/or can be compensated for by adequate debriefing.
- *Right to withdraw* – Participants should have the right to withdraw from a study if they are uncomfortable in any way. However, the loss of participants may bias the study's findings.
- *Protection from harm* – Participants should not experience negative physical effects (e.g. physical injury) or negative psychological effects (e.g. lowered self-esteem). However, it may not be possible to estimate harm before conducting a study.
- *Confidentiality* – A participant's right to have personal information protected.
- *Privacy* – A person's right to control the flow of information about themselves.

Dealing with ethical issues...

Debriefing...

A post-research interview to inform participants about the true nature of a study, and restore them to the state they were in at the start of the study.

Ethical committee...

A group of people within a research institution that must approve a study before it begins. May consist of both professional and lay people.

Ethical guidelines...

Concrete, quasi-legal documents that establish principles for standard practice and competence. The current British Psychological Society (BPS) code of ethics and conduct:

- *Respect* for the dignity and worth of all persons, including standards of privacy and confidentiality and informed consent. Observations of behaviour in public are only acceptable in situations where people would reasonably expect to be observed by strangers. Intentional deception (lack of informed consent) is only acceptable when it is necessary to protect the integrity of research and when the nature of the deception is disclosed to participants at the earliest opportunity.
- *Competence* – Psychologists should maintain high standards in their professional work.
- *Responsibility* – Psychologists have responsibility to clients, the general public and the science of psychology. This includes protecting participants from physical and psychological harm, and debriefing participants to inform them of the nature and conclusions of the research, to identify and deal with any unforeseen harm.
- *Integrity* – Psychologists should be honest and accurate. This includes reporting research findings accurately and bringing instances of misconduct by other psychologists to the attention of the BPS.

Punishment...

A professional organisation, such as the BPS, punishes psychologists who contravene the code with disbarment from the society.

Socially sensitive research

'Studies in which there are potential social consequences or implications, either directly for the participants in research or the class of individuals represented by the research' (Sieber and Stanley), e.g. research on inter-racial differences in IQ.

Dealing with such issues...

Psychologists may prefer to avoid socially sensitive research, but this means that such groups may miss out on any of the potential benefits from the research (e.g. increased funding or wider public understanding). Ignoring these important areas of research would amount to an abdication of the 'social responsibilities' of the psychological researcher (i.e. their duty to society to study important areas of human behaviour).

Ethical issues with non-human animals

Reasons for conducting research using non-human animals

- Animals may be studied because they are interesting in their own right and such research may benefit animals.
- Animals offer the opportunity for greater control and objectivity in research procedures.
- Animals may be used when we can't use humans, e.g. research on the effects of emotional deprivation or on effects of drugs to treat mental illness.
- Human beings and non-human animals have sufficient of their physiology and evolutionary past in common to justify conclusions drawn from the one being applied to the other. However, it can be argued that animals tested under stressful conditions may provide very little useful information.

Is 'science at any cost' ever justifiable?...

Sentient beings...

Animals do respond to pain, but there is little evidence that animals other than primates have self-awareness. However, equally, some humans lack sentience (e.g. some brain-damaged individuals).

Speciesism...

Discrimination on the basis of species is no different to racism or sexism (Singer). However, Gray argues that we have a special duty of care to humans so speciesism is not equivalent to, for example, racism.

Animal rights...

Singer's view is a utilitarian one, i.e. if animal research can alleviate pain and suffering it is justifiable. Regan argues that there are no circumstances under which animal research is acceptable.

Existing constraints...

- The BPS publishes guidelines for research with animals.
- The UK *Animals (Scientific Procedures) Act* (1986) requires that animal research only takes place at licensed laboratories with licensed researchers on licensed projects.
- The 3 Rs (reduction, replacement, refinement) is a means of protecting animals, as the need for animal research continues, e.g. British law requires that new drugs are tested on at least two species of live mammal.

Chapter 16

Inferential analysis, probability and significance

The application of scientific method in psychology Descriptive and inferential statistics
Designing psychological investigations Analysis and interpretation of qualitative data
Research methods > Data analysis and reporting on investigations > Designing and reporting investigations

Inferential analysis, probability and significance

Significance and probability

Significance

A statistical term indicating that a set of research findings is sufficiently strong for us to accept the research hypothesis under test.

Example: Consider the ability of men and women to read maps accurately.

Null hypothesis (H_0): There is no difference between men and women in terms of their ability to read maps.

Alternative hypothesis (H_1): Women are better than men in terms of their ability to read maps.

We conduct a study and find that there is a difference between men and women in terms of their ability to read maps. There are two possible explanations for this difference:
- This pattern could have arisen by chance. Then it would be incorrect to conclude that there is a real difference between the groups. We should accept H_0.
- This pattern did *not* arise by chance and is described as *significant*. We conclude that there is a real difference between the groups. We reject H_0 and accept H_1.

Probability

A numerical measure of the likelihood or chance that certain events will occur.

We cannot be certain that an observed effect was due to chance but we can state how certain we are in terms of probability.

In general, psychologists use a probability level of $p \leq 0.05$.

This means that there is less than (or equal to) a 5% possibility that the results did occur by chance.

It also means that the likelihood of obtaining this result if the null hypothesis was true is less than (or equal to) 5%.

In other words, less than (or equal to) a 5% probability of the results occurring even if there was no real difference in the population from which the samples were drawn (ultimately we are interested in populations rather than samples).

Significance level

The level of probability (p) at which it has been agreed to reject the null hypothesis.

In some studies psychologists want to be more certain – such as when they are conducting a replication of a previous study or considering the effects of a new drug on health.

Then, researchers use a more stringent probability level, such as $p \leq 0.01$ or even $p \leq 0.001$.

In other studies a less stringent level of $p \leq 0.10$ might be used, such as when conducting research into a new topic.

Type 1 and Type 2 errors

A researcher may erroneously accept a hypothesis that is false.

Type 1 error – Rejecting a null hypothesis that is true. This is more likely to happen if the significance level is too high (lenient, e.g. 10%).

Type 2 error – Accepting a null hypothesis that is in fact not true. This is more likely to happen if the significance level is too low (stringent, e.g. 1%).

Inferential analysis

Inferential tests

Procedures for drawing logical conclusions (inferences) about the population from which samples are drawn.

In order to work out whether a difference is or is not significant we use inferential tests. Such tests permit us to work out, at a given probability, whether a pattern in the data from a study could have arisen by chance or whether the effect occurred because there is a real difference/correlation in the populations from which the samples were drawn.

Different inferential tests are used for different research designs, for example:
- Spearman's *rho*: correlation, data is ordinal or better.
- Chi-square: difference or association, nominal data only.
- Mann–Whitney *U*: difference, independent groups, data is ordinal or interval.
- Wilcoxon *T*: difference, repeated measures, data is ordinal or interval.

Observed and critical values

Two values used to determine whether the results of a study occurred by chance or are significant.

The value that is calculated for any set of data is called the *observed value* (so called because it is based on the observations made). It is also sometimes called the *calculated value* – because it is calculated.

To decide if this observed (calculated) value is significant it is compared to the *critical value*, found in a table of critical values. This is the number that the observed value must reach in order for the null hypothesis to be rejected.

There are different tables of critical values for each different inferential test. To find the appropriate critical value in a table we typically need to know:
- *Degrees of freedom* (*df*) – In most cases we get this value by looking at the number of participants in the study (*N*).
- *One- or two-tailed test* – If the hypothesis was a directional hypothesis, then we use a one-tailed test, if it was non-directional we use a two-tailed test.
- *Significance level* – The researcher decides on a suitable probability, usually $p \leq 0.05$.
- *Greater or less than* – Whether the observed value needs to be greater than or less than the critical value for significance to be shown. This information is stated with each table of critical values.

Chapter 16

Inferential analysis, probability and significance

The application of scientific method in psychology

Descriptive and inferential statistics

Designing psychological investigations

Analysis and interpretation of qualitative data

Research methods > Data analysis and reporting on investigations > Designing and reporting investigations

Descriptive statistics

Measures of central tendency inform us about central (middle or average) values for a set of data.

- *Mean* – Calculated by adding up all the scores and dividing by the number of scores. It makes use of the *values* of all the data but can be unrepresentative of the data as a whole if there are extreme values. It is not appropriate for nominal data.
- *Median* – The middle value in an ordered list. It is unaffected by extreme scores because not all values are reflected in the median. It is not appropriate for nominal data.
- *Mode* – The value that is most common in a data set. It is the only method appropriate when the data are in categories, i.e. nominal data, but can be used for all kinds of data. It is not a useful way of describing data when there are several modes.

Measures of dispersion inform us about the spread of data.

- *Range* – Calculated by finding the difference between the highest and lowest score in a data set. This is easy to calculate but may be affected by extreme values.
- *Standard deviation* – Expresses the spread of the data around the mean. This is a more precise measure because all of the values of the data are taken into account. However, some characteristics of the data are not expressed, such as the influence of extreme values.

Graphs provide a means of 'eyeballing' the data and seeing the results at a glance.

- *Bar chart* – The height of the bar represents frequency. Suitable for words and numbers, i.e. all levels of measurement.
- *Scattergram* – Suitable for correlational data, a dot or cross is shown for each pair of values. If the dots form a pattern going from bottom left to top right this indicates a positive correlation, whereas top left to bottom right suggests a negative correlation. If there is no detectable pattern there is a zero correlation.

Levels of measurement

When deciding which test to use you may need to identify the level of measurement that was used.

- *Nominal* –The data are in separate categories, e.g. grouping your class into people who are tall, medium or short.
- *Ordinal* – Data are ordered in some way, e.g. lining your classmates up in order of height. The 'difference' between each item is not the same.
- *Interval* – Data are measured using units of equal intervals, e.g. when counting correct answers or measuring your classmates' height.
- *Ratio* – There is a true zero point as in most measures of physical quantities.

Inferential statistics

1. Selecting the right test

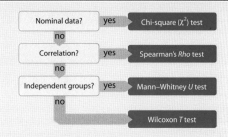

2. Justifying your choice

Below is a variety of possible justifications that could be used in an exam question. In each case, full reference to the data has been made, as well mentioning other important criteria for deciding which test to use. In an exam question we must shape our justification to fit the particular scenario presented.

Spearman's rho

A test of correlation is needed as the hypothesis predicted a correlation. The data involved ratings made by participants that are ordinal data. This means we should use Spearman's rho (test of correlation, ordinal data).

Chi-squared

As the data have been put into categories, they are classified as nominal data. The results are independent in each cell, and the expected frequencies in each cell are greater than 4. The appropriate inferential test to use is therefore a chi-squared test (test of association, independent groups, nominal data).

Mann–Whitney

A test of difference is required because the hypothesis predicts that there will be a difference between the two groups. The design is independent groups as participants were allocated to one of two treatment groups, and the data were scores on a test (ordinal data). Therefore the Mann–Whitney test is suitable (test of difference, independent groups, ordinal data).

Wilcoxon

A test of difference is required because the hypothesis predicts that there will be a difference between the two conditions. The design is repeated measures as all the participants were tested twice. The data were scores on a memory test, which are interval data. Therefore a Wilcoxon test was chosen (test of difference, related groups, interval data).

3. Stating conclusions

- State the observed value.
- Say whether it is greater than or less than the critical value.
- State whether the null hypothesis can be rejected or must be accepted.
- State the hypothesis you are accepting.

Analysis and interpretation of qualitative data

Summarising qualitative data

Qualitative data is difficult to summarise. Quantitative data can be readily summarised with measures of central tendency and measures of dispersion, and also with the use of graphs.

Qualitative data is summarised by identifying repeated themes.

Inductive or deductive

Most qualitative analysis aims to be inductive or 'bottom-up' – the categories ('themes') that emerge are based in the data. The categories/themes may lead to new theories (called 'emergent theories').

A less common approach to the analysis of qualitative data is a deductive or 'top down' one, where the researcher starts with preselected categories/themes. Such categories are likely to be generated by previous theories/research studies. The researcher would aim to see if the data are consistent with the previous theoretical viewpoint.

An iterative process

Qualitative analysis is a very lengthy process. The data are worked through repeatedly (iterations). The main intention is to impose some kind of order on the data and ensure that the 'order' represents the participants' perspective.

1. Read and re-read the data, making no notes, to try to understand the meaning.
2. Break data into meaningful units, each with a particular meaning.
3. Assign a code or label to each unit. If using a top-down approach the code will be determined by pre-existing categories.
4. Combine simple codes into larger themes.
5. Check the emergent categories by using the scheme to code a new set of data. They should fit the data well.
6. Conclusions can be drawn, including new theories.

Validity and reflexivity

One real world, or not – The traditional approach in psychology claims there is one 'real' world and quantitative research seeks to discover that reality or 'truth' – validity is a measure of the extent to which that has been achieved.

The qualitative approach denies the existence of any one real world. It aims to view phenomena from the perspective of those who experience it.

Subjective bias – The process of analysis depends on the researcher's perceptions. The term *reflexivity* is used to describe the extent to which the process of research reflects a researcher's values and thoughts.

In order to enhance the scientific nature of qualitative research this inevitable subjective bias must be recognised. Instead of trying to minimise or remove subjectivity, this is dealt with by acknowledging that the subjective nature is part of the research itself.

Demonstrating validity – The validity of qualitative research findings may be demonstrated using triangulation, comparing the results from a variety of different studies of the same thing or person. The studies are likely to have used different methodologies. If the results agree this supports their validity.

If the results differ then this can lead to further research to enhance our understanding.

Comparing quantitiative and qualitative data

Qualitative data

Advantages
- Represents the true complexities of human behaviour, rather than reducing information to a small set of variables.
- Gains access to thoughts and feelings, which may not be assessed using quantitative methods with closed questions.
- Provides rich details of what people think and say.

Weaknesses
- More difficult to detect patterns in the data because there is so much information. This may mean that simple conclusions are not possible.
- Subjective analysis can be affected by personal expectations and beliefs, (although quantitative methods may only appear to be objective but are equally affected by bias).

Quantitative data

Advantages
- Easier to analyse because data in numbers and statistics, such as measures of central tendency, can be calculated and graphs drawn.
- Produces neat conclusions because only a small set of variables considered.

Weaknesses
- Oversimplifies reality and human experience (statistically significant but humanly insignificant).

hapter 16

The application of scientific method in psychology | Inferential analysis, probability and significance
Designing psychological investigations | Descriptive and inferential statistics
| Analysis and interpretation of qualitative data

esearch methods > Data analysis and reporting on investigations > Designing and reporting investigations

Design and report your own study

Design involves decisions about research aims/hypotheses, research method, target population, sampling method and materials. Also issues related to validity, reliability and ethics. Actual procedural detail needs to be identified and piloted. Finally decide what statistics to use.

Report

Abstract – Summary of study covering aims/hypothesis, method/procedures, results and conclusions.

Introduction/Aim – Review previous research (theories/studies). State research prediction(s) and/or a hypothesis/es.

Method – Provide enough information for replication. Include details of participants (the sample), testing environment, procedures, instructions and debrief.

Results – Descriptive statistics (tables, averages and graphs) and inferential statistics. State conclusions.

Discussion – Summarise results, explain relationship between the results and past research findings. Consider problems with the methodology, implications for psychological theory, real-world applications, and suggestions for future research.

References – Full details of journal articles or books.

Additional research methods terms

Cohort effects occur because group of participants that has unique characteristics because of time-specific experiences during their development, such as growing up during the Second World War. This can affect both *cross-sectional studies* (because one group is not comparable with another) and *longitudinal studies* (because the group studied is not typical).

Control condition/group The condition (in a repeated measures design) or group (in an independent groups design) that provides a baseline measure of behaviour without the experimental treatment (IV), so that the effect of the experimental treatment may be assessed.

Correlation coefficient A number between −1 and +1 that tells us how closely the co-variables in a correlational analysis are related.

Counterbalancing An experimental technique used to overcome order effects. Counterbalancing ensures that each condition is tested first or second in equal amounts.

Covert observations Observing people without their knowledge, e.g. using one-way mirrors. Knowing that your behaviour is being observed is likely to alter your behaviour.

Critical value The value that a test statistic must reach in order for the null hypothesis to be rejected.

Cross-sectional study One group of participants of a young age is compared with another, older group of participants, with a view to investigating the effect of age on the behaviour in question.

Dependent variable (DV) A measurable outcome of the action of the *independent variable* in an experiment.

Experimental realism The extent to which participants become involved in an experiment and are less influenced by cues about how to behave.

Experimenter effect See investigator effect (below).

Hawthorne effect The tendency for participants to alter their behaviour merely as a result of knowing that they are being observed.

Independent variable (IV) An event that is directly manipulated by an experimenter in order to test its effect on another variable – the *dependent variable* (DV).

Investigator effect Anything that the investigator does which has an effect on a participant's performance in a study, other than what was expected. This includes investigator/experimenter bias.

Longitudinal study Observation of behaviour over a long period of time, possibly looking at the effects of age on a particular behaviour (such as moral development) by repeatedly testing/interviewing a group of participants at regular intervals.

Operationalised Providing variables in a form that can be easily tested.

Order effect In a repeated measures design, an extraneous variable arising from the order in which conditions are presented, e.g. a *practice effect* or *fatigue effect*.

Participant variables Characteristics of individual participants (such as age, intelligence, etc.) that might influence the outcome of a study.

Peer review The practice by academic journals and research assessments of using scientific experts to assess other scientific experts.

Pilot study A small-scale trial of a study run to test any aspects of the design, with a view to making improvements.

Presumptive consent A method of dealing with lack of informed consent or deception, by asking a group of people who are similar to the participants whether they would agree to take part in a study. If this group of people consents to the procedures in the proposed study, it is presumed the real participants would have agreed.

Quasi-experiments Studies that are 'almost' experiments (e.g. natural experiment) but lack one or more features of a true experiment, such as full experimenter control over the IV or *random allocation* of participants to conditions. Quasi-experiments cannot therefore claim to demonstrate causal relationships.

Role play A controlled observation in which participants are asked to imagine how they would behave in certain situations and act out the part. This method has the advantage of permitting the study of certain behaviours that might be unethical to study or difficult to find in the real world.

Single blind A type of research design in which the participant is not aware of the research aims or of which condition of the experiment they are receiving. *See also* double blind

Situational variables Factors in the environment that could affect the DV, such as noise, time of day or the behaviour of an investigator.

Structured interview Any interview in which the questions are decided in advance.

Structured (systematic) observations An observer uses various 'systems' to organise observations, such as behavioural categories and sampling procedures. Unstructured observations are when an observer records all relevant behaviour but has no system. This technique may be chosen because the behaviour to be studied is largely unpredictable.

Systematic sample A method of obtaining a representative sample by selecting every fifth or tenth person. This can be a random sample if the first person is selected using a random method and then every 5th or 10th person is selected.

Zero correlation In a correlation co-variables are not linked at all.

Glossary

Page numbers are provided for most terms, except those that are common throughout the book

Acculturation effect Adopting the characteristics and behaviours of the surrounding culture (particularly among non-natives). Page 40

ACTH (adrenocorticotropic hormone) A hormone released by the pituitary gland, which stimulates the adrenal glands. Page 8

Adaptive Any physical or psychological characteristic that enhances an individual's survival and reproduction, and is thus likely to be naturally selected. Pages 9, 13, 18, 20, 38, 42, 43, 45, 50, 62, 77, 83, 89, 95, 105, 110, 119

Adrenaline A hormone associated with arousal of the autonomic nervous system, and also a neurotransmitter. Pages 89, 91

Agonistic buffering Refers to situations where a male (e.g. a baboon) carries an infant as a signal to inhibit aggression from dominant animals, thus allowing them to approach individuals to which they normally have no access. Page 63

Agonist A drug that binds to and alters the activity of a receptor, as distinct from an antagonist drug. Page 77

Agoraphobia A fear of being in places or situations from which escape might be difficult (or embarrassing). Pages 88, 89, 90, 91

Alternative hypothesis A testable statement about the relationship between two variables. Page 128

Amphetamines A group of drugs that increase focus and wakefulness by increasing levels of adrenaline, serotonin and dopamine in the brain. Pages 35, 77

Amygdala A group of nuclei in the brain forming part of the limbic system and involved in emotional processing and memory. Pages 20, 42, 89

Anomalous experience An umbrella term for experiences that do not currently have a scientific explanation. Page 116

ANS (autonomic nervous system) Governs the body's involuntary activities (e.g. stress, digestion, heart beat) and is self-regulating (autonomous). Page 89

Antagonist A drug that binds to a receptor but which does not alter the activity of the receptor, as distinct from an agonist. Pages 77, 114

Antipsychotic drugs Medication used with schizophrenia and other psychotic conditions. Pages 35, 77, 79, 80

Anxious-ambivalent (resistant) attachment A form of insecure attachment where an infant feels uneasy about strangers and about exploring their environment, even with their attachment figure present. The infant will be ambivalent when the mother returns (seeking closeness but also rejecting when approached). Page 105

Appearance–reality distinction The ability (or inability) to understand that what something looks like (its appearance) does not represent how things really are (reality). Page 68

Attachment disorder A disorder characterised by an inability to interact or relate to others, associated with a lack of early attachments. Page 29

Attachment style The characteristic way an individual responds in relationships, such as being trusting and close (secure attachment) or wary and sometimes rejecting (insecure attachment). Pages 105, 106

Attribution theory or **attributional style** An account of how, or the manner by which, we explain the causes of our own and other people's behaviour to ourselves. Pages 14, 84

Attrition The loss of participants from a study over time, which is likely to leave a biased sample or a sample that is too small. Page 86

Autism A mental disorder that usually appears in early childhood and typically involves avoidance of social contact, abnormal language, and so-called 'stereotypic' or bizarre behaviours. Pages 50, 72, 73, 74, 95

Barnum effect Tendency for people to accept general statements (Barnum statements) as an accurate description of themselves. Page 121

Basal ganglia 'Basal' refers to the fact this region is found in the 'basement' of the brain. Pages 45, 95

Behavioural categories Dividing a target behaviour (such as attachment or sociability) into a subset of behaviours. Pages 125, 131

Behaviourist An approach to explaining behaviour which holds the view that all behaviour can be explained in terms of learning (i.e. nurture or environment), referring only to the behaviours themselves rather than any internal mechanisms – thus 'behaviourism'. Pages 74, 90, 98, 119

Beta-blockers (BBs) Decrease anxiety by reducing the activity of adrenaline and noradrenaline, which are part of the sympathomedullary response to stress. Pages 89, 91

Biological 'preparedness' The ability of some organisms to associate significant (i.e. in terms of survival) combinations of stimuli, responses and reinforcers. Pages 43, 60, 89, 90

Bipolar disorder A mental illness that includes both manic and depressive episodes. Mania is characterised by an elevated and expansive mood, delusions, overactivity and impulsive behaviour. Page 76

Bottom-up Processing which starts from the base elements of the system (the physical stimulus or data itself), as distinct from top-down processing. Pages 17, 18

Broca's area An area in the frontal lobe of the forebrain, usually in the left hemisphere, related to speech production. Page 74

Caudate nucleus A region of the brain located in the basal gangia and an important part of the brain's learning and memory system. Pages 95, 97

CBT *see* cognitive-behavioural therapy

Circadian rhythm A pattern of behaviour that occurs or recurs approximately every 24 hours, such as the sleep–wake cycle. Pages 8, 9, 10

Circular reactions A feature of the sensorimotor stage in Piaget's theory, to describe the repetitive actions which enable an infant to learn new schema linking sensory and motor experiences. Page 68

Classical conditioning Learning that occurs through association. A neutral stimulus is paired with an unconditioned stimulus, resulting in a new stimulus-response (S-R) link. Pages 24, 90, 96

Clinical Refers to medical practice, thus a non-clinical population refers to a group of people with no incidence of the target illness, a sub-clinical population refers to a group of people who have some of the symptoms of the target illness but not enough to be diagnosed with the disorder. Pages 40, 88, 89, 96, 106

Clinician A health professional, such as a doctor, psychiatrist, psychologist or nurse, who deals with the diagnosis and treatment of mental disorder. Pages 88, 94, 114

Closed questions Questions that have a range of answers from which respondents select one; produces quantitative data. Pages 125, 130

Cognitive style An individual's characteristic way of thinking. Page 90

Cognitive therapy (CT) A form of psychotherapy which attempts to change a client's thoughts and beliefs as a way of treating maladaptive behaviour. It differs from cognitive-behavioural therapy because the latter involves some element of behavioural techniques. Pages 80, 84, 114

Cognitive-behavioural therapy (CBT) An approach to the treatment of mental disorders combining both cognitive and behavioural approaches. Pages 80, 86, 90, 92, 97, 108, 109, 114

Coincidence When two events happen at about the same time (they are co-incidents). Page 118

Collectivist A culture characterised by the extent to which things are shared – groups live and work together sharing tasks, belongings and valuing interdependence. Japan and Israel are examples of collectivist societies. Pages 30, 72

Comorbidity The presence of two or more coexisting morbid conditions or diseases. Pages 76, 82, 83, 88, 94, 95

Compound conditioning Where an unconditioned stimulus is associated with two or more neutral stimuli so that either will produce the conditioned response. Page 62

Concordance rate A measure of similarity (usually expressed as a percentage) between two individuals or sets of individuals on a given trait. Pages 15, 65, 77, 83, 89, 95

Concurrent validity A means of establishing validity by comparing an existing a test/questionnaire with the one you are interested in. Pages 82, 88, 126

Conditioned A response that has been created through classical or operant conditioning. Pages 19, 89, 98

Conditioned response (CR) In classical conditioning, the response elicited by the conditioned stimulus, i.e. a new association has been learned so that the neutral stimulus (NS) now produces the unconditioned response (UCR), now called the CR. Pages 60, 90

Conditioned stimulus (CS) In classical conditioning, the neutral stimulus (NS) after it has been paired with the unconditioned stimulus. The NS now elicits the unconditioned response UCR, now called a conditioned response (CR). Pages 60, 90

Confederate An individual in a study who is not a real participant and has been instructed how to behave by the investigator/experimenter. May act as the independent variable. Page 119

Configural process Using the relationship between separate features (i.e. the configuration) to help in recognising an object or a face. Page 22

Conservation The ability to distinguish between reality and appearance, e.g. to understand that quantity is not changed even when a display is transformed. Pages 52, 68

Construct validity A means of assessing the validity or trueness of a psychological test by demonstrating the extent to which performance on the test measures an identified underlying construct. Page 88

Content validity A means of assessing the internal validity of a questionnaire or psychological test. It aims to demonstrate that the content (e.g. questions) of the test/measurement represents the area of interest. Page 82

Contingent regulations The relation between a behaviour and what has come before and/or after the consequences. Page 70

Cortisol A hormone produced by the adrenal gland that is associated with stress. Pages 7, 10, 35, 50, 83, 108

Counterconditioning Being taught a new association that runs counter to the original association, thus removing the original association. Page 92

Covert desensitisation Using the principles of systematic desensitisation but only imagining the hierarchy of situations from least to most fearful. Page 92

CR *See* conditioned response

Critical period A limited window in biological development during which certain characteristics develop. Page 45

Cross-cultural research A type of natural experiment in which the IV is different cultural practices and the DV is a behaviour such as attachment. Pages 20, 30, 46, 72, 125

CS *See* conditioned stimulus

Cuckoldry The reproductive cost inflicted on a man as a result of his partner's infidelity. The consequence of cuckoldry is that the man might unwittingly invest his resources in offspring that are not his own. Page 37

Culture-bound syndrome Any form of abnormal behaviour that is found only in certain cultures and does not conform to the Western classification of mental disorders. Page 46

D_2 dopamine receptor One of at least five different dopamine receptor subtypes. A receptor is located at the receiving end of a synapse to receive neurotransmitters being transmitted across the synapse. Pages 77, 79

Decentration The ability to focus on more than one aspect of a problem, overcoming the problem of centration (thinking focused on one aspect of a problem, e.g. height, and ignoring other features, e.g. width). Page 68

Defence mechanism In psychoanalytic theory, the strategies used by the ego to defend itself against anxiety, such as repression, denial and projection. Pages 96, 119, 120

Degrees of freedom (*df*) The number of values which are free to vary given that the overall total values are known. Page 128

Delayed sleep phase syndrome A disorder where a person's major sleep episode is delayed by two or more hours of the desired bedtime. Pages 9, 11

Demand characteristic A cue that makes participants unconsciously aware of the aims of a study or how the researchers expect the participants to behave. This may act as a confounding variable. Pages 34, 68, 101, 132

Depressive attributional style An individual's preferred method of explaining what has caused their own or another person's behaviour. Page 84

Descriptive statistics Methods of summarising a data set such as measures of central tendency and dispersion, and the use of graphs. Page 129

Determinist The view that an individual's behaviour is shaped or controlled by internal or external forces rather than an individual's will to do something. Pages 8, 29, 45, 46, 49, 50, 51, 56

Diathesis-stress model The view that individuals inherit a susceptibility for a disorder (diathesis) which develops only if the individual is exposed to certain environmental conditions (stress). Pages 14, 15, 44, 45, 83, 84, 89, 90

Directional hypothesis States the direction of the predicted difference between two conditions or two groups of participants. Page 128

Discovery learning Learning through personal enquiry and constructing your own knowledge, rather than being told the answers to questions and presented with pre-constructed categories. Page 70

Dissociative identity disorder Characterised by the presence of at least two clear personality states (called alters) in the individual, which may have different reactions and emotions. Page 76

Dopamine A neurotransmitter produced in the brain, involved in sexual desire and the sensation of pleasure. Unusually high levels of dopamine can be associated with schizophrenia. Pages 35, 45, 46, 77, 78, 79, 89, 91, 95, 108, 111, 114, 118, 119

Double blind Neither the participant nor the experimenter is aware of the research aims and other important details, and thus have no expectations. Pages 85, 131

DSM (The Diagnostic and Statistical Manual of Mental Disorders) This is a classification system of mental disorders published by the American Psychiatric Association. It contains typical symptoms of each disorder and guidelines for clinicians to make a diagnosis. The most recent version is DSM-IV-TR. Pages 76, 88

DZ (dizygotic) twins Non-identical twins formed from two fertilised eggs (or zygotes). Pages 15, 36, 65, 77, 83, 89, 95

Ecological Factors in the environment. Page 56

Ecological approach Explanations based on observations of animals in their natural environment. Pages 18, 126

Ecological validity A form of external validity, concerning the ability to generalise a research effect beyond the particular setting in which it is demonstrated, to other settings. Ecological validity is established by representativeness (mundane realism) and generalisability (to other settings). Page 125

ECT *See* electroconvulsive therapy

EEA (environment of evolutionary adaptation) The environment to which a species is adapted and the set of selection pressures that operated at this time. For humans, this is thought to be the African savannah approximately 2 million years ago. Pages 50, 105

EEG (electroencephalograph) A method of detecting activity in the living brain, electrodes are attached to a person's scalp to record general levels of electrical activity. Pages 8, 11, 15

Effect size A measure of the strength of the relationship between two variables. Page 117

Ego Part of Freud's conception of the structure of the personality, the ego is driven by the reality principle, which makes the child accommodate to the demands of the environment. Pages 78, 90

Egocentric Seeing things from your own viewpoint and being unaware of other possible viewpoints. Pages 68, 69, 73

Eidolic An image that represents objects in three dimensions, as if it were the real thing. The opposite is an epitomic image. Page 20

Electro-convulsive therapy (ECT) The administration of a controlled electrical current through electrodes placed on the scalp. The electrodes induce a convulsive seizure which can be effective in relieving an episode of major depression. Pages 79, 85

Empathy Being aware of and identifying with another person's feelings. Pages 72, 73, 74, 100

Empirical A method of gaining knowledge which relies on direct observation or testing. Pages 92, 116, 124

Endogenous Internal. Page 9

Endorphins Neurotransmitters released in response to pain that act as the body's natural painkiller. Page 122

Entrain The process of bringing bodily rhythms into synchronisation with an external influence. Pages 7, 8, 9, 10

Epitomic An image which extracts the basic elements, i.e. the 'epitome', or perfect example, of the object. Epitomic images are easier to draw than eidolic ones. Page 20

ESP (extrasensory perception) The ability to acquire information without the direct use of the five known physical senses. Pages 116

Event sampling An observational technique in which a count is kept of the number of times a certain behaviour (event) occurs. Page 125

Exogenous External. Page 8

Experimenter bias See investigator bias

Extraneous variables In an experiment, any variable other than the independent variable that might potentially affect the dependent variable and thereby confound the results. Pages 125, 131

Extravert/extraversion Exhibited by an individual who is outgoing and impulsive, and seeks greater excitement and more dangerous pastimes. This is possibly because they have a lower level of cortical arousal and therefore need more

stimulation to experience the same sense of excite-ment as introverts. Pages 69, 105

Face validity A means of establishing validity by considering the extent to which a test/questionnaire looks as if it is measuring what it intends to measure. Page 126

Factor analysis A statistical technique used to identify the variables that explain correlations between scores on tests of different abilities. Page 58

False belief A mistaken opinion arising from incorrect reasoning. Pages 72, 73

Falsify The attempt to prove something wrong. Pages 124

First-degree relatives Closest genetic relatives – parent, sibling, or offspring. Pages 83, 95

fMRI (functional magnetic resonance imaging) A method used to scan brain activity while a person is performing a task. It enables researchers to detect which regions of the brain are rich in oxygen and thus are active. Pages 22, 74

Frontal cortex The front (anterior) region of the cerebral cortex, containing the motor cortex and prefrontal cortex. Involved in fine motor movement and thinking. Pages 42, 95, 97

Frontal lobe A region in each hemisphere of the frontal cortex. It is located in front of (anterior to) the central sulcus and above the lateral fissure. It contains the prefrontal cortex. Pages 58, 74

GABA (Gamma-amino-butyric-acid) A neurotransmitter that regulates excitement in the nervous system, thus acting as a natural form of anxiety reducer. Pages 91, 97

Gambler's fallacy The mistaken belief that the probability of an event occurring increases or decreases depending on recent events. Pages 109, 118

Gender The psychological characteristics associated with being male or female, as distinct from 'sex' which is a biological fact.

Gender dysphoria Having negative or conflicting feelings about one's sex or gender role. Page 52

Gender identity disorder (GID) The psychiatric classification for people experiencing gender dysphoria. Page

Gene A unit of inheritance which forms part of a chromosome.

Generalised anxiety disorder An anxiety disorder that involves excessive worry about anything and everything. Page 83

Genetic engineering The deliberate manipulation of the genes of an unborn child, with the intent of making them 'better' in some way, e.g. less aggressive. Page 36

Ghrelin A hormone produced by the stomach cells, and thought to increase feelings of hunger. Page 42

Glutamate The most common excitatory neurotransmitter in the brain which is thought to be involved in learning and

memory. Excessive amounts, caused by brain injury or illness, cause neuronal damage and cell death. Page 122

Growth hormone A hormone that stimulates growth and cell reproduction. Pages 7, 8, 11

GSR (galvanic skin response) A measure of ANS activity indicating emotional arousal (increased sweatiness of the skin increases electrical conductivity). Page 89

Habituation method A method of testing infants' perceptual abilities by exposing them to a certain stimulus until they get used to it (i.e. habituate) and show less interest when later shown the same stimulus because it is no longer novel. Page 19

Heritability The ratio between (a) genetic variability of the particular trait and (b) total variability in the whole population. Pages 65, 89, 108

Holistic process Perceiving the whole display rather than the individual features and/or the relations between them. Page 22

Horizon-ratio relation The proportion of an object that is above the horizon divided by the proportion below. Two objects of the same size on a flat surface will have the same horizon ratio. Page 18

Hormone Hormones are chemical substances that circulate in the blood and only affect target organs. They are produced in large quantities but disappear very quickly. Their effects are slow in comparison to the nervous system, but very powerful. Pages 7, 8, 11, 41, 42, 46, 47, 49, 50, 51, 52, 53

Hypocretin A neurotransmitter that regulates sleep, appetite and energy conservation. Page 15

Hypothalamus A part of the brain that functions to regulate bodily temperature, metabolic processes such as eating, and other autonomic (ANS) activities including emotional responses. Page 9

Hypothetico-deductive reasoning An approach to problem-solving where a person starts with many possible hypotheses and eliminates erroneous ones through testing, thus arriving at the correct solution. Page 68

ICD (International Classification of Disease and Related Health Problems) The classification scheme produced by the World Health Organisation for both physical and mental disorders. Page 76

Idealistic thinking Thinking in terms of abstract principles such as love, liberty and justice. Page 68

Independent variable (IV) An event that is directly manipulated by an experimenter in order to test its effect on another variable – the *dependent variable* (DV).

Idiographic An approach to research that focuses more on the individual case as a means of understanding behaviour rather than a way of formulating general laws of behaviour (the nomothetic approach). Page 124

Immature *See* mature

Imposed etic A technique or theory developed in one culture and then used to study the behaviour of people in a different culture with different norms, values, experiences etc. Pages 20, 56, 66

Insecure attachment A form of attachment between infant and caregiver that develops as a result of the caregiver's lack of sensitive responding to the infant's needs. There are two main subtypes: insecure-avoidant (children who tend to avoid social interaction and intimacy with others) and insecure-resistant (ambivalent) (children who both seek and reject intimacy and social interaction). Insecure attachment is associated with poor subsequent cognitive and emotional development. Pages 29, 46

***In vivo* desensitisation** Using principles of systematic desensitisation where a patient has direct experience of the hierarchy of situations from least to most fearful (as distinct from covert desensitisation). Page 92

Independent groups design An experimental design where participants are allocated to two (or more) groups representing different experimental conditions. Allocation is usually done using random techniques. Pages 125, 128, 129

Indigenous psychologies The study of human behaviour that is specific to a particular culture. The methods of research used are not transported from other regions but are designed specifically for the people of that culture. Page 30

Individualist A culture that values independence rather than reliance on others, in contrast to many non-Western cultures that could be described as collectivist. Pages 25, 30, 69, 70, 72

Inferential statistics Procedures for making inferences about the population from which samples are drawn. Pages 129, 130

Information-processing theory An approach to explaining behaviour based on a computer analogy, i.e. the concept that mental processes are similar to computer processes. Page 58

Infradian rhythm A pattern of behaviour that occurs less often than once a day, such as the human female menstrual cycle. Page 8

Ingroup Those individuals who, for whatever reason, are part of or accepted by the group of people with whom we usually identify. Pages 54, 105

Innate Behaviours that are a product of genetic factors. These may be apparent at birth or appear later through the process of maturation.

Insomnia Problems with falling asleep or staying asleep despite the opportunity to do so. Pages 10, 11, 14, 91, 97

Inter-interviewer reliability The extent to which two interviewers produce the same outcome from an interview. Page 125

Inter-rater/inter-observer reliability The extent to which there is agreement between two or more observers or raters involved in observations of a behaviour. Pages 76, 82, 88, 94, 125, 126

Internal working model A mental model of the world that enables individuals to predict and control their environment. Page 29

Intersex A person who has a mismatch between internal genitalia, external genitalia and/or gender identity. Pages 49, 52

Interval data A level of measurement where units of equal value are used, such as counting correct answers or any 'public' unit of measurement. Pages 128, 129

Intervening variable A variable that comes between two other variables that can explain the relationship between those two variables. Page 11

Interviewer bias The effect of an interviewer's expectations, communicated unconsciously, on a respondent's behaviour. Pages 30, 122, 125

Inversion effect When viewing a face upside down the ability to recognise facial features is affected. For example, if the person's eyes are upside down people do not normally notice this (the *Thatcher effect*). Page 22

Investigator/experimenter bias The effect that an investigator/experimenter's expectations has on the participants, and thus on the results of a research study. Pages 19, 117, 124, 125

IQ test A test of intelligence, IQ is the score derived from such tests, the letters stand for 'intelligence quotient' because the score used to be calculated by dividing test score by age. More recent tests use norms to work out a person's IQ based on their score and age. Pages 7, 58, 65, 72, 97, 126, 127

Jealousy A state of fear or suspicion caused by a real or imagined threat to one's current status. Page 72

Jet lag A physiological condition caused by desychronisation of the body clock as a consequence of travelling across time zones. Pages 8, 9

Just world hypothesis The belief that people will get what they deserve. As a result, an individual may rationalise an injustice by identifying things the victim might have done to deserve it. Page 109

Ketamine A drug used medically as an anaesthetic and also used as a recreational, hallucinogenic drug. Page 122

Klüver-Bucy syndrome A syndrome caused by injury to the temporal lobes of the brain and characterised by memory defects, hypersexuality and diminished fear reactions. Page 42

Lateral hypothalamus Part of the hypothalamus, stimulation of which is thought to lead to the onset of eating behaviour. Damage to the lateral hypothalamus leads to reduced food intake. Page 42

Learned helplessness Occurs when an animal finds that its responses are ineffective, and thus it learns that there is no point in responding and behaves passively in future. Page 84

Leptin A hormone produced by fat cells and involved in the regulation of appetite. Page 47

Life event Commonplace experiences that involve change from a steady state. Pages 78, 84, 86

Limbic system A system of structures lying beneath the cortex (subcortical), including the amygdala, hippocampus and hypothalamus. The region is associated with emotional behaviour. Pages 91, 97

Linear perspective Parallel lines that recede into the distance appear to get closer together, providing information about depth. Page 20

Locus of control An aspect of our personality; people differ in their beliefs about whether the outcomes of their actions are contingent on what they do (internal control) or on events outside their personal control (external control). Page 120

Machiavellian intelligence The ability to intentionally deceive another individual. It requires a Theory of Mind in order to comprehend what the other knows or doesn't know. Pages 63, 64, 73

Magical thinking Meaning is attached to objects or actions so that the objects/actions gain special (magical) properties. Page 119

Major depressive disorder (MDD) Also known as 'major depression', 'clinical depression', or 'unipolar disorder', MDD is a condition characterised by a long-lasting depressed mood or marked loss of interest or pleasure in all or nearly all activities. Page 82

MAOI (Monoamine oxidase inhibitor) Creates higher levels of neurotransmitters of the monamine group such as serotonin, noradrenaline and dopamine. Pages 12, 91

Mark test *See* mirror test

Mature/maturation The process of ripening. In psychological terms it means a change that is due to innate factors rather than learning. Pages 11, 12, 19, 45, 64, 68, 72

Melatonin A hormone mainly produced in the pineal gland which induces sleep. Pages 7, 8, 9, 10, 11

Mental module The assumption within evolutionary psychology that the human mind comprises a number of innate 'structures' that have evolved because they had adaptive functions for our ancestors. Pages 73, 95

Meta-analysis A researcher looks at the findings from a number of different studies in order to reach a general conclusion about a particular hypothesis. Pages 29, 33, 35, 36, 41, 61, 65, 66, 77, 78, 79, 92, 101, 102, 104, 117, 120

Metabolic processes The chemical processes that occur within any living organism to produce energy. Pages 8, 13

Microsleep Small periods of sleep during the day which possibly enable some physiological recovery to take place. The individual may not be aware they have been asleep. Page 12

Mirror neuron (MN) A neuron that responds to actions performed by oneself as well as when the same actions are performed by others. Page 74

Mirror test An investigative technique used to assess self-awareness by, for example, putting red colour on an individual's nose and showing them their image in a mirror. The individual demonstrates self-awareness if they touch their nose. Page 72

Modelling The process of imitating another's behaviour, which involves cognitive representations of the modelled activities as well as abstractions of the underlying rules of the modelled behaviours. Pages 34, 40, 55, 90, 92, 101

Motion parallax As we move, objects that are closer to us move farther across our field of vision than more distant objects, providing information about depth. Page 19

MRI (magnetic resonance imaging) Produces a three-dimensional image of the static brain which is very precise. A magnetic field causes the atoms of the brain to change their alignment when the magnet is on and emit various radio signals when the magnet is turned off. A detector reads the signals and uses them to map the structure of the brain. Page 64

Müller-Lyer illusion Illusion created by fins at the end of a line such that one line looks longer (fins pointing out) than the other (fins pointing in). Pages 17, 18, 20

Mundane realism Refers to how a study mirrors the real word. The experimental environment is realistic to the degree to which experiences encountered in the environment will occur in the real world. Pages 24, 125, 126

MZ (monozygotic) twins Identical twins formed from one fertilised egg (or zygotes). Pages 14, 36, 65, 77, 83, 89, 95

Narcolepsy A disorder in which individuals experience sudden and uncontrollable attacks of sleep, lasting seconds or minutes at irregular or unexpected times. Page 15

Nativist The view that development is determined by innate factors, that most abilities simply need fine tuning but do not depend on experience for their development. Page 68

Natural selection The major process that explains evolution whereby inherited traits that enhance an animal's reproductive success are passed on to the next generation and thus 'selected', whereas animals without such traits are less successful at reproduction and their traits are not selected. Pages 45, 51, 64, 73, 77

Nature Those aspects of behaviour that are innate and inherited. Nature does not simply refer to abilities present at birth but to any ability determined by genes, including those that appear through maturation. Pages 14, 18, 19, 49, 72, 73, 74

Need for cognition (NC) A personality variable describing people who enjoy tasks that involve high cognitive effort, such as analysing arguments and brain teasers. Page 103

Negative correlation Describes a correlation where, as one co-variable increases, the other decreases. Pages 13, 125, 129

Negative reinforcement Increases the probability that a behaviour will be repeated because it leads to escape from an unpleasant situation. Pages 40, 61, 90, 96, 98, 119

Neocortex or 'new' cortex is the six-layered covering of the brain. About 95% of the cerebral cortex is neocortex so that gradually the terms have come to mean the same. The 'old' cortex or 'archicortex' is mainly the limbic system and basal ganglia. Page 64

Neuropeptide Y (NPY) A neurotransmitter believed to be important in the control of appetite and eating behaviour, especially in response to leptin. Page 42

Neuroticism The tendency to experience negative emotional states such as anxiety, anger, guilt and depressed mood. Individuals cope poorly with stress and are often self-conscious and shy. Pages 105, 111

Neurotransmitters Chemical substances, such as serotonin or dopamine, which play an important part in the workings of the nervous system by transmitting nerve impulses across a synapse. Pages 12, 79, 83, 85, 91, 95, 119

Neutral stimulus (NS) In classical conditioning, the stimulus that initially does not produce the target response i.e. it is neutral. Through association with the unconditioned stimulus (UCS), the NS acquires the properties of the UCS and becomes a conditioned stimulus (CS) producing a conditioned response (CR). Pages 60, 90, 96

Night terrors A parasomnia related to sleep walking, where nightmares occur during slow wave sleep. It may not be possible to wake a person suffering from night terrors. Page 11

Nominal data A level of measurement where data are in separate categories. Pages 128, 129

Nomothetic An approach to research that focuses more on general laws of behaviour than on the individual, possibly unique, case (the idiographic approach). Page 124

Non-clinical See clinical

Non-directional hypothesis Predicts that there will be a difference between two conditions or two groups of participants, without stating the direction of the difference. Page 128

Noradrenaline A neurotransmitter found mainly in areas of the brain that are involved in governing autonomic nervous system activity, e.g. blood pressure and heart rate. Pages 46, 83, 85, 97

NREM sleep Non-rapid eye movement sleep, which includes slow wave sleep. Pages 11, 13

NS See neutral stimulus

Null hypothesis An assumption that there is no relationship (difference or association) in the population from which a sample is taken with respect to the variables being studied. Pages 118, 119, 128, 129

Nurture Those aspects of behaviour that are acquired through experience i.e. learned from interactions with the physical and social environment. Pages 14, 18, 19, 49, 72, 73, 74

Object permanence A child's understanding that objects that are no longer visible nevertheless continue to exist. Page 68

Observer bias The tendency for observations to be influenced by expectations or prejudices. Pages 125, 126

Occam's razor The principle that simpler explanations are preferable, if everything else is equal. Page 51

Occlusion Objects that are closer block out (or occlude) objects that are more distant, providing information about depth. Pages 19, 20

Oestrogen The primary female hormone, though also present in males in small amounts. Regulates the menstrual cycle and female development in puberty. Pages 8, 41, 51

One-tailed test Form of test used with a directional hypothesis. Page 128

Open questions Questions that invite respondents to provide their own answers rather than to select an answer that has been provided. Tend to produce qualitative data. Page 125

Operant conditioning Learning that occurs when we are reinforced for doing something, which increases the probability that the behaviour in question will be repeated in the future. Conversely, if we are punished for behaving in a certain way, there is a decrease in the probability that the behaviour will recur. Pages 24, 34, 61, 62, 90, 96, 110, 119

Orbitofrontal cortex (OFC) A region of the frontal cortex, lying just above the eyes, involved in cognitive processes such as decision-making. Pages 95, 97

Ordinal data A level of measurement where data are ordered in some way. Pages 128, 129

Outgroup Those individuals who, for whatever reason, are not part of or accepted by the group of people with whom we usually identify. Page 54

Oxytocin A hormone that also acts as a neurotransmitter. Its effect is to promote feelings of pleasure and its release is associated with bonding, trust and also orgasm. Page 50

Panic disorder Unexpected and repeated episodes of intense fear accompanied by physical symptoms. Page 91

Paranormal A general term to describe experiences that lack a scientific explanation. The term 'anomalous experience' is preferred because it has fewer negative connotations.

Parasocial relationship A one-sided relationship with someone you haven't met, such as a celebrity, which creates the illusion of a friendship. Pages 104, 105, 106

Parasomnias Sleep disorders that revolve around sleep, such as sleep walking and night terrors, as distinct from disorders of sleep, such as insomnia. Page 14

Paraventricular nucleus (PVN) An area in the anterior (towards the front) part of the hypothalamus, damage to which is more recently thought to cause hyperphagia. The PVN also detects the specific foods our body needs, and seems to be responsible for many food 'cravings'. Page 42

Parental investment Any investment by a parent in an offspring that increases the chance that the offspring will survive at the expense of that parent's ability to invest in any other offspring (alive or yet to be born). Pages 27, 28

Participant effects A general term used to acknowledge the fact that participants react to cues in an experimental situation, and that this may affect the validity of any conclusions drawn from the investigation. Page 125

PET scan (positron emission tomography) A brain scanning method used to study activity in the brain. Radioactive glucose is ingested and can be detected in the active areas of the brain. Pages 58, 77, 95

Pheromones Chemical substances that are transmitted from one animal to another animal of the same species, affecting the other animal's behaviour. Page 8

Phototherapy The use of very bright lights to treat disruptions to biological rhythms, such as SAD and jet lag. The aim is to entrain biological rhythms and reduce levels of melatonin. Page 8

Phylogenetic signal This refers to the behavioural similarities between species that are genetically similar, i.e. close on the phylogenetic scale. Page 13

Pineal gland Small gland in the brain that is stimulated by darkness or by the SCN to release melatonin, inducing sleep. Page 8

Pituitary gland Known as the 'master gland', the pituitary releases a variety of hormones that act on other glands throughout the body. Page 8

Placebo A substance or treatment which 'pretends' to be the real thing so we can observe the psychological effects of the treatment. Pages 8, 46, 77, 79, 83, 85, 86, 91, 97, 98, 114, 119, 212

Population In psychological research, all the people about whom we wish to make a statement, also called the 'target population'. Page 101

Positive correlation Refers to when, in a correlation, co-variables both increase together. Pages 13, 35, 36, 40, 58, 63, 64, 95, 104, 120, 125

Post traumatic stress disorder A condition triggered by a terrifying event (such as combat or rape). Symptoms may include flashbacks, nightmares and severe anxiety, as well as uncontrollable thoughts about the event. Pages 102, 111

Pre-operational A stage in Piaget's theory of cognitive development where a child (aged between two and seven years) is able to use symbols to represent experience (e.g. language) but lacks the ability to operate on concepts with internally consistent, adult logic. Pages 53, 68, 73

Predictive validity A means of assessing the validity or trueness of a psychological test by correlating the results of the test with some later behaviour; the ability to predict something it should theoretically be able to predict. Page 76

Prefrontal cortex Section of the cerebral cortex at the front of the brain associated with working memory and planning. Pages 66, 74

Premotor cortex A region of the motor cortex responsible for the sensory guidance of movement. Page 74

Probability judgement Refers to making estimations of how likely a particular event is, i.e. judging their probability. Page 118

Proband The first person who seeks treatment for a genetic disorder; other relatives are then contacted to see if they also have the disorder in order to investigate genetic factors. Pages 83, 89, 118

Progesterone A female hormone that increases after ovulation and is important in pregnancy. Page 8

Prosopagnosia A form of visual agnosia where an individual cannot recognise familiar faces, though they can respond to facial expressions and may be able to identify individual features. Page 22

Pseudoscience A practice or approach that claims to be scientific but does not adhere to the key principles of the scientific process. Pages 116, 124

Psychosurgery Surgery that involves severing fibres or removing brain tissue with the intention of treating disturbed behaviour for which no physical cause can be demonstrated. Modern psychosurgery techniques, such as deep brain stimulation, do not involve permanent damage. Pages 91, 97

Psychotic A loss of contact with reality, consistent with serious mental illness, which typically includes delusions, hallucinations and disordered thinking. Pages 12, 77, 111, 120

Psychokinesis (PK) The ability to move or change objects using the mind only. Pages 116, 120

Publication bias A tendency to publish research findings that are in the direction of the preferred result, usually a positive one. Page 109

Qualitative data Data that expresses the 'quality' of things involving descriptions, words, meanings, pictures, texts and so on. Qualitative data cannot be counted or quantified but they can be turned into quantitative data by placing them in categories. Pages 44, 124, 125, 130

Quantitative data Data that represent how much or how long, or how many, etc. there are of something; i.e. a behaviour is measured in numbers or quantities. Pages 125, 130

Reductionist An approach which breaks complex phenomenon into more simple components, implying that this is desirable because complex phenomena are best understood in terms of a simpler level of explanation. Pages 77, 96, 108, 122

Regression A form of defence mechanism where an individual deals with anxiety by returning to an earlier ego state rather than coping with unacceptable impulses in an adult way. Pages 78, 119

Reliability A measure of consistency both within a set of scores or items (internal reliability) and also over time so that it is possible to obtain the same results on subsequent occasions when the measure is used (external reliability). Pages 41, 76, 82, 88, 94

REM sleep Rapid eye movement sleep, during which the body is paralysed except for the eyes. REM sleep is often equated with dreaming, though dreams also occur in NREM sleep. Pages 8, 11, 13, 15

Repeated measures design An experimental design where each participant takes part in every condition under test. Pages 125, 128, 129

Replication If a finding from a research study is true (valid) then it should be possible to obtain the same finding if the study is repeated. This confirms the validity of the finding. Pages 3, 108, 109, 116, 121, 124, 125, 126, 128, 130

Representative sample A sample selected so that it accurately stands for or represents the population being studied. Pages 101, 126, 131

Repressed A form of defence mechanism whereby anxiety-provoking material is kept out of conscious awareness as a means of coping. Pages 90, 96

Reproductive fitness A measure of the success of an individual in passing on their genes to the next generation and beyond. Page 64

Retinal disparity The difference in the images received by the retina in the right and left eye. Page 19

Retinal image The image formed on the retina, a region of the eye containing photosensitive cells (rods and cones) which record light energy. Page 17

Retinal size The true size of an object as recorded on the retina, as opposed to the perceived size when factors such as distance are taken into account. Page 17

Sally Anne test A method used to assess an individual's understanding of false beliefs and Theory of Mind. Sally puts a ball in her basket and leaves the room, Anne moves the ball to her box. When Sally returns, where does she think her ball is? The answer is 'in the basket' but some children, after observing Anne's actions, would say Anne's box because they don't comprehend that someone else may be thinking something different to themselves. Page 73

Sampling The process of taking a sample intended to be a representative selection of a target population. Pages 36, 126, 131

Scaffolding An approach to instruction that aims to support a learner only when absolutely necessary i.e. to provide a support framework (scaffold) to assist the learning process. Page 70

Schema A cluster of related facts based on previous experiences, and used to generate future expectations. Pages 54, 68, 84

Selective pressure In evolutionary theory, demands made by the environment resulting in one set of genes being favoured over another. This is the mechanism of natural selection. Pages 13, 51, 64

Self-actualisation A person's motivation to maximise their achievements and fulfill their potential. Page 120

Self-efficacy The belief that we can perform competently in a given situation. Pages 55, 110, 113, 114, 119

Self-esteem The feelings that a person has about their self-concept. Pages 44, 46, 72, 102, 106

Self-fulfilling prophecy A prediction that comes true simply because of the expectations generated by the prediction that was made. Our beliefs generate expectations which affect our own perceptions and other people's behaviour. Pages 14, 78, 119

Self-monitoring The extent to which an individual is able to observe their own behaviour to check that their behaviour is appropriate and/or desirable. Page 104

Semi-structured interview An interview that combines both structured and unstructured interviews. The interviewer has some pre-established questions but also develops questions in response to the answers given. Page 88

Sensorimotor The co-ordination of sensory and motor experiences, such as hand–eye coordination. Page 68

Serotonin A neurotransmitter found in the central nervous system and implicated in many different behaviours and physiological processes, including aggression, eating behaviour, sleep and depression. Pages 8, 35, 36, 45, 83, 85, 89, 91, 95, 97, 114

Sex A biological fact, as opposed to gender.

Sexual selection A key part of Darwin's theory explaining how evolution is driven by competition for mates, and the development of characteristics that ensure reproductive success. Pages 46, 64, 105

Sheep–goat effect The observation that people who believe in paranormal phenomena (sheep) are more likely to produce evidence that supports the reality of such phenomena, whereas sceptics (goats) tend to produce evidence againt the existence of paranormal phenomena. Page 117

Shift lag A physiological condition caused by dyschronisation of the body clock as a consequence of working shifts at different times of day and night. Pages 9, 10

Sleep walking A parasomnia that occurs during slow wave sleep and entails a range of activities normally associated with wakefulness (e.g. eating, getting dressed, walking about); the person has no conscious knowledge of what they are doing. Pages 11, 14, 15

SLT See social learning

SNS (sympathetic nervous system) The part of the autonomic nervous system that is associated with physiological arousal and 'fight or flight' responses. Pages 89, 91

Social cognition The study of how cognition (i.e. thinking, beliefs, perception) influences social behaviour. Page 74

Social constructionist An approach to studying and explaining human behaviour in terms of its social context rather than any objective reality. Social constructionists believe that, if behaviour is separated from social context, then its true meaning is lost. Page 51

Social desirability bias A tendency for respondents to answer questions in a way that they think will present them in a better light. Pages 37, 125

Social identity theory An important part of our personal identity is determined by the various social groups to which we belong. Page 111

Social learning (social learning theory, SLT) Learning through observing the behaviour of others, mentally rehearsing the behaviours they display, then later imitating them in similar situations. Pages 32, 36, 40, 52, 55, 64, 90, 111

Social phobia A phobia of situations involving other people, such as speaking in public or being part of a social group. Pages 88, 89, 91, 92

Socioeconomic status (SES) A measure of an individual's or family's social and economic position, based on income, education, and occupation. Pages 66, 89, 100

Specific phobia A phobia of specific activities or objects, such as bathing or spiders. Page 88

Split-half method A method of assessing internal reliability by comparing two halves of, for example, a psychological test to see if they produce the same score. Page 126

SSRIs (selective serotonin re-uptake inhibitors) Commonly prescribed drugs for treating depression. They work by selectively preventing the re-uptake of serotonin from the synaptic gap, thus leaving more serotonin available at the synapse to excite surrounding neurons. Pages 45, 46, 83, 85, 91, 95, 97, 114

Sub-clinical See clinical

Superstition Beliefs that are not based on reason or knowledge. Page 119

SWS (slow wave sleep) Stages 3 and 4 of NREM sleep when brain waves have low frequency and high amplitude. This stage of deep sleep is associated with bodily growth and repair, such as the production of growth hormones. Pages 8, 11

Symbolic Learning or thinking using abstract symbols. Page 68

Synapse A small gap separating neurons. It consists of the presynaptic membrane (which discharges neurotransmitters), the postsynaptic membrane (containing receptor sites for neurotransmitters) and a synaptic gap between the two. Pages 77, 85, 97

Systematic desensitisation A process by which a patient is gradually exposed to (or imagines) a threatening situation under relaxed conditions until the anxiety reaction is extinguished. Pages 90, 92, 98

Target population In a research study, the group of people that the researcher is interested in. The group of people from whom a sample is drawn. The group of people about whom generalisations can be made. Page 126

Test–retest reliability A method used to check external reliability. The same test or interview is given to the same participants on two occasions to see if the same results are obtained. Pages 76, 82, 88, 94, 126

Testosterone Hormone produced mainly by the testes in males, but also occurring in females. It is associated with the development of secondary sexual characteristics in males (e.g. body hair), but has also been implicated in aggression and dominance behaviours. Pages 35, 49, 51, 52, 53

Texture gradient Objects that are closer to the viewer appear more widely spaced, providing a cue to depth or distance. Pages 18, 20

Thalamus A structure lying under the cortex (subcortical) that has been described as the great relay station of the brain because most sensory information first goes to the thalamus, where it is processed and sent on to the cerebral cortex. Page 95

Theory of Mind (ToM) An individual's understanding that other people have separate mental states and that they see the world from a different point of view from their own. Pages 50, 74

'Theory' theory (TT) A theory of human development that proposes a middle ground between pure innateness, on the one hand, and the role of experience, on the other. Pages 74

Three mountains task Designed by Piaget to investigate perceptual perspective-taking ability in children. A child is asked to identify the hypothetical view of three mountains seen by a doll placed in different positions. Pages 68, 73

Time sampling An observational technique in which the observer records behaviours in a given time frame, e.g. noting what a target individual is doing every 30 seconds. Page 125

Tolerance The progressive reduction of the effect of a drug (or other addiction) due to its continued use. Page 114

Top-down Processing that starts from an overview of a system, as opposed to bottom-up processing, such as using previous experience and context to enrich sensory input. Pages 17, 18, 19

Tourette's syndrome A neurological disorder characterised by tics (sudden involuntary movements or vocalisations (such as swear words) which are repeated excessively. Pages 95, 96

Transcranial magnetic stimulation (TMS) A technique used to trigger brain activity in target areas using an electric current to create a magnetic field. Page 122

Tryptophan An essential amino acid found in the diet, particularly in milk, cheese, fish, nuts and chocolate. Tryptophan is a precursor of the neurotransmitter serotonin, and melatonin, a hormone related to sleep. Pages 46, 83

Two-tailed test Form of test used with a non-directional hypothesis. Page 128

Type 1 error Rejecting a null hypothesis that is true. This is more likely to happen if significance level is too high (lenient, e.g. 10%). Pages 118, 119, 128

Type 2 error Accepting a null hypothesis that is in fact not true. This is more likely to happen if the significance level is too low (stringent, e.g. 1%). Pages 118, 119, 128

UCR See unconditioned response

UCS See unconditioned stimulus

Ultradian rhythm A pattern of behaviour that occurs more often than once a day, such as the cycle of sleep stages that occurs every 90 minutes during sleep Page 8

Unconditioned response (UCR) In classical conditioning, the innate reflex response to a stimulus, such as salivating when presented with food. Page 90

Unconditioned stimulus (UCS) In classical conditioning, the stimulus that inevitably produces an innate reflex response, such as food producing a salivation response. Pages 60, 90

Unstructured interview An interview that starts out with some general aims and possibly some questions, and lets the interviewee's answers guide subsequent questions. Page 125

Validity Refers to the legitimacy of a study, the extent to which the findings can be applied beyond the research setting as a consequence of the study's internal and/or external validity. Pages 34, 36, 76, 78, 80, 82, 88, 94, 130

Ventromedial hypothalamus Part of the hypothalamus, stimulation of which

is thought to lead to the termination of eating behaviour. Damage to the ventromedial hypothalamus leads to excessive food intake. Page 42

Vicarious reinforcement Learning not through direct reinforcement of behaviour, but through observing someone else being reinforced for that behaviour. Page 34

Visual agnosia The brain's inability to recognise objects, including words (alexia) and faces (prosopagnosia) despite being able to see them (intact visual system). Page 22

Visual cliff A laboratory apparatus to investigate depth perception in babies and other young animals. It consists of a large glass sheet with patterned material directly below the glass on one side, and a foot below on the other. This apparatus creates the visual illusion of a cliff, while protecting the subject from injury. Pages 19

Visual constancy We continue to see the shape, size, colour etc. of familiar objects as being the same despite changing retinal images due to perspective and/or lighting conditions. Pages 19, 20

Volunteer bias A form of sampling bias caused by the fact that volunteer participants are usually more highly motivated than randomly selected participants. Page 126

Working memory An area of memory that deals with information that is being worked on, equivalent to short-term memory. It is divided into separate stores representing different modalities. Pages 78

Xenophobia A fear and distrust of strangers, although this is now popularly recognised as a fear and distrust of foreigners. Page 38

Zero correlation In a correlation co-variables are not linked at all. Page 125

Notes

Notes

Notes

Complete Companions
for AQA A Psychology

There's more online…

The free **Psychology: The Online Companion** blog is packed with up-to-date research, helpful resources and useful psychology links for students and teachers. Written by leading authors and examiners **Cara Flanagan, Mike Cardwell, Adrian Frost, Evie Bentley, Jean-Marc Lawton** and **Mike Griffin**.

Visit www.oxfordschoolblogs.co.uk

el 01536 452620   **email** schools.enquiries.uk@oup.com
ax 01865 313472   **web** www.oxfordsecondary.co.uk/psychology

The Complete Companions for A Level Psychology

Written by an expert team of experienced authors and editors led by **Mike Cardwell** and **Cara Flanagan**

For AQA A

The Student Books

978 019 912981 2

978 019 912984 3

The Exam Companions

978 019 912982 9

978 019 912985 0

The Mini Companions

978 019 912983 6

978 019 91298

The AS Visual Companion

978 185 008548 5

The Teacher's Companions

978 185 008295 8

978 185 008396 2

The AS Digital Companion

978 185 008394 8

The AS Audio Companion
CD-ROM with printable activity sheets and site licence

978 019 912972 0

For WJEC

The Student Books

978 185 008440 2

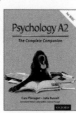
978 185 008571 3

The AS Revision Companion

978 019 913617 9

For all A Level courses

Research Methods Companion

978 019 912962 1

Order your copies now

tel 01536 452620
fax 01865 313472

email schools.enquiries.uk@oup.com
web www.oxfordsecondary.co.uk/psychology

OXFORD
UNIVERSITY PRESS